BUILDING A SERVER WITH FREEBSD 7

BUILDING A SERVER WITH FREEBSD 7

A MODULAR APPROACH

by Bryan J. Hong

NO STARCH
PRESS

San Francisco

Printed on recycled paper in the United States of America

12 11 10 09 08   1 2 3 4 5 6 7 8 9

ISBN-10: 1-59327-145-X
ISBN-13: 978-1-59327-145-9

Publisher: William Pollock
Production Editor: Riley Hoffman
Cover Design: Octopod Studios
Developmental Editor: William Pollock
Technical Reviewer: Dru Lavigne
Copyeditor: David Erik Nelson
Compositor: Riley Hoffman
Proofreader: Rachel Kai

For information on book distributors or translations, please contact No Starch Press, Inc. directly:

No Starch Press, Inc.
555 De Haro Street, Suite 250, San Francisco, CA 94107
phone: 415.863.9900; fax: 415.863.9950; info@nostarch.com; www.nostarch.com

Library of Congress Cataloging-in-Publication Data

```
Hong, Bryan J. (Bryan Johnathan)
   Building a server with FreeBSD 7 : a modular approach / Bryan J. Hong.
      p. cm.
   Includes index.
   ISBN-13: 978-1-59327-145-9
   ISBN-10: 1-59327-145-X
 1.  FreeBSD. 2.  Free computer software. 3.  Operating systems (Computers)
4.  Client/server computing.  I. Title.
   QA76.76.O63H6694 2008
   005.4'3--dc22
                                                          2007000276
```

Thanks, Mom and Dad . . . for everything

ACKNOWLEDGMENTS

Lindsay, thanks for being so patient while I did computer nerd stuff in the middle of the night. Rachael, maybe now I'll have time to put that wheel cap on your car. Michelle, thanks for leaving your plasma TV with me when you move to Hawaii?

I'd like to thank Bill Pollock, Elizabeth Campbell, Ellen Har, Patricia Witkin, Leigh Poehler, and Tyler Ortman of No Starch Press for all of their hard work and dedication. They did an amazing job of transforming what was once a pile of notes into a truly useful book. Special thanks to Riley Hoffman of No Starch Press for wearing so many hats. She did a phenomenal job; I am forever grateful. Thanks again, Bill, for all of your input and guidance.

Thanks to Dru Lavigne for providing her technical expertise and guidance. Your commitment to FreeBSD and open source software is a source of inspiration for me. Thanks to Michael Lucas for the words of wisdom and for writing one of the best FreeBSD books around.

I'd also like to thank Richard Bejtlich for reviewing the first incarnation of this book; his suggestions led to improvements to this edition. Thanks to Derek Yee of Octopod Studios for the clever cover graphics. Thanks to Joseph Koshy and the other members of the FreeBSD community who donate their time selflessly. Lastly, thanks to all of the open source developers who created the excellent software mentioned in this book. I hope this book brings more people to appreciate the work you do.

Bryan J. Hong
San Francisco, CA
February 29, 2008

BRIEF CONTENTS

CONTENTS IN DETAIL

PART I: THE BASE SYSTEM

PART II: THIRD-PARTY APPLICATIONS

PREFACE

Without question, the Internet-connected computer has become an essential tool in today's society. Most people know what the Internet is, but few know that open source software has played an important role in making it all work, powering services on the Internet for over a decade. Now you can leverage that same open source software. Think of this book as a field guide to installing open source software on FreeBSD.

FreeBSD is the powerful UNIX-like operating system derived from BSD Unix. BSD Unix was developed at the University of California, Berkeley in the early '80s. Historically, software installation on Unix-based systems has been a challenging task, but FreeBSD mitigates this issue with its ports collection.

The FreeBSD ports collection is a system for installing programs that uses scripts to automate the process of building software from source code. The success of this system has caused it to be propagated to other operating systems, including NetBSD, OpenBSD, and Gentoo Linux. The ports collection simplifies the process of building software, but new users are often left in the dark once the build process is complete. This is especially true in the case of server applications. Server applications require custom configuration, and most books lack detail in that area.

If you've installed software via the FreeBSD ports collection, you're probably familiar with post-installation messages instructing you to make a copy of a sample configuration file and then modify it to fit your setup. This can be a bewildering task for those who are new to FreeBSD or used to graphical interfaces. This book's aim is to take you through this process step by step in as little time as possible. I designed this book to get readers "up and running" quickly. Once you have a working system, you're free to experiment, extend, and customize as you please.

This book attempts to fill the void for those of us who prefer the do-it-yourself approach. If you're on a limited budget, the knowledge you gain here may help you become less dependent on costly commercial solutions. Whether you're a small business owner looking for a reliable email server, a curious Windows administrator, or a geek who wants to put that old computer in the closet to work, this book is a natural first step to discovering open source server applications on FreeBSD.

THIS BOOK'S ROOTS

I graduated with an aeronautical science degree and flew airplanes for a regional airline based on the east coast of the United States. I wanted a way to centrally host a personal website, retrieve email, and access files while I was away from home. There were many sites offering these services at the time, but I wanted something free, centralized, and feature-rich. I decided that the way to accomplish this was to host it on my own server. There were a few solutions to choose from. . . .

First, I looked at proprietary software like Microsoft Windows Server, but it was cost-prohibitive. On top of that, the hardware I possessed didn't have the extra horsepower necessary for a GUI solution like Windows. I was left with two choices: Linux, or one of the three major BSD variants. I decided to forgo Linux because, although it is popular and widely supported as a whole, I didn't feel there was a specific distribution that matched the completeness of FreeBSD.

I began the task of installing and configuring FreeBSD and an array of third-party server applications. As a new user to FreeBSD, I struggled to learn the new concepts and commands. I visited forums, read articles, and bought books. I found a lot of information online, but many of the how-to guides were outdated or incomplete. The constant search for information consumed a lot of time. Many late nights ensued, but after much perseverance, the server went live—a month after the project began.

The server performed for months without a hitch, so well that I forgot what I had learned during its initial inception. Six months later, I wanted to add additional server software to the system, and I couldn't remember how to do it! This presented a problem because I didn't want to spend time relearning all the steps I had taken months before. I began to document my efforts so I could accelerate this process later when I needed to install something else. The documentation project grew into the book that is now before you. With it, you'll minimize frustration and be able to consolidate what took me months (collectively) into a weekend.

HOW TO USE THIS BOOK

The guides in this book are constructed to provide information in a standard format. The book consists of two parts: Part I, "The Base System," and Part II, "Third-Party Applications."

Part I provides information on installing the FreeBSD operating system. This section of the book also contains important information on setting up your base FreeBSD environment and updating the ports collection. If you need more information on the FreeBSD operating system, consult the *FreeBSD Handbook*. It is an invaluable resource and can be found on the Web at *http://freebsd.org/doc/en/books/handbook*.

Part II constitutes the bulk of this book. This section provides the information you'll need to install and configure software using the ports collection. Applications are divided into individual modules that are arranged alphabetically, minimizing the need to search indexes or tables of contents.

The applications covered in this book were carefully selected. A balance between stability and available support were determining factors in choosing which applications would be included. Stability is paramount in server environments. Community support is also very important for long-term viability of an application; a well-supported application means that resources will be available to you if you need help. Community support also encourages development efforts, which may lead to faster responses to bugs or security issues.

FORMAT

Let's examine the standardized guide format used throughout. The following figure shows the information given in the headers and title of each module.

❶ Title of the module: This dictionary-style header makes it easy to find the project you're looking for by flipping through the pages.

❷ File paths: The paths to the Makefile and other associated files in the FreeBSD ports tree are given here.

❸ Protocol(s) and port(s) used by the application: If services provided by the application need to be available to clients on the Internet, you may need to configure your router to forward these ports to your FreeBSD server. Check your router's documentation for details on port forwarding.

❹ Level of effort: This value is an estimate of the time and effort required to complete the module, on a scale of 1 to 5. Level 1 requires the least effort, while level 5 requires the most.

❺ Application version covered in the module and the developer's website: The applications covered in this book are under continuous development, so version numbers will change, but the installation procedures described should stay relatively constant. The URL of the developer's website is provided for reference.

Each module contains some or all of the following sections:

Summary This section explains what the application covered in the module does, the service or solution it provides, and its history.

Resources This section shows websites that provide further information about the application covered or the protocol(s) it employs.

Required This section specifies modules or tasks that need to be installed or completed prior to beginning the module.

Optional This section lists modules or items that enhance or extend the application's functionality.

Preparation This section contains instructions and tasks to complete before beginning the application installation process.

Install This section contains instructions and/or commands that compile the source code of an application into binary form using scripts called *Makefiles.*

Configure This section contains important post-installation instructions that prepare configuration files for use by the installed application.

Testing If applicable, this section gives steps to test the installation of an application or service. Details for enabling automatic startup of server applications are also mentioned here.

Utilities This section contains important commands or programs that are useful for system administration purposes.

NOTE *Commonly used options (or switches) are provided here for quick reference. Consult the manual page for the command or utility for full documentation. See "Manual Pages" on page 234 for more information.*

Config Files This section contains a list of important configuration files with short descriptions and their default locations.

Log Files This section contains a list of logs that record information about the application; these can be useful for diagnosing problems and monitoring activity.

Notes This section contains information that may be useful for extending the functionality and security of the application. Options that depend on personal preference may also reside here.

WHERE TO START

Below is a visual representation of the modules included in this book and their relationships. Server roles are organized vertically with associated modules beneath.

Arrows represent the logical order that should be taken when using the modules in this book. Solid lines connecting modules show relationships between modules. You can use this as a starting point, or you can develop your own build strategy.

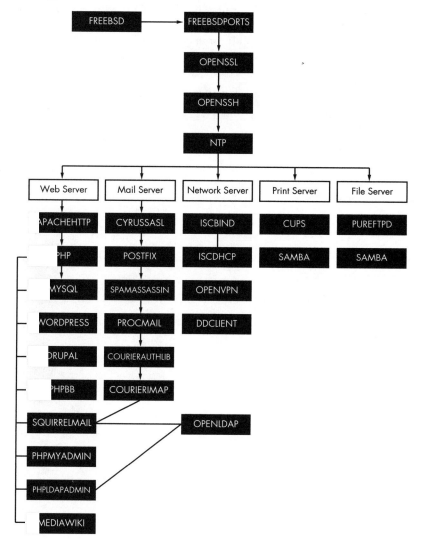

BECOMING THE SUPERUSER

The direction "become the superuser" is used throughout the book, and I want to clarify its meaning early on. The term *superuser* is synonymous with the root account on other UNIX-like systems. The *root account* is a special user account that has full administrative rights to the system. Most of the modules in this book require you to execute commands as the superuser.

To become the superuser, you can log in at the console (using the *console* means you are using the monitor and keyboard attached to the system) with the username root. There may be times when you need to log in remotely via SSH (Secure Shell). For security reasons, FreeBSD does not allow the root user to log in via SSH. You must first log in as a normal user, then switch to the superuser account with the su command. Only user accounts that belong to the wheel group may switch to the superuser account. The FreeBSD module in this book explains how to add your initial user to the wheel group during the installation process. If you don't follow that module or if you want to verify your group memberships, log in and then type:

```
# id
uid=1001(john) gid=1001(john) groups=1001(john), 0(wheel)
```

You can see above that the user john is a member of the wheel group. To become the superuser, John would type:

```
# su
```

After John enters the superuser (root) password, he will be switched to the superuser account. He could verify this by typing:

```
# whoami
root
```

Once logged in as the superuser, you may add other users to the wheel group with the following command:

```
# pw user mod uname -G wheel
```

Replace *uname* with the username of the user you want to add.

EASY EDITOR

Like on other UNIX-like platforms, FreeBSD configuration is controlled by the contents of various text configuration files. These configuration files dictate how the system behaves, so the ability to edit them is critical. FreeBSD includes ee (Easy Editor), which is easy to learn and has the basic functionality needed to perform administrative tasks. To start Easy Editor, simply type **ee** at the command prompt. Here is an example of the interface:

```
^[ (escape) menu ^y search prompt ^k delete line    ^p prev li  ^g prev page
^o ascii code    ^x search        ^l undelete line ^n next li  ^v next page
^u end of file   ^a begin of line ^w delete word    ^b back 1 char
^t top of text   ^e end of line   ^r restore word   ^f forward 1 char
^c command       ^d delete char   ^j undelete char ^z next word
============================================================================
```

The carat symbols indicate that the [CTRL] key should be pressed in combination with the adjacent letter. For example, to search the current text file for a certain word, press [CTRL-Y]. You will see the following search prompt:

```
search for:
```

Easy Editor shows prompts and status messages at the bottom of the screen. To access the menu system, press [ESC]:

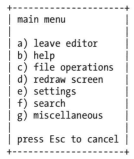

```
+---------------------+
| main menu           |
|                     |
| a) leave editor     |
| b) help             |
| c) file operations  |
| d) redraw screen    |
| e) settings         |
| f) search           |
| g) miscellaneous    |
|                     |
| press Esc to cancel |
+---------------------+
```

The interface is intuitive and doesn't require much effort to learn. Take some time to familiarize yourself with Easy Editor once you complete the initial FreeBSD installation.

PART I

THE BASE SYSTEM

FREEBSD 7.0
HTTP://WWW.FREEBSD.ORG

SUMMARY

FreeBSD is a free, UNIX-like operating system based on BSD (the Berkeley Software Distribution), which was originally developed at the University of California, Berkeley. FreeBSD is open source software; the *source code* (software blueprint) is freely available to the public to be modified or improved upon.

FreeBSD is developed as an entire operating system that includes the *kernel* (the core of the operating system), a *shell* (the user interface), and *device drivers* (software that controls hardware). The Linux kernel, on the other hand, is developed separately from the Linux userland. In other words, the shell, system utilities, and applications are developed separately and are packaged with the kernel as various distributions (Ubuntu, Red Hat, SUSE, and so on).

License

Linux is licensed under version 2 of the GPL (the GNU General Public License); FreeBSD is released under the new BSD license. Visit *http://www.opensource.org* for details about the GPL and BSD licenses.

The Ports Collection

The standard FreeBSD distribution includes a proven array of powerful utilities together with a massive library of dynamically developed third-party software known as the *ports collection*.

The ports collection is one of the most convenient features of FreeBSD. It is laid out as a hierarchy of categorical directories containing *makefiles* (scripts that build software from source code). Each makefile contains scripts that patch, compile, and install applications automatically, making it relatively easy to install and track software.

FreeBSD's Roots, Briefly

FreeBSD had its beginnings when Bell Labs employees Ken Thompson and Dennis Ritchie presented a paper on UNIX at the ACM (Association for Computing Machinery) Symposium on Operating Systems Principles in 1973. A UC Berkeley professor, Robert Fabry, heard their presentation and convinced staff at UC Berkeley to purchase a PDP-11 (a 16-bit computer built by Digital Equipment Corporation, costing nearly $11,000 at the time) to run Thompson's AT&T UNIX. The system's popularity grew and Berkeley faculty and students set up a system to share time on the PDP-11.

With UNIX running on the PDP-11, two Berkeley graduate students, Bill Joy and Chuck Haley, began to write programs for UNIX. UNIX development at Berkeley eventually caught the eye of the US government, and the Department of Defense awarded UC Berkeley a contract to create a customized version of UNIX for use by its contractors working with DARPA (the Defense Advanced Research Projects Agency). Code developed at Berkeley was integrated into the existing AT&T UNIX system to meet the needs of the DARPA project, and Joy was chosen to lead the project, which he did until mid-1982 when he left to co-found Sun Microsystems. (Bill Joy was also the creator of the vi text editor and developed the TCP/IP stack for UNIX.)

Corporate interest in using Berkeley's BSD Unix grew. However, at the time, BSD Unix contained source code from AT&T UNIX, requiring that a license fee be paid to AT&T for its use. This fee was cost-prohibitive for many small companies and liberation from AT&T's license became a priority. Developers were called upon en masse to rewrite and replace the AT&T kernel and utilities.

After considerable coding effort, BSD Unix was free of AT&T code in 1991, but it still lacked six kernel files needed to make it fully functional. These files, originally coded by AT&T, were not easily rewritable. In late 1991, Bill and Lynne Jolitz (two UC Berkeley alumni) coded the six missing files and released 386/BSD. The FreeBSD Project, responsible for development of the FreeBSD operating system, was formed a few months later and based its initial code on the Jolitzes' 386/BSD.

In January of 1992, Berkeley Software Design Inc. (BSDI) began to sell a commercial version of Unix that was also based on 386/BSD. In late 1992 UNIX System Labs (a subsidiary of AT&T responsible for UNIX development) filed a lawsuit against both BSDI and UC Berkeley citing copyright infringement and unauthorized release of trade secrets. A settlement was reached in January of 1994 that required small modifications to be made to the Berkeley code. The resultant code, released as 4.4BSD-Lite, is the foundation of the current FreeBSD.

RESOURCES

Official FreeBSD Handbook
  http://www.freebsd.org/doc/en/books/handbook

Why FreeBSD by Frank Pohlmann
  http://www.ibm.com/developerworks/opensource/library/os-freebsd

A Brief History of FreeBSD by Jordan Hubbard
  http://www.freebsd.org/doc/en_US.ISO8859-1/books/handbook/history.html

REQUIRED

The following are minimum hardware and software requirements needed for a CD install of the FreeBSD operating system. For an official list of supported hardware, visit *http://www.freebsd.org/releases/7.0R/hardware.html*.

☑ x86 based computer with a i80486 processor or higher, or an AMD Am486 processor or higher; 32MB of RAM; at least 2GB hard drive space; a system BIOS that supports booting from CD

☑ CD drive

☑ FreeBSD 7.0-RELEASE install CD1 (ISO image available at *http://www.freebsd.org/where.html*)

OPTIONAL

The following are not required for a basic installation of FreeBSD, but may be needed to run a functional network server:

☑ Network adapter and Internet connection, if you wish to use the ports collection

☑ Registered domain name, if you wish to host a server on the Internet

☑ A second physical hard drive of comparable size to store backups or to mirror the primary hard drive

PREPARATION

Back up all data you wish to retain on the system in which you intend to install FreeBSD. This guide assumes that FreeBSD will be the sole operating system in use on the computer. Make sure that booting from CD is enabled in your system's BIOS settings.

INSTALL

Below are the steps needed to begin the FreeBSD installation process.

1. Insert the FreeBSD CD into the system and reboot. A Welcome to FreeBSD menu should appear. You can either press [ENTER] or let the timer run down to zero.

2. After booting, the country selection menu should appear. Choose your country using the arrow keys and press [ENTER].

3. The sysinstall Main Menu should appear. Choose the **Standard Install** option with the arrow keys and press [ENTER].

4. A message should appear with details about different partitioning schemes. Press [ENTER]. You may see another dialog appear with a warning about incorrect geometry; if so, sysinstall should automatically adjust this. Press [ENTER].

5. For simplicity's sake, we will devote the entire disk to FreeBSD. To do so, press **A**, then press **Q** to finish.

6. Select **Standard** in the Boot Manager dialog to make the drive we just partitioned bootable.

7. The next dialog will explain that we need to create BSD partitions inside the new partition. Press [ENTER], then press **A** to have the editor automatically create the standard partitions. Press **Q** to exit and continue.

8. A dialog will appear asking you to select a distribution type. Scroll down to **User** and press [SPACEBAR] to select it. Another dialog will appear asking if you would like to install the FreeBSD ports collection. Select **yes** and press [ENTER] to proceed. After returning to the Choose Distributions menu, press [TAB] to highlight **OK** and press [ENTER].

9. The next screen will ask you to choose installation media. Since we are using the CD, choose **CD/DVD** and press [ENTER].

10. Finally, you are asked to confirm that you are ready to install. Choose **yes** if you are and press [ENTER]. sysinstall should copy all necessary files to your hard drive.

CONFIGURE

Once sysinstall finishes copying the necessary files to the hard drive, it is time to configure FreeBSD's options.

1. The Congratulations dialog should appear. Press [ENTER].

2. Now you may configure your Ethernet adapter. If you have one installed, select **yes** and press [ENTER]. Otherwise select **no** and proceed to step 5.

3. The next dialog lists the available interfaces. Your installed Ethernet adapter is most likely at the top of the list. If so, simply press [ENTER]; if not, select it and press [ENTER]. sysinstall will ask you if you want to try IPv6 configuration. Select **no** and press [ENTER].

4. You are asked if you want to try DHCP (Dynamic Host Configuration Protocol). Choose **yes** and press [ENTER]. (To do this manually, select **no** and enter your settings.) A screen appears with the cursor at the position labeled *host*. Enter the fully qualified domain name (FQDN) here (for example, *server.example.com*). Replace *server* with a name of your choice and *example.com* with your registered domain name. If this computer will be a server on a domain, enter the domain name in the domain field. If you have not registered a domain name yet or want to set this up later, just leave the domain name field blank and continue (see "Configuring a Static IP" on page 16 to configure later). Finally, press [TAB] until **OK** is highlighted, then press [ENTER] to continue.

5. When asked if you want the machine to be a network gateway, choose **no** and press [ENTER]. A dialog asking if you would like to configure inetd should appear. Choose **no** and press [ENTER].

6. sysinstall will ask if you want to enable SSH (secure shell) login. Choose **yes** and press [ENTER].

7. When asked if you would like to allow anonymous FTP access, choose **no** and press [ENTER].

8. When asked if you would like to configure the machine as an NFS server, choose **no** and press [ENTER].

9. When asked if you want to configure the machine as a NFS client, choose **no** and press [ENTER]. sysinstall will ask to customize system console settings. Choose **no** and press [ENTER].

10. When asked to set the time zone, choose **yes** and press [ENTER]. A dialog appears asking if the CMOS clock is set to UTC. Most likely it is not, so choose **no** and press [ENTER]. Choose the region/country/time zone that your computer is set to and press [ENTER]. sysinstall will ask you to confirm your selections; choose **yes** if everything looks okay and press [ENTER].

11. When asked if you would like to enable Linux binary compatibility, choose **no** and press [ENTER].

12. You are asked if you have a mouse. Since this install is from the command line, choose **no** and press [ENTER].

13. When asked if you would like to browse the applications, choose **no** and press [ENTER].

14. The next dialog asks if you want to add a user account. Choose **yes** and press [ENTER]. Select **user** from the menu and press [ENTER]. The cursor should now be at the login ID field in the following screen. Enter a username of your choice (this will be the account you will use to manage the system), then press [TAB] until the cursor is at the password field and enter a password for this account (a strong one, preferably a combination of numbers and letters, avoiding guessable words), then press [TAB] until the cursor is at the full name field and type in your full name. Now tab again to the field labeled **member groups** and enter the word wheel to allow the user to become root/ administrator with the su command (see "su" on page 225 for details). Tab to **OK** and press [ENTER].

15. You are returned to the User/Group Management menu. Select **exit** and press [ENTER]. A notification will come up telling you to set the system manager's (i.e., *root*) password. Press [ENTER] and enter a password of your choice. (Use a strong one, preferably a combination of numbers and letters, avoiding guessable words.) Retype your password for verification.

16. Finally, sysinstall asks if you would like to set any last options. Choose **no** and press [ENTER]. You should now be at the main menu. Press [TAB] until **exit install** is highlighted and press [ENTER]. When asked if you are sure, choose **yes** before removing the FreeBSD CD from the CD drive. The system should now reboot.

Logging In

Once the system reboots, a login prompt will appear. You may log in as root to perform administrative tasks. When logging in remotely through SSH, you will need to log in as a normal user and then switch user identity to that of the root user using the su command (see "su" on page 225 for details).

Default Search Path

When you type a command at the command prompt, FreeBSD looks in a list of directories for the name of the command you entered and runs the program if a match is found. This list of directories is called the *default search path* or *path environment variable*.

The order in which FreeBSD searches this path is important when installing third-party software, which this book concentrates on. Most third-party program files are put into subdirectories of */usr/local*. The default position of the */usr/local* directory is near the end of the path statement. If a command that is part of a third-party application has the same name as a command that is part of the base FreeBSD command set, it will never run because the FreeBSD command will be found first and always take precedence. Since we'll be installing third-party applications to extend and/or update FreeBSD's base system, it is beneficial to invert the order of the search path. Let's change the order of the default search path for the root user using Easy Editor:

```
# cd /root
# ee .cshrc
```

We'll *comment out* (disable) the default set path statement and enter our own customized one. Scroll down to the set path declaration (~17) and precede it with a hash mark (#) to disable it, then add the alternative path below so that your third-party programs will run even if they have the same names as native FreeBSD commands. The set path statement should now appear as follows:

```
#set path = (/sbin /bin /usr/sbin /usr/bin /usr/games
/usr/local/sbin /usr/local/bin /usr/X11R6/bin)

set path = (/usr/local/sbin /usr/local/bin /usr/sbin
/usr/bin /sbin /bin $HOME/bin)
```

NOTE *The text is wrapped above but each* set path *statement should only occupy a single line in the .cshrc file.*

Save, exit, log out, and log in. You can display the current search path with this command:

```
# echo $path
```

By default, non-root users use the sh *shell* (interface), and root defaults to the tcsh shell. The default search path can be modified for non-root users in the same way. The sh shell stores this setting in the *.profile* file of each user's home directory.

Limiting SSH Access

By default, all users (except the root account) have remote SSH access. To limit SSH access to specific users add `AllowUsers` *username* to the */etc/ssh/sshd_config* file, separating multiple users with spaces. Only users who appear on this line will have remote SSH access.

To do so, open *sshd_config* with Easy Editor:

```
# ee /etc/ssh/sshd_config
```

Add the following line (substitute your names for the usernames in italics):

```
AllowUsers curly larry moe
```

Save and exit (press [ESC] for Easy Editor's main menu). For the above setting to take effect you'll need to reboot (see below) or restart the ssh daemon using the following command:

```
# /usr/rc.d/sshd restart
```

Shutting Down

When shutting down the system, use the `shutdown` command to safely flush the filesystem cache to disk and allow processes to properly terminate. If your system's BIOS supports ACPI (Advanced Configuration and Power Interface), power will also be removed. Log in as root, then enter:

```
# shutdown -p now
```

Rebooting

To reboot the system you may use the `reboot` command as shown below (you will need to be logged in as root).

```
# reboot
```

CONFIGURING A STATIC IP

It is important for a server to have a static IP or permanent address for much the same reason a person needs a phone number: It allows callers or clients to reach the recipient. FreeBSD uses a file named *rc.conf* to establish the system's IP address, among other settings, during system startup. In this section we'll customize the *rc.conf* file to reflect your server's intended configuration.

The *rc.conf* file contains configuration settings for the computer's hostname, network interface cards, and which services to start at boot time. It is important that the settings in this file are correct; a typo here could hamper the system's functionality.

NOTE *The following discussion assumes that you're building your FreeBSD system to function as an Internet server. If this is not the case, then the options we selected during installation should be sufficient and you can skip this section.*

We will cover two scenarios for configuring a static IP address:

- Server behind a NAT (Network Address Translation) router
- Server directly connected to the Internet

A. FreeBSD Server Behind a NAT Router

A small office or home network commonly has one Internet connection that needs to be shared by multiple computers. A NAT router allows the sharing of a single Internet connection within the local (private) network. The router functions as a *firewall*, creating a protected zone in the private network by allowing all traffic out, but only allowing known or solicited traffic in.

Port Forwarding

Most NAT routers provide a port-forward function that forwards traffic received at the router to a computer with a static IP address inside the private network. If, for example, you were hosting a web server, you would need to forward TCP port 80 (the IANA standard for HTTP) to the IP address of your FreeBSD server. (See your router's documentation for details on port forwarding.)

Most NAT routers that support port forwarding have built-in DHCP servers that assign computers in the private network a *dynamic* IP address, one that may change each time the computer logs on to the network.

DHCP works when machines simply need to connect to a network and get the first available IP address, but it's no help to you if you want to use your FreeBSD system as a server. You'll need a *static* (permanent) IP address so that information destined for your server will arrive.

Modifying rc.conf to Specify a Static IP Address

To specify your server's static IP address you'll modify *rc.conf*. But first you need to tell the DHCP server to assign IP addresses in a range that doesn't conflict with the server's IP address.

Your router's DHCP options should allow you to set the starting IP address (consult your router's documentation for details). For this example, we'll use 192.168.1.12 as the starting address for the range of addresses that can be assigned to machines, knowing that numbers are assigned from this address up (.13, .14, .15, and so on). We'll assign 192.168.1.11 as your server's static IP address since it is outside the range of the DHCP server.

Now let's set this in *rc.conf*. Open *rc.conf*:

```
# ee /etc/rc.conf
```

You should see something like the following in your *rc.conf* file (~7). Your FQDN should be here if specified during setup; the *xl0* may be different.

```
hostname="host.example.com"
ifconfig_xl0="DHCP"
```

NOTE   *If you don't already have the hostname set, be sure to set it correctly. The hostname should be your system's fully qualified domain name;* host *is the name of the machine and* example.com *is your registered domain name.*

Insert your router's IP address in the `defaultrouter` statement as shown below (~7). Using our example scenario above, the `hostname`, `ifconfig`, and `defaultrouter` statements should now look like this:

```
hostname="host.example.com"
ifconfig_xl0="inet 192.168.1.11 netmask 255.255.255.0"
defaultrouter="192.168.1.1"
```

Notice that we have replaced "DHCP" with our static IP address and added the netmask address (255.255.255.0 is the default netmask address in most configurations).

We've also added a `defaultrouter` line which points to the NAT router's IP address. This address, 192.168.1.1, will be the IP address you enter into your web browser to access the router web configuration; this is also called the *default gateway*.

Now save and exit. (Skip to "Dynamic DNS" on page 18.)

B. FreeBSD Server Connected Directly to the Internet

If your FreeBSD system is connected directly to a cable or DSL modem and you have correctly entered your FQDN during configuration step 4 above, no further configuration is necessary. However, if you did not enter a hostname during the DHCP configuration, then you will need to edit */etc/rc.conf* to include your FQDN.

Open *rc.conf* with Easy Editor:

```
# ee /etc/rc.conf
```

rc.conf (~7) should look like this (replace *host.example.com* with your FQDN):

```
hostname="host.example.com"
```

Dynamic DNS

Dynamic DNS is a service provided by third-party companies that keeps track of a computer's public IP address. These providers automatically update your domain name's associated IP address if it changes for any reason. Most Internet service providers use DHCP servers to assign public IP addresses to their customers dynamically. Unless you pay for a static IP address, this dynamically assigned address may change from time to time.

When you register your domain name, you can specify the target IP address of your server if you wish to host your own services. Many people mistakenly assume that their current, dynamic IP address will be theirs indefinitely. When your dynamic IP address changes (which may happen frequently or once every few months), you appear to "drop off" the Internet since your domain registrar's records point to the previous IP address, which is no longer valid. You would then have to go back to your domain registrar and notify them of your new IP address to regain your Internet presence (this is usually accomplished through a web-based control panel).

This is where dynamic DNS service providers become useful. These third-party companies allow you to keep your IP address updated by using a client program on your server to detect when the IP changes. When it does, the client program automatically contacts the dynamic DNS service to update your DNS record so you stay "live." When using these services you need to point your domain registrar to your dynamic DNS service's servers, which then point to your updated IP address. Most dynamic DNS providers charge a fee for their services, though there are a few free ones, like ZoneEdit (*http://zoneedit.com*). By combining a dynamic DNS service provider with a dynamic DNS updating client like ddclient, you can provide a static IP–like Internet presence. See "ddclient 3.7.3" on page 65 for information on ddclient.

HOSTS AND RESOLV.CONF

The *hosts* and *resolv.conf* files are used to control how FreeBSD performs DNS lookups. A DNS lookup is like calling a telephone operator: You give the operator a person's name and she gives you a phone number in return. For example, if a web page like *http://www.google.com* is requested, FreeBSD (by default) first consults the *hosts* file (*/etc/hosts*), then the DNS servers specified in *resolv.conf* in order to translate *www.google.com* into an IP address like 66.102.7.99.

Let's take a closer look at each of these files and see how to set them up.

hosts

The *hosts* file *resolves* (translates) hostnames to IP addresses. At minimum, the *hosts* file should be modified to reflect your system's domain name and hostname.

Open the *hosts* file in a text editor:

```
# ee /etc/hosts
```

Your *hosts* file (~14) should look like this (replace *example.com* with your domain name, *host.example.com* with your hostname, and *192.168.1.11* with your IP address):

```
::1             localhost localhost.example.com
127.0.0.1       localhost localhost.example.com
192.168.1.11    host.example.com
```

Save and exit.

Settings in this file only affect the local system. The *hosts* file supplies basic hostname resolution for daemons and other system processes. If you need to provide DNS services, you'll need to use a DNS server. (See "ISC BIND DNS Server 9.4.2" on page 73 for more information.)

resolv.conf

The *resolv.conf* file contains the IP addresses of the DNS servers that your system will query when trying to resolve any hostname whose IP address is not found in the *hosts* file. The addresses in this file are automatically set if you chose DHCP to configure your network adapter during the initial FreeBSD installation. To set this file manually, open it:

```
# ee /etc/resolv.conf
```

The *resolv.conf* file should look something like this, where *example.com* is your domain name, *206.12.29.11* is the IP address of the DNS server, and *192.168.1.11* is the IP address of the backup DNS server (both IP addresses are provided by your ISP):

```
domain example.com
nameserver 206.12.29.11
nameserver 192.168.1.11
```

CONFIG FILES

Following are a few common FreeBSD configuration files important to basic FreeBSD administration:

/etc/rc.conf

Contains most of the common configuration and startup options for *daemons*, which are programs that run in the background to provide a service, such as a web server (Apache) or mail server (Postfix).

/etc/resolv.conf

The resolver configuration file. This contains the DNS servers to query when resolving a hostname to an IP address.

/etc/hosts

The system's hostname to IP address table. This file contains manually entered hostnames and their associated IP addresses. FreeBSD will look at this file prior to querying a DNS server listed in the *resolv.conf* file.

The following two directories contain startup scripts that execute automatically at boot time. These scripts are designed to consult the *rc.conf* file for instructions on whether or not to start services. For example, the */etc/rc.d/sshd* script will look for SSHD_ENABLE="YES" in *rc.conf*. If an enable line exists, rc starts the specified service; otherwise it does not.

/etc/rc.d

This directory contains system startup scripts that execute at boot time.

/usr/local/etc/rc.d

This directory contains third-party startup scripts that execute at boot time.

NOTES

- If you aren't familiar with Unix commands, make sure you consult Appendix A before attempting to go any further in this guide. You'll save yourself a lot of time and frustration. Appendix B contains details on backup and restore, which are very important to any server setup. Appendix D contains details on protocols and terms mentioned throughout this book.

- It is important to monitor FreeBSD security advisories for up-to-date information on known security issues. *Security advisories* are documents that detail security issues with the FreeBSD operating system. To have FreeBSD security advisories emailed to you, visit *http://lists.freebsd.org/mailman/listinfo/ freebsd-security-notifications.*

  Additionally, check FreeBSD's security page: *http://www.freebsd.org/security.*

If a security issue requires a software update, you can update your system with the `freebsd-update` command instead of compiling the source manually.

NOTE *This is meant for binary installations of FreeBSD as mentioned in this book. Visit* http://www.daemonology.net/freebsd-update *for additional information on freebsd-update. It is prudent to back up your system before any update.*

```
# freebsd-update fetch
# freebsd-update install
# reboot
```

After rebooting, display the release level using the following command:

```
# uname -r
```

The release level should match or supersede the release level mentioned in the security advisory.

- See "FreeBSD Ports Collection" on page 23 for more information on the ports collection.

FREEBSD PORTS COLLECTION
HTTP://WWW.FREEBSD.ORG/PORTS

SUMMARY

As you learned in "FreeBSD 7.0" on page 9, the ports collection provides a simple and centralized way of installing software on FreeBSD. It consists of categorized directories containing makefiles that are used by the make command to compile source code into executable programs or libraries. The ports collection is designed to be automated and relatively easy to use.

Ports are maintained by designated port administrators who are responsible for ensuring that each port stays current with the latest version available from the original software author.

Installing software from a port builds the program from its source code; if the source code isn't already on the system, it is downloaded from a site designated in the makefile. The system verifies the contents of the downloaded source code, typically using an MD5 (Message-Digest algorithm 5) hash to ensure its authenticity. An *MD5 hash* is a 32-character alphanumeric string that is like a fingerprint for the file. A typical MD5 hash might look like this: e6c75c12f663a484ee3157ab058cfc9e.

Once the authenticity of the source code has been assured, the make program checks the makefile to see if the port requires any other software. If it does, FreeBSD installs those dependencies as well. Next, patches are applied to the source code, as necessary, before it is compiled and installed.

Once all processes are complete, the port is treated as a FreeBSD package and recorded in the installed packages database, *pkgdb.db*, which is stored in the */var/db/pkg* directory. Information on the FreeBSD package system can be found at *http://www.freebsd.org/doc/en_US.ISO8859-1/books/handbook/ports-overview.html.*

RESOURCES

Using the Ports Collection (FreeBSD Handbook)
   http://www.freebsd.org/doc/en/books/handbook/ports-using.html

Search FreeBSD Ports Collection
   http://www.freebsd.org/ports

portmaster
   http://dougbarton.us/portmaster.html

REQUIRED

☑ FreeBSD 7.0-RELEASE (see "FreeBSD 7.0" on page 9)

☑ FreeBSD 7.0-RELEASE install CD1

☑ Internet connection (you will need to be online if you want to use the ports collection to install applications)

PREPARATION

Become the superuser.

INSTALL

If you installed the ports collection when you installed FreeBSD (as discussed in the previous chapter), skip to the "Configure" section below. Otherwise, insert the FreeBSD CD into the CD drive, then enter the following commands to mount the FreeBSD CD, change to the correct working directory, and install the ports collection to the */usr/ports* directory.

```
# mount /cdrom
# cd /cdrom/7.0-RELEASE/ports
# ./install.sh
```

CONFIGURE

Keeping the ports collection up to date ensures that applications you install via the ports system are the latest versions available. To update the ports collection:

1. Modify the file *ports-supfile*. Specify the server to contact when downloading updates via csup, then copy this configuration file into the */root* directory so that you can find it easily later. To copy the example *ports-supfile* to the */root* directory, enter:

```
# cp /usr/share/examples/cvsup/ports-supfile /root
```

2. Before editing *ports-supfile*, choose a suitable update server. FreeBSD maintains cvsup servers with names like *cvsup2.freebsd.org*, *cvsup3.freebsd.org*, and so on. For a complete list of worldwide CVSup servers, visit *http://www.freebsd.org/doc/en/books/handbook/cvsup.html*.

Using the following command, ping a few servers to find one that is relatively fast.

```
# ping -c 5 cvsup2.freebsd.org
PING cvsup2.us.freebsd.org (130.94.149.166): 56 data bytes
64 bytes from 130.94.149.166: icmp_seq=0 ttl=48 time=85.607 ms
```

The rightmost column in the last line above (time=85.607 ms) displays the time it takes each packet to reach the server and return. The lower the number, the better. Repeat this for a few servers and pick the one with the shortest time.

3. Open the *ports-supfile* and add the name of the server you have chosen. Scroll down to and replace CHANGE_THIS in the *default host declaration with the name of your chosen server. The command below opens *ports-supfile* in Easy Editor:

```
# ee /root/ports-supfile
```

The *default host declaration should appear as follows around line 49 of */root/ports-supfile*:

```
*default host=cvsup4.FreeBSD.org
```

Replace *cvsup4* with the server you chose earlier, then save and exit.

4. To update the ports collection, use this command:

```
# csup -g -L 2 /root/ports-supfile
```

5. Before continuing, we will install the Perl programming language from the ports collection so that we can create the ports index file. To begin the installation, enter the following commands:

```
# cd /usr/ports/lang/perl5.8
# make install clean
# rehash
```

6. After installing Perl, update the ports index and README files with the following commands:

```
# cd /usr/ports
# make readmes && make index
```

This may take more than half an hour to complete, depending on the speed of your system.

You can search the ports collection with the following commands:

```
# cd /usr/ports
# make search name=portname
```

Replace *portname* with the name of an application you would like to find. The output of this command will provide the port name, path, description, and dependencies, among other information. You can also search for ports on the Internet by visiting *http://www.freebsd.org/ports/* or *http://www.freshports.org*.

If you have a web browser like Lynx (see "Lynx 2.8.6" on page 91) installed, you may browse the ports collection via an HTML interface. The following command will use Lynx to open this file.

```
# lynx /usr/ports/README.html
```

portmaster

The portmaster utility allows you to upgrade most installed ports to the current version available in the ports collection without breaking dependencies or links to other programs. For example, the Apache HTTP Server relies on the port eXpat for XML (Extensible Markup Language) support. Upgrading to the latest version of eXpat manually involves removing the previous installation and reinstalling. Doing this will break the Apache HTTP Server install, because its link with eXpat is lost. portmaster will allow you to remove and reinstall eXpat without changing this dependency or the link with the Apache HTTP Server.

To install portmaster from the ports collection, enter the following commands:

```
# cd /usr/ports/ports-mgmt/portmaster
# make install clean
# rehash
```

NOTE *Back up your system before performing any software installation or upgrade. Upgrading installed ports can break things, and having a fresh backup will allow you to revert relatively painlessly. (See Appendix B for information on backup and restore.)*

A list of installed ports that have new versions available in the ports tree can be shown with this command:

```
# portmaster -L | grep -B1 "New version"
===>>> expat-1.95.8
        ===>>> New version available: expat-2.0.0
```

It is a good idea to read */usr/ports/UPDATING* prior to upgrading a port. This text file contains known issues when upgrading certain ports.

To upgrade a specific port (eXpat for example), run the portmaster command as shown below:

```
# portmaster -b expat-1.95.8
```

NOTE *You must specify the old port name as shown in italics above.*

By default, portmaster will prompt you prior to upgrading the specified port. Type **Y** and press [ENTER] to commence the upgrade. Once portmaster completes, you should have a current version of eXpat installed without affecting the Apache HTTP installation.

The -b switch above tells portmaster to keep a backup of the old port in the */root* directory. This can prove useful if you need to revert to the old version of the port. For example, if the new version of eXpat that was installed was 2.0.0 we could use the following commands to revert to the old version:

```
# pkg_delete -f expat-2.0.0
# pkg_add /root/expat-1.95.8.tbz
```

NOTE *The ports collection is constantly updated and changes frequently. Trying to keep your installed ports up to date can be challenging. You should use portmaster only when necessary (e.g., for security updates; see the "portaudit" section below), because incompatibilities may appear when running the latest version of a program in conjunction with software that expects an older version for functionality. To minimize this effect, the* portmaster *command can be run with the* -r *switch, which will upgrade the specified port and any port that depends on it. This switch should be used with caution as it can affect more than the port being upgraded.*

portaudit

The portaudit utility allows you to check your installed ports against a database of published security vulnerabilities. This database is maintained by the FreeBSD port administrators and the FreeBSD Security Team. If a security advisory exists for an installed port, a web link to the security advisory is provided for more information.

To install portaudit, enter:

```
# cd /usr/ports/ports-mgmt/portaudit
# make install clean
# rehash
```

To check installed ports against the current portaudit database, enter:

```
# portaudit -Fda
```

NOTE *When building ports,* make *will check the vulnerability database to ensure that the port you are installing does not have any known security vulnerabilities. If it does, the port will not install and references to the vulnerability (or vulnerabilities) will be provided. If you determine that the installation of the port does not pose a security risk to your system, you may allow installation of the affected port by disabling the vulnerability check temporarily. To disable vulnerability checking when running* make*:*

```
# make -D DISABLE_VULNERABILITIES install clean
```

UTILITIES

Once a port is successfully installed, it is registered in the package database located in */var/db/pkg*. A *package* is a group of files that are installed by a software application. Installed ports are treated as packages after being installed and should be managed as such. The utilities below are used to manage installed packages.

pkg_info

This utility is used to display information about packages installed on the system.

Command   pkg_info

Syntax   pkg_info *-option pkgname*

Options

-a   Shows all installed packages

-r   Shows a list of dependent packages

Examples

To show a list of all installed packages in two-column format, issue the following command:

```
# pkg_info
```

To show the dependencies of a package named *perl-5.8.8*, issue the following command:

```
# pkg_info -r perl-5.8.8
```

To list dependencies of all installed packages, enter:

```
# pkg_info -a -r
```

NOTE   *Output from pkg_info may span several pages. As such, it may be wise to use a text display utility like* less *when dealing with long file listings. The* less *command would allow you to view a long document page by page. See "less" on page 223 for details.*

pkg_delete

This utility is used to remove installed packages or ports.

Command pkg_delete

Syntax pkg_delete *-option pkgname*

Options

-f Forces removal of the installed package, even if it contains dependencies

-r Recursive removal; deletes specified package and dependent packages

Examples

To remove a package named *perl-5.8.8*, enter:

```
# pkg_delete perl-5.8.8
```

To force the removal of a package named *perl-5.8.8* that contains dependencies, enter:

```
# pkg_delete -f perl-5.8.8
```

To remove a package named *perl-5.8.8* along with its dependencies, enter:

```
# pkg_delete -r perl-5.8.8
```

CONFIG FILES

ports-supfile
The configuration file for the optional CVSup system. You'll find an example at */usr/share/examples/cvsup*.

NOTES

Before you install applications via the ports system, make a full backup of the system. This is a good habit, in case the installation doesn't perform the way you expected. (See Appendix B for details on backup procedure.)

PART II

THIRD-PARTY
APPLICATIONS

LEVEL
3

APACHEHTTP
FreeBSD port path: /usr/ports/www/apache22
TCP ports used – HTTP (80), HTTPS (443)

APACHE HTTP SERVER 2.2.8

HTTP://HTTPD.APACHE.ORG

SUMMARY

Apache HTTP Server is an open source web server application regarded as one of the most efficient, scalable, and feature-rich web servers available. Apache is also highly customizable, with numerous third-party modules available to extend its functionality. You'll find modules that add support for SSL (Secure Sockets Layer) encryption over HTTP (HyperText Transfer Protocol), PHP support (PHP is a server-side scripting language), and authentication support for password protecting a site or page.

Apache was born at the NCSA (National Center for Supercomputing Applications) in 1993 when Rob McCool developed a public domain HTTP *daemon* (background process) that would later become the foundation of the Apache project. Apache version 1.3 still contains code from the original NCSA-developed HTTP daemon, while version 2 was rewritten from scratch and contains no NCSA code.

Apache HTTP Server is installed on nearly 53 percent of the world's web servers. Microsoft's Internet Information Server is in second place, with more than a 32 percent share of the server market.[1]

The FreeBSD port of the Apache HTTP server documented here includes support for SSL over HTTP using the mod_ssl module. The module was created by Ralf S. Engelschall in 1998; it is based on software developed by Ben Laurie.

RESOURCES

Official Apache HTTP Server Online Documentation
http://httpd.apache.org/docs/2.2

RFC 2616 – Hypertext Transfer Protocol – HTTP/1.1
http://tools.ietf.org/html/rfc2616

REQUIRED

☑ FreeBSD 7.0-RELEASE (see "FreeBSD 7.0" on page 9)

☑ Updated ports collection (see "FreeBSD Ports Collection" on page 23)

☑ Internet connection

---

[1] Netcraft Ltd., "Netcraft: July 2007 Web Server Survey," *http://news.netcraft.com/archives/2007/07/09/july_2007_web_server_survey.html*

APACHEHTTP
FreeBSD port path: /usr/ports/www/apache22
TCP ports used – HTTP (80), HTTPS (443)

OPTIONAL

☑ OpenSSL with a signed SSL Certificate (if you wish to enable secure HTTP connections; see "OpenSSL 0.9.8g" on page 127)

☑ Registered domain name

PREPARATION

Become the superuser and then make sure your server's hostname is resolvable locally. This should already be the case if you are running your own DNS server and have it configured properly.

If you aren't running your own DNS server, make sure you have an entry in your */etc/hosts* file that points to your server's IP address; this will ensure that your server's hostname is resolvable locally. To do so, open the *hosts* file in a text editor:

```
# ee /etc/hosts
```

You should find something like the following around line 14 of the */etc/hosts* file; replace *example.com* with your domain name, *host.example.com* with your hostname, and *192.168.1.11* with your server's local IP address:

```
::1             localhost localhost.example.com
127.0.0.1       localhost localhost.example.com
192.168.1.11    host.example.com
```

INSTALL

To begin the Apache installation process, enter the following commands:

```
# cd /usr/ports/www/apache22
# make config ; make install clean
# rehash
```

A menu should appear showing options for Apache. We'll leave the settings at their defaults, so press [TAB] to highlight **OK** and then press [ENTER].

CONFIGURE

Once the installation process completes, it is time to configure Apache for use on your system.

1. Open the *httpd.conf* file located in */usr/local/etc/apache22*:

```
# ee /usr/local/etc/apache22/httpd.conf
```

2. We'll edit a few entries in *httpd.conf* to get the HTTP daemon up and running. To do so, scroll to the ServerAdmin declaration (~138) and replace

APACHEHTTP
FreeBSD port path: /usr/ports/www/apache22
TCP ports used — HTTP (80), HTTPS (443)

you@example.com with the email address of the person who will be maintaining the server. The line should appear as follows:

    ServerAdmin *you@example.com*

3. Scroll to the `ServerName` declaration (~147), *uncomment* (remove the leading hash mark), and replace *host.example.com*:80 with the hostname of your server. The line should now appear as follows:

    ServerName *host.example.com*:80

NOTE   *If you do not wish to set up SSL over HTTP, save, exit, and proceed to "Testing" on page 36.*

4. To enable SSL support, uncomment the Secure (SSL/TLS) connections declaration (~449) by removing the hash mark. The line should now appear as follows:

    Include etc/apache22/extra/httpd-ssl.conf

5. Save, exit, and open Apache's SSL configuration file:

    # ee /usr/local/etc/apache22/extra/httpd-ssl.conf

6. Scroll to the `ServerName` and `ServerAdmin` declarations (~78) and replace *host.example.com* with your server's hostname. Replace *you@example.com* with the email address of the person who will be maintaining the server. The two lines should now appear as follows:

    ServerName *host.example.com*:443
    ServerAdmin *you@example.com*

7. Go to the `SSLCertificateFile` declaration (~99) and input the path and filename of your server's SSL Certificate. The line should now appear as follows (replacing the path and filename shown in italics with the path and filename of your SSL Certificate):

    SSLCertificateFile */usr/local/openssl/certs/host.example.com-cert.pem*

8. Go to the `SSLCertificateKeyFile` declaration (~107) and input the path and filename of your server's private SSL key. The line should now appear as follows (replacing the path and filename shown in italics with the path and filename of your private key):

SSLCertificateKeyFile */usr/local/openssl/certs/host.example.com-unencrypted-key.pem*

NOTE   *It is highly recommended that you specify your unencrypted key file here. An encrypted key file will cause Apache to prompt for a password that may interfere with the startup of other critical services. See "OpenSSL 0.9.8g" on page 127 for details on decrypting your key file if you haven't already done so.*

9. Save and exit.

APACHEHTTP
FreeBSD port path: /usr/ports/www/apache22
TCP ports used – HTTP (80), HTTPS (443)

TESTING

In this section, we'll perform some basic tests to confirm that Apache answers HTTP requests properly.

1. Apache includes a utility called apachectl that is capable of testing your configuration files for syntax errors. Let's run this program to check for syntax errors:

```
# apachectl configtest
```

If apachectl returns Syntax OK, continue below. If apachectl finds a problem, it will list the filename, line number, and possible reasons for the error. Be sure to resolve any issues prior to continuing below.

2. We'll configure Apache to start automatically at boot time. To do so, open the *rc.conf* file located in */etc*:

```
# ee /etc/rc.conf
```

Then add the following lines in */etc/rc.conf*:

```
apache22_enable="YES"
apache22_http_accept_enable="YES"
```

Save, exit, and start Apache with this command:

```
# /usr/local/etc/rc.d/apache22 start
```

3. You can choose to conduct your tests via a standard web browser, but the instructions below will conduct tests via the command line. Enter the following commands to connect directly to the HTTP service listening on port 80:

```
# telnet localhost 80
Trying 127.0.0.1...
Connected to localhost.
Escape character is '^]'.
```

The GET command below is case sensitive. Be sure to press [ENTER] twice and input a space before and after the first slash:

```
GET / HTTP/1.0
HTTP/1.1 200 OK
Date: Sat, 01 Mar 2008 02:00:30 GMT
Server: Apache/2.2.8 (FreeBSD) mod_ssl/2.2.8 OpenSSL/0.9.8g DAV/2
Last-Modified: Sat, 20 Nov 2004 20:16:24 GMT
ETag: "cf597-2c-4c23b600"
Accept-Ranges: bytes
Content-Length: 44
Connection: close
Content-Type: text/html
<html><body><h1>It works!</h1></body></html>Connection closed by foreign host.
```

APACHEHTTP
FreeBSD port path: /usr/ports/www/apache22
TCP ports used – HTTP (80), HTTPS (443)

If you see the It works! text in the last line of output then Apache does indeed work!

4. If you configured Apache SSL support, enter the following command to connect to the HTTP server via SSL:

```
# openssl s_client -connect localhost:443
```

The GET command is case sensitive; press [ENTER] twice:

```
GET / HTTP/1.0
```

The output should be identical to the output you received over the unencrypted connection.

UTILITIES

Following is brief information on the apache22 script that should be used to control the Apache daemon on FreeBSD.

apache22

This script is used to control the HTTP daemon.

Command   /usr/local/etc/rc.d/apache22

Syntax   /usr/local/etc/rc.d/apache22 *option*

Options

start   Launches the Apache HTTP server

stop   Stops the Apache server

configtest   Parses the configuration files for syntax errors

restart   Restarts the Apache server

Example

To start the HTTP daemon, issue the following command at the prompt:

```
# /usr/local/etc/rc.d/apache22 start
```

NOTE   *apache22_enable="YES" must exist in* /etc/rc.conf *in order for this script to function.*

CONFIG FILES

/usr/local/etc/apache22/httpd.conf
   The Apache HTTP server's main configuration file

/usr/local/etc/apache22/extra/httpd-ssl.conf
   The Apache HTTP server's SSL configuration file

APACHEHTTP
FreeBSD port path: /usr/ports/www/apache22
TCP ports used – HTTP (80), HTTPS (443)

LOG FILES

/var/log/httpd-access.log
    Contains a log of IP addresses, times, and activity on the HTTP server

/var/log/httpd-error.log
    Contains a log of error messages produced by the HTTP server

/var/log/httpd-ssl_request.log
    Contains a log of IP addresses, times, and activity on the HTTPS server

NOTES

- The HTTP server uses the default port 80 for non-secure communications. The SSL-enabled HTTP server uses the default port 443 for secure communications. If you are behind a NAT router, be sure to forward these ports to your server. (Refer to your router's documentation for details on port forwarding.)

- The default root folder of the HTTP server is *parallel/usr/local/www/apache22/data*. Web content must be placed here unless you change the document root directory in *httpd.conf*.

COURIER-AUTHLIB 0.60.2
HTTP://WWW.COURIER-MTA.ORG/AUTHLIB

SUMMARY

Courier-authlib (the Courier Authentication Library) provides authentication functionality for Courier-IMAP Server (see "Courier-IMAP Server 4.3.0" on page 43). This package makes it possible for Courier-IMAP to authenticate users against the system password file in */etc/master.passwd*. The master password file stores passwords for all user accounts on the system.

Courier-IMAP Server includes both an IMAP (Internet Message Access Protocol) and POP3 (Post Office Protocol version 3) server implementation, and both rely on Courier-authlib for authentication. Username and password information is compared against the system password file located in */etc/master.passwd* using Courier-authlib's `authpam` authentication module. Courier-authlib then consults FreeBSD's built-in PAM (Pluggable Authentication Modules) library to authenticate. If authentication is successful, the user is allowed to access services offered by Courier-IMAP.

RESOURCES

Courier Authentication Library Documentation
http://www.courier-mta.org/authlib/documentation.html

REQUIRED

☑   FreeBSD 7.0-RELEASE (see "FreeBSD 7.0" on page 9)

☑   Updated ports collection (see "FreeBSD Ports Collection" on page 23)

☑   Internet connection

PREPARATION

Become the superuser.

INSTALL

To begin the Courier-authlib installation process, enter the following commands:

```
# cd /usr/ports/security/courier-authlib
# make config ; make install clean
# rehash
```

A menu should appear showing options for Courier-authlib. We will not need any of these optional authentication modules, so press [TAB] to highlight **OK** and then press [ENTER].

CONFIGURE

Once the installation process is complete, it's time to configure the authentication daemon for use on your system.

We will only use the authpam method of authentication.

The next steps remove extraneous authentication modules listed in the *authdaemonrc* configuration file to prevent authdaemond from generating errors in the *maillog* file.

1. Open *authdaemonrc*:

```
# ee /usr/local/etc/authlib/authdaemonrc
```

2. Remove the names of all authentication modules in the authmodulelist declaration (~27) except for authpam. The authmodulelist declaration should now look like this:

```
authmodulelist="authpam"
```

3. Save and exit.

TESTING

In this section, we'll perform a basic test to confirm that Courier-authlib starts properly.

1. Configure Courier-authlib to start automatically at system startup. To load the Courier-authlib daemon at boot time, open *rc.conf*:

```
# ee /etc/rc.conf
```

and add the following line:

```
courier_authdaemond_enable="YES"
```

Save and exit.

2. Start the Courier-authlib daemon and verify that it is running:

```
# /usr/local/etc/rc.d/courier-authdaemond start
# /usr/local/etc/rc.d/courier-authdaemond status
```

If startup is successful, the output of the second command should read:

```
courier_authdaemond is running as pid 12073.
```

Your *pid* (process ID) will be different.

CONFIG FILES

/usr/local/etc/authlib/authdaemonrc
Contains configuration information for authdaemond

LOG FILES

/var/log/maillog
A general log of email activity that includes information from authdaemond

LEVEL
4

COURIERIMAP
FreeBSD port path: /usr/ports/mail/courier-imap
TCP ports used – IMAP (143), IMAP-SSL (993)

COURIER-IMAP SERVER 4.3.0

HTTP://WWW.COURIER-MTA.ORG/IMAP

SUMMARY

Courier-IMAP is an open source IMAP (Internet Message Access Protocol) server that functions in conjunction with an MTA (Mail Transfer Agent) such as Postfix. Courier-IMAP provides access to Maildir mailboxes, a system for email storage first introduced in Qmail.

Courier-IMAP also includes a POP3 (Post Office Protocol version 3) server that provides POP3 protocol access to Maildir mailboxes. POP3 is currently the most popular email retrieval protocol; virtually all email providers support it. A POP3 mail transaction consists of a client-initiated connection to the server, the downloading of messages, deletion of those messages from the server, and connection termination. This method of email retrieval is well suited to users who access their email from the same computer on a consistent basis, but it can be cumbersome for users who need email access from a variety of different computers (e.g., work, home, Internet café, etc.).

IMAP was written by Mark Crispin in 1986 to provide an alternative to POP. Some advantages IMAP provides over POP are on-demand message downloading (only selected messages are downloaded to the client instead of the whole mailbox), support for multiple mailboxes (IMAP users can create and move messages between folders on the server), and portable mailbox access (IMAP users may move between different computers and have full access to their mail; POP users are restricted to the machine where their email was downloaded).

Sam Varshavchik wrote Courier-IMAP in 1999. He did so to provide IMAP support to MTAs employing the Maildir format; none existed at the time.

RESOURCES

Official Courier-IMAP Documentation
http://www.courier-mta.org/imap/documentation.html

RFC 3501 – Internet Message Access Protocol (IMAP)
http://tools.ietf.org/html/rfc3501

RFC 1939 – Post Office Protocol – Version 3 (POP3)
http://tools.ietf.org/html/rfc1939

COURIERIMAP
FreeBSD port path: /usr/ports/mail/courier-imap
TCP ports used – IMAP (143), IMAP-SSL (993)

REQUIRED

☑ FreeBSD 7.0-RELEASE (see "FreeBSD 7.0" on page 9)

☑ Updated ports collection (see "FreeBSD Ports Collection" on page 23)

☑ MTA configured to deliver to Maildir (see "Postfix SMTP Server 2.5.1" on page 163)

☑ Courier-authlib (see "Courier-authlib 0.60.2" on page 39)

☑ Internet connection

OPTIONAL

☑ OpenSSL with a signed SSL Certificate (see "OpenSSL 0.9.8g" on page 127); if you need secure communication between the email client and the server, OpenSSL should be installed before starting

PREPARATION

Become the superuser.

INSTALL

To begin the installation of Courier-IMAP, enter the following commands:

```
# cd /usr/ports/mail/courier-imap
# make config ; make install clean
```

A menu with a list of options for Courier-IMAP will appear. Leave the options at their defaults; press [TAB] to select **OK** and then press [ENTER] to start the installation.

NOTE *Courier-IMAP includes both an IMAP and a POP3 server. This guide will configure both services; if you do not wish to enable a particular server, simply skip to the appropriate part of the "Testing" section (beginning on page 45).*

CONFIGURE

Once the installation process is complete, it's time to configure Courier-IMAP for use on your system.

1. To enable secure communications between Courier-IMAP and email clients, you need to configure SSL Certificates. If you do not wish to enable secure communications, skip to "Testing" on page 45. Courier-IMAP needs the private server key and the server's SSL Certificate combined into a single file. We will assume your private key and server certificates reside in the */usr/local/openssl/certs* directory.

COURIERIMAP
FreeBSD port path: /usr/ports/mail/courier-imap
TCP ports used – IMAP (143), IMAP-SSL (993)

The following commands will merge your private key with your server certificate into a single file that Courier-IMAP can use:

```
# cd /usr/local/openssl/certs
# cp host.example.com-unencrypted-key.pem\
? host.example.com-key-cert.pem
# chmod 400 host.example.com-key-cert.pem
# cat host.example.com-cert.pem >> host.example.com-key-cert.pem
```

host.example.com-unencrypted-key.pem is your server's unencrypted private key file.

host.example.com-key-cert.pem is the combined key and certificate file.

host.example.com-cert.pem is the server's public certificate file.

Change these example filenames to match the naming conventions you used when you created your server key and certificate files with OpenSSL.

2. You will need to tell Courier-IMAP where the combined key-certificate file (the one created in step 1) resides by editing the *imap-ssl* and *pop3d-ssl* files located in */usr/local/etc/courier-imap*. Open and modify the *imap-ssl* file as follows (~257):

```
# ee /usr/local/etc/courier-imap/imapd-ssl

TLS_CERTFILE=/usr/local/openssl/certs/host.example.com-key-cert.pem
```

Save and exit.

3. Open and modify the *pop3d-ssl* file as follows (~244):

```
# ee /usr/local/etc/courier-imap/pop3d-ssl

TLS_CERTFILE=/usr/local/openssl/certs/host.example.com-key-cert.pem
```

Save and exit.

Substitute the appropriate filename for *host.example.com-key-cert.pem* if you used a different naming convention. If the path to this file is different than above, be sure to change that as well. Your certificate file must be in the format *key followed by certificate* (as demonstrated in step 1), with no extraneous text.

TESTING

In this section we'll perform some basic tests to confirm that Courier-IMAP is answering requests properly.

IMAP

You will need the username and password of an account on your system to test IMAP functionality. Ensure the user account you select has an existing Maildir directory. This directory is automatically created by Postfix when it delivers mail to users. If a user has not yet received email, the Maildir directory will be

COURIERIMAP
FreeBSD port path: /usr/ports/mail/courier-imap
TCP ports used – IMAP (143), IMAP-SSL (993)

absent. Use the `maildirmake` command to manually create a Maildir directory in this case. See "maildirmake" on page 48 for details.

1. Check that Courier-IMAP starts and handles requests properly. To enable the IMAP service, modify *rc.conf*. Open the *rc.conf* file located in */etc*:

```
# ee /etc/rc.conf
```

and add one or both of the following lines:

```
courier_imap_imapd_enable="YES"
courier_imap_imapd_ssl_enable="YES"
```

NOTE *If you did not configure Courier-IMAP to use SSL for secure communications, omit the second line.*

To start the IMAP service, enter:

```
# /usr/local/etc/rc.d/courier-imap-imapd.sh start
# /usr/local/etc/rc.d/courier-imap-imapd-ssl.sh start
```

2. Enter the following command to connect to the IMAP server on port 143:

```
# telnet localhost 143

Connected to localhost.
Escape character is '^]'.
* OK [CAPABILITY IMAP4rev1 UIDPLUS CHILDREN NAMESPACE THREAD=ORDEREDSUBJECT
THREAD=REFERENCES SORT QUOTA IDLE ACL ACL2=UNION STARTTLS] Courier-IMAP
ready. Copyright 1998-2005 Double Precision, Inc.  See COPYING for
distribution information.
```

NOTE *This output, the IMAP server connection banner, will appear on a single line.*

Log in using a valid username and password for your system.

```
aa login username password

aa OK LOGIN Ok.
```

The next command is typically sent by mail clients prior to retrieving messages from the mailbox; you'll want to see a response similar to that shown below.

```
ab select inbox

* FLAGS (\Draft \Answered \Flagged \Deleted \Seen \Recent)
* OK [PERMANENTFLAGS (\* \Draft \Answered \Flagged \Deleted \Seen)] Limited
* 2 EXISTS
* O RECENT
* OK [UIDVALIDITY 1129543635] Ok
* OK [MYRIGHTS "acdilrsw"] ACL
ab OK [READ-WRITE] Ok

ac logout
```

COURIERIMAP
FreeBSD port path: /usr/ports/mail/courier-imap
TCP ports used – IMAP (143), IMAP-SSL (993)

```
 * BYE Courier-IMAP server shutting down
ac OK LOGOUT completed
Connection closed by foreign host.
```

If your session looked similar to the one above, then Courier-IMAP is functional.

3. Testing Courier-IMAP with SSL is similar, but uses the OpenSSL command-line tool. (If you did not choose to configure secure communications with SSL, you may proceed to the "POP3" section below.) The following command begins an IMAP session with SSL:

```
# openssl s_client -connect localhost:993
```

Once the connection is established, you may issue the same commands as above to test IMAP-SSL functionality, starting with the command aa login *username password*.

POP3

You will need the username and password of an account on your system to test POP3 functionality. Ensure the user account you select has an existing Maildir directory. This directory is automatically created by Postfix when it delivers mail to users. If a user has not yet received email, the Maildir directory will be absent. Use the maildirmake command to manually create a Maildir in this case. See "maildirmake" on page 48 for details.

1. Check that Courier-IMAP starts and handles requests properly. To enable the POP3 service, open the *rc.conf* file located in */etc*:

```
# ee /etc/rc.conf
```

and add one or both of the following lines:

```
courier_imap_pop3d_enable="YES"
courier_imap_pop3d_ssl_enable="YES"
```

NOTE *If you did not configure Courier-IMAP to use SSL for secure communication, omit the second line.*

To start the POP3 service, enter:

```
# /usr/local/etc/rc.d/courier-imap-pop3d.sh start
# /usr/local/etc/rc.d/courier-imap-pop3d-ssl.sh start
```

2. Enter the following command to connect to the POP3 server on port 110:

```
# telnet localhost 110
```

```
Connected to localhost.
Escape character is '^]'.
+OK Hello there.
```

COURIERIMAP
FreeBSD port path: /usr/ports/mail/courier-imap
TCP ports used – IMAP (143), IMAP-SSL (993)

Log in using a valid username and password for your system.

    user *username*

    +OK Password required.

    pass *password*

    +OK logged in.

The stat command triggers the POP3 server to return what is known as a *drop listing*. The seven (in the drop listing below) signifies the number of messages in the mailbox, followed by the number of bytes these messages consume on disk (in octets). Your output will certainly be different depending on the contents of your mailbox.

    stat

    +OK 7 19775

    quit

At this point, we can assume the POP3 server is functioning correctly.

3. You can test the POP3 daemon with SSL the same way, using the OpenSSL command-line utility. The following command begins a POP3 session over SSL:

    # openssl s_client -connect localhost:995

Once the connection is established, you may issue the same commands as above, starting with the command user *username*, to test POP3 SSL functionality.

UTILITIES

Following is brief information on the maildirmake program, which is used to create a user's initial Maildir directory structure or to add subdirectories to an existing Maildir.

maildirmake

This utility is used to create a user's Maildir directory and subdirectories.

Command   maildirmake

Syntax   maildirmake *-options* Maildir

Options

-f   Create a subdirectory within an existing Maildir

COURIERIMAP
FreeBSD port path: /usr/ports/mail/courier-imap
TCP ports used – IMAP (143), IMAP-SSL (993)

Examples

The following examples assume you are the root user and in the appropriate user's home directory.

To create a new Maildir, enter:

```
# su user
# maildirmake Maildir
# exit
```

In place of *user*, substitute the username of the account for which you are creating the Maildir.

To create a subdirectory named *Junk* within an existing Maildir, use the command:

```
# su user
# maildirmake -f Junk Maildir
# exit
```

In place of *user*, substitute the username of the account for which you are creating the subdirectory.

CONFIG FILES

/usr/local/etc/courier-imap/imapd
The main IMAP configuration file

/usr/local/etc/courier-imap/imapd-ssl
Supplements the main IMAP configuration file with options pertaining to SSL

/usr/local/etc/courier-imap/pop3d
The main POP3 configuration file

/usr/local/etc/courier-imap/pop3d-ssl
Supplements the main POP3 configuration file with options pertaining to SSL

LOG FILES

/var/log/maillog
General log of email activity

COURIERIMAP
FreeBSD port path: /usr/ports/mail/courier-imap
TCP ports used – IMAP (143), IMAP-SSL (993)

NOTES

- If you installed Courier-IMAP without SSL support, be aware that port 143 transmits login and password information "in the clear." This means that it can be obtained by unauthorized persons. If all of your users will be using email clients with SSL support, it may be a good idea to run only the SSL-enabled instance of Courier-IMAP by removing the non-SSL startup line from the /etc/rc.conf file.

  If your server is behind a NAT router, you can enable port forwarding to only port 993. This would allow only SSL connections from outside the local network. Local traffic would still be vulnerable unless you have Standard IMAP disabled as mentioned above.

  If you intend to install a webmail client that uses IMAP (such as Squirrel-Mail; see "SquirrelMail 1.4.13" on page 207) then *do not* disable Standard IMAP functionality on port 143.

  If you choose to remove the non-SSL imapd line from *rc.conf*, remember to stop the non-SSL daemon like this:

  ```
  # /usr/local/etc/rc.d/courier-imap-imapd.sh stop
  ```

- Similarly, if you installed POP3 without SSL support, be aware that port 110 transmits login and password information "in the clear." This means that that it can be obtained by unauthorized persons. If all of your users will be using email clients with SSL support, it may be a good idea to run only the SSL-enabled instance of the POP3 daemon by removing the non-SSL startup line from the /etc/rc.conf file.

  If your server is behind a NAT router, you can enable port forwarding to only port 995. This would allow only SSL connections from outside the local network. Local traffic would still be vulnerable unless you have non-SSL POP3 disabled as mentioned above.

  If you choose to remove the non-SSL pop3d line from *rc.conf*, remember to stop the non-SSL daemon like this:

  ```
  # /usr/local/etc/rc.d/courier-imap-pop3d.sh stop
  ```

LEVEL
4

CUPS
FreeBSD port path: /usr/ports/print/cups
TCP port used – IPP (631)

CUPS PRINT SERVER 1.3.3
HTTP://CUPS.ORG

SUMMARY

The *Common Unix Printing System (CUPS)* is an open source printing system that provides a common interface to support printers in Unix-based systems. It also provides a standardized and modular platform that allows the use of external filters like Foomatic and Ghostscript for expanded printer compatibility. CUPS is licensed under the GNU GPL and has become the standard printing system for a large number of Linux distributions as well as Mac OS X.

CUPS is composed of a print spooler, filters, and backends. It uses the Internet Printing Protocol (IPP) to accept print jobs from clients on the network. The print data is then stored in a print spool or queue until the printer is ready to accept a print job. When the printer is ready, CUPS sends the print job through filters that convert the print job data into a language the printer understands. The converted data then travels through a backend to the intended printer. Common backends include Universal Serial Bus (USB) and parallel interfaces.

Most printers communicate using either PostScript or Printer Control Language (PCL). PostScript was developed at Adobe Systems in the mid-1980s to create a standard language for both document exchange and printer communication. CUPS can print to virtually all printers that support PostScript. However, PostScript printers are notoriously expensive due to the cost of licensing the technology from Adobe. PCL was created by Hewlett-Packard in 1984 and didn't carry the licensing restrictions of PostScript. This has created a large market of low cost PCL printers. To support this large market, projects like Gimp-Print were started to develop Unix drivers for PCL printers. HP has responded to the need for Unix-based drivers with the Hewlett-Packard Inkjet Driver Project. Gimp-Print and the HP Inkjet Driver Project greatly expand CUPS support for non-PostScript printers.

CUPS was created by Michael Sweet and first released in 1999 by Easy Software Products, a company he co-founded with Andrew Senft. CUPS was originally designed around the 30-year-old Line Printing Daemon (LPD) protocol common in Unix systems. The emergence of IPP ultimately resulted in the switch from the LPD protocol to the more scalable IPP protocol.

CUPS
FreeBSD port path: /usr/ports/print/cups
TCP port used – IPP (631)

RESOURCES

CUPS 1.3 User Documentation
http://cups.org/documentation.php

REQUIRED

☑ FreeBSD 7.0-RELEASE (see "FreeBSD 7.0" on page 9)

☑ Updated ports collection (see "FreeBSD Ports Collection" on page 23)

☑ Internet connection

☑ Supported parallel or USB printer (see "Printer Types" on page 58)

☑ Lynx (see "Lynx 2.8.6" on page 91) or other web browser

OPTIONAL

☑ OpenSSL (see "OpenSSL 0.9.8g" on page 127) if you wish to enable secure HTTP connections to the web administration interface

☑ Registered domain name

☑ Local Authoritative DNS server (see "ISC BIND DNS Server 9.4.2" on page 73) if you wish to assign the print server a hostname

PREPARATION

See "Printer Types" on page 58 for information on printer compatibility before proceeding.

Become the superuser.

INSTALL

Enter the following commands to begin the CUPS installation process:

```
# setenv XORG_UPGRADE yes
# cd /usr/ports/print/cups
# make config ; make install clean
# rehash
```

A menu will appear displaying options for cups-base. We will leave these at their defaults, so press [TAB] to select **OK** and then press [ENTER] to continue the installation process.

A GNU Ghostscript driver configuration menu will also appear (more than 30 minutes into the build process). Leave the selections at their defaults unless you have a specific reason to change them. Press [TAB] to select **OK** and then press [ENTER] to continue the installation process.

CUPS
FreeBSD port path: /usr/ports/print/cups
TCP port used – IPP (631)

CONFIGURE

Once the installation process is complete, it's time to configure CUPS for use on your system.

1. FreeBSD includes a print spooling system that utilizes the same command names as CUPS. If the search path has not been modified from its default, the FreeBSD spooler will run instead of CUPS. See "Default Search Path" on page 14 for details on changing the default search path.

2. The phrase "NO_LPR = YES" must be added to the *make.conf* file in */etc*. This tells the FreeBSD make command to skip compilation of the print spooler if you choose to recompile the base operating system. CUPS can be considered a drop-in replacement for the FreeBSD print spooler. The following commands will add this line to *make.conf*:

```
# cp /etc/make.conf /etc/make.conf.old
# echo "NO_LPR = YES" >> /etc/make.conf
```

3. In order to allow print clients to send raw print data to the connected printer you must uncomment a line in the *mime.convs* file located in */usr/local/ etc/cups*. Open *mime.convs* like this:

```
# ee /usr/local/etc/cups/mime.convs
```

Scroll down to the application/octet-stream declaration (~109) and remove the hash mark (#) to uncomment the line. It should now appear as follows:

```
application/octet-stream   application/vnd.cups-raw    0     -
```

Save and exit.

4. You are now ready to modify the main configuration file, *cupsd.conf*, located in */usr/local/etc/cups*. To open *cupsd.conf*, enter:

```
# ee /usr/local/etc/cups/cupsd.conf
```

Change the Listen localhost:631 declaration (~18) to Listen *:631. This allows external clients access to the CUPS web administration page. This line should appear as follows after the modification:

```
Listen *:631
```

5. By default, access to CUPS services is restricted and needs to be relaxed to enable printing support to computers on the local network. Change the Allow localhost declaration (~32) within the Location / container to Allow @LOCAL. The line should appear as follows after the modification:

```
# Restrict access to the server...
<Location />
  Order allow,deny
  Allow @LOCAL
</Location>
```

53

CUPS
FreeBSD port path: /usr/ports/print/cups
TCP port used – IPP (631)

6. By default, access to the administrative web interface is closed to the local network and can only be accessed from the server itself. To allow access from the local network, change the `Allow localhost` declaration (~39) within the `Location /admin` container to `Allow @LOCAL`. You should also add `Require user @SYSTEM` to require authentication for access to the web administration page. The lines should appear as follows after the modification:

```
# Restrict access to the admin pages...
<Location /admin>
  Encryption Required
  Require user @SYSTEM
  Order allow,deny
  Allow @LOCAL
</Location>
```

NOTE *The root account and users that are members of the wheel group will be able to log in to the web administration page at* https://host.example.com:631/admin *(substitute your server's hostname or IP address for* host.example.com*) to manage printers and print jobs. CUPS will encrypt authentication credentials using a self-signed certificate. You may specify your own SSL Certificate if you like. See "SSL Certificates" on page 60 for details.*

7. Save and exit.

TESTING

In this section we'll perform some basic tests to confirm that CUPS starts properly before attempting to configure printers.

1. To configure CUPS to start automatically at system startup, open the *rc.conf* file located in */etc*:

```
# ee /etc/rc.conf
```

then add the following line:

```
cupsd_enable="YES"
```

Save your changes and run the startup script:

```
# /usr/local/etc/rc.d/cupsd start
```

2. Test the server by pointing a web browser to *http://host.example.com:631* (substituting your server's hostname or IP address for *host.example.com*). You should see a Common Unix Printing System Welcome! page if the server started successfully; if you don't, check your *cupsd.conf* file for typographical errors.

3. If you are using a PostScript printer, have its PPD (PostScript Printer Description) file handy and skip to step 8. If you don't have your printer's PPD file, check *http://openprinting.org*.

CUPS
FreeBSD port path: /usr/ports/print/cups
TCP port used – IPP (631)

NOTE *PPD files are usually shipped with the software that came with the printer. You may be able to find them on the manufacturer's website or at* http://linuxprinting.org. *CUPS stores these files in the* /usr/local/share/cups/model *directory.*

4. If you are going to be using a non-PostScript printer with CUPS, you will need to install printer drivers. If your printer is supported by either the Gutenprint or HPLIP (Hewlett-Packard Linux Imaging and Printing) driver, proceed to the appropriate section. If your printer is not supported by either of these two drivers, skip to step 7 and specify *Raw* as the printer make in step 10.

Gutenprint Driver

5. The Gutenprint driver contains extensive support for Epson printers (among others). Visit *http://gutenprint.sourceforge.net* for a complete list of supported printers. The following commands will install the Gutenprint driver from the ports collection (this may take 30 minutes or more to complete):

```
# cd /usr/ports/print/gutenprint
# make install clean
```

A menu will appear containing options for Gutenprint; highlight **Gutenprint Cups Drivers** and press [SPACEBAR] to put a tick in its box. Leave the other options at their defaults: Press [TAB] to highlight **OK** and then press [ENTER]. Once the installation is complete, proceed to step 8 below. You may install the HPLIP driver as well, if you wish.

HPLIP Driver

6. The HP Linux Imaging and Printing driver was developed at Hewlett-Packard, and it contains support for virtually all HP printers. Visit *http://hplip.sourceforge.net* for a complete list of supported printers. The following commands will install the HPLIP printer driver from the ports collection (this may take 60 minutes or more to complete):

```
# cd /usr/ports/print/hplip
# make config ; make install clean
```

A menu will appear containing options for HPLIP. Leave them at their defaults: Press [TAB] to highlight **OK** and then press [ENTER] to continue installation.

Finishing Printer Setup

7. Ensure that your printer is powered on and connected to the CUPS server via a USB or parallel cable. Reboot the system. Log in as root to the web administration interface *https://host.example.com:631/admin* (substitute your server's hostname or IP address for *host.example.com*).

8. Select **Add Printer**. Choose a name for the connected printer (write this name down; you will need it when you set up client printing). You may enter a

CUPS
FreeBSD port path: /usr/ports/print/cups
TCP port used – IPP (631)

location if you wish (e.g., upstairs office). Enter a description of the printer (e.g., HP LaserJet 1100). Click **Continue**.

9. There should be a pull-down menu on the next page. Select either USB or LPT (parallel) as appropriate and then click **Continue**.

10. Select the correct brand (make) of your printer on the next page, then click **Continue**.

11. Choose the correct model from the list presented on the next page, then click **Continue**.

12. Your printer should be ready to accept print jobs. You can print a test page from the Printers page of the CUPS web interface.

Proceed to the appropriate section to set up client printing.

Printing from Windows XP

1. To print to a CUPS printer from Windows XP, click the **Start** menu and select **Control Panel**.

2. Double-click the Printers and Faxes icon.

3. Click **Add a Printer** at the left side of the window. The Welcome to the Add Printer Wizard dialog will appear; click **Next**.

4. Click the *Network Printer* radio button, then click **Next**.

5. Click the *Connect to a Printer on the Internet or on a Home or Office Network* radio button. In the URL field, use the following syntax to specify the server address: *http://host.example.com:631/printers/printername* (substitute the hostname or IP address of your CUPS server for *host.example.com* and replace *printername* with the name you assigned the printer during the CUPS printer setup).

6. After clicking **Next**, you will be required to select the printer make and model from a list. If you have a Windows driver from the manufacturer, use it; otherwise select it from the given list and click **OK**.

7. You should be able to print via the CUPS print server from Windows applications.

Printing from Mac OS X

1. Open an application capable of printing (e.g., Safari).

2. In the **File** menu, select **Print**.

3. Select the **Printer** pull-down menu to display a list of available printers. You should see Shared Printers in the lower half of the menu.

CUPS
FreeBSD port path: /usr/ports/print/cups
TCP port used – IPP (631)

4. Hover the mouse over **Shared Printers** to display the submenu.

5. Select the appropriate CUPS printer from the list. The CUPS printer will be added to your permanent list of printers.

6. You can print the current document by clicking **Print** on the lower-right side of the dialog box.

Printing from the FreeBSD Command Line

You can print the contents of a file to the CUPS-configured printer at the FreeBSD command line with the following command:

```
# lp -d printername filename
```

Replace *printername* with the name of the CUPS printer you'd like to print to. Replace *filename* with the path and filename of the file you wish to print.

ADMINISTRATION

To administer CUPS, enter one of the following URLs, replacing *host.example.com* with your hostname or CUPS server IP address.

http://host.example.com:631 (printer and print job status)

https://host.example.com:631/admin (CUPS administration over SSL)

CONFIG FILES

/usr/local/etc/cups/cupsd.conf
The main configuration file of the CUPS print server

LOG FILES

/var/log/cups/access_log
Contains IP addresses, times, and activity on the CUPS web interface

/var/log/cups/error_log
Contains error and status messages produced by the CUPS print server

/var/log/cups/page_log
Contains a log of printers, who printed to them, when, number of pages, and their IP addresses

CUPS
FreeBSD port path: /usr/ports/print/cups
TCP port used – IPP (631)

NOTES

The following sections include a brief explanation of the two general classes of printers, some options for printing restrictions, and coverage of SSL Certificates and the lptcontrol utility.

Printer Types

In general, two categories of printers exist, PostScript and PCL. PostScript is an industry-standard page description language. The language was developed by Adobe Systems in the mid-1980s to allow the sharing of electronic documents while preserving formatting and appearance. It is similar to the PDF (Portable Document Format), also developed by Adobe. PostScript printers are usually more expensive than non-PostScript printers. High-end business laser printers usually include PostScript support. PCL printers include most consumer-oriented inkjet and laser printers. Most low-cost printers do not support the PostScript language. This means drivers must be installed that are specific to the make and model of the printer. Finding and installing drivers compatible with the CUPS system can be a challenging task. This guide provides installation instructions for the Gutenprint and HPLIP drivers. Many popular consumer printers are covered by at least one of these two drivers.

The CUPS system contains native support for virtually all PostScript printers provided you have the matching PostScript Printer Description file for the printer. The PPD file is usually included with the software that is bundled with the printer. Many PPD files are also freely available at *http://linuxprinting.org*.

If you own an Epson, Canon, Lexmark, or other PCL-based printer, check *http://gutenprint.sourceforge.net* to see if your printer is supported by the Gutenprint driver. If you own an HP printer, check *http://hplip.sourceforge.net* to see if your printer is supported by the HPLIP driver. If your printer is from another manufacturer, check *http://linuxprinting.org* to see if your printer is supported by another CUPS-compatible driver.

If your printer is not supported by a CUPS-compatible driver, you may still print to it using the CUPS server, provided:

- All intended print clients are running Microsoft Windows
- A Windows-compatible printer driver is available on each system

This is possible because CUPS has the capability to send raw data to the connected printer. The Windows driver sends the data to be printed in the correct printer language; CUPS then relays this data to the connected printer.

To configure CUPS to send raw data to the connected printer, select **Raw** when specifying the printer make in step 10 of "Testing" (page 56). Complete the rest of the guide normally.

CUPS
FreeBSD port path: /usr/ports/print/cups
TCP port used – IPP (631)

Printing Restrictions

Restrictions to printing may be enforced with authentication and/or access rules based on client IP address. For example, to restrict printing to authenticated users only, add the lines below to the end of the *cupsd.conf* file in */usr/local/etc/cups*. To open *cupsd.conf*, enter:

```
# ee /usr/local/etc/cups/cupsd.conf
```

Scroll down to the bottom of the *cupsd.conf* file using [CTRL-U] and add the following lines:

```
<Location /printers>
AuthType Basic
AuthClass User
</Location>
```

Save and exit.

With these settings in place, users will be required to provide a username and password to send jobs to any printer.

NOTE   *Users must have their own system-level account to authenticate. Username and password information is sent in the clear; consider using access rules if you do not want authentication information sent insecurely over the network.*

Access rules may be used to allow access to printers based on a client's originating IP address. For example, to restrict printing to IP addresses 192.168.0.1 and 192.168.0.2 only, add the lines below to the end of the *cupsd.conf* file in */usr/local/etc/cups*. To open *cupsd.conf* enter:

```
# ee /usr/local/etc/cups/cupsd.conf
```

Scroll down to the bottom of the *cupsd.conf* file using [CTRL-U] and add the following lines:

```
<Location /printers>
Order Deny,Allow
Deny From All
Allow From 192.168.0.1
Allow From 192.168.0.2
</Location>
```

Save and exit.

The aforementioned methods of print restrictions are very basic. If you need more functionality or flexibility, consider using Samba to manage print privileges. See "Samba 3.0.28" on page 185 for more information.

CUPS
FreeBSD port path: /usr/ports/print/cups
TCP port used – IPP (631)

SSL Certificates

You can use an existing SSL Certificate with CUPS instead of the self-signed certificate CUPS generates for use with the secure web administration interface. Add the following lines to *cupsd.conf* in */usr/local/etc/cups*. Substitute the path- and filenames of your server certificate and key files.

```
ServerCertificate /usr/local/openssl/certs/host.example.com-cert.pem
ServerKey /usr/local/openssl/certs/host.example.com-unencrypted-key.pem
```

host.example.com-cert.pem is the server's public SSL Certificate file.

host.example.com-unencrypted-key.pem is the server's private unencrypted key file.

lptcontrol

The lptcontrol utility controls how the LPT printer driver sends data to the printer. This does not apply to USB printers. By default, the LPT printer driver uses interrupt-driven mode. This works satisfactorily with most printers. Some printers, however, exhibit problems with this mode. If you experience slower than typical print times, you might try changing the default interrupt-driven mode to polling mode with the following command:

```
# lptcontrol -p -d /dev/lpt0
```

You may add this line to */etc/rc.local* to automatically set LPT port polling mode at boot time, if necessary.

CYRUS SASL 2.1.22

HTTP://ASG.WEB.CMU.EDU/SASL

SUMMARY

SASL (Simple Authentication and Security Layer) is a system for adding authentication support to connection-based protocols. For the purposes of this book, we will be using this mechanism for the Simple Mail Transfer Protocol (SMTP). The Postfix MTA employs SMTP to transfer Internet email. Adding authentication support to Postfix is important for users who wish to relay email through their server from an unsecured public network. A secure mail relay can be attained by coupling SASL with SSL/TLS-based encryption.

By default, the Postfix MTA is not an open email relay. While this prevents unauthorized users from using the server to relay spam, it also prevents legitimate users from sending email from a location other than the local private network. Cyrus SASL allows the SMTP server to verify the identity of remote users. Once authenticated, users are allowed remote relay privileges.

John Myers, a former systems architect at Carnegie Mellon University, published the SASL specification in October 1997. Cyrus SASL is maintained under Project Cyrus at Carnegie Mellon.

RESOURCES

Official Cyrus SASL Website at Carnegie Mellon University
http://asg.web.cmu.edu/sasl/

REQUIRED

☑   FreeBSD 7.0-RELEASE (see "FreeBSD 7.0" on page 9)

☑   Updated ports collection (see "FreeBSD Ports Collection" on page 23)

☑   Internet connection

PREPARATION

Become the superuser.

NOTE   *This guide is relevant for the configuration of Cyrus SASL with the Postfix MTA, and it assumes that you intend to utilize SASL with SMTP coupled with SSL/TLS encryption to secure the PLAIN and/or LOGIN authentication methods.*

INSTALL

You will be installing the Cyrus SASL authentication server, which includes Cyrus SASL. To begin the installation of the Cyrus SASL authentication server, type the following commands:

```
# cd /usr/ports/security/cyrus-sasl2-saslauthd
# make config ; make install clean
# rehash
```

A menu should appear showing options for Cyrus SASL. We will leave these settings at their defaults, so press [TAB] to highlight **OK** and then press [ENTER].

CONFIGURE

Once the installation process is complete, it's time to configure Cyrus SASL for use on your system.

1. Create a file named *smtpd.conf.* The *smtpd.conf* file is used by Cyrus SASL when it is configured to work with the Postfix MTA. Create the file:

```
# ee /usr/local/lib/sasl2/smtpd.conf
```

and add these two lines to it:

```
pwcheck_method: saslauthd
mech_list: plain login
```

The first line directs Cyrus SASL to use the SASL authentication server that you installed. The second line tells Cyrus SASL to announce only PLAIN and LOGIN methods when a client initially connects to the SMTP server.

2. Save and exit.

TESTING

In this section, we'll enable the SASL authentication server to start at boot time, then perform a test to confirm that it is running.

1. To configure the SASL authentication server to start automatically at boot time, open *rc.conf.*

```
# ee /etc/rc.conf
```

and add the following startup lines:

```
saslauthd_enable="YES"
saslauthd_flags="-a pam"
```

2. Save your changes and test by running the startup script:

```
# /usr/local/etc/rc.d/saslauthd start
# /usr/local/etc/rc.d/saslauthd status
```

If the SASL authentications server is running, you'll see:

```
saslauthd is running as pid 1234.
```

The pid (process ID) will vary.

CONFIG FILES

/usr/local/lib/sasl2/smtpd.conf

This file controls the behavior of the SASL daemon when used with the Postfix MTA. It stores parameters that tell Cyrus SASL what method of authentication to announce to SMTP clients.

DDCLIENT 3.7.3

HTTP://DDCLIENT.SOURCEFORGE.NET

SUMMARY

ddclient is an open source program written in Perl. It is used to automatically update dynamic DNS (domain name system) entries for a variety of dynamic DNS service providers. When ddclient detects that the system's IP address has changed, it sends the new IP address information to your designated dynamic DNS service provider. This enables systems with dynamically assigned IP addresses to maintain resolvability (stay reachable) by the Internet domain name system, regardless of IP address changes made by their ISPs.

ddclient supports many dynamic DNS service providers, including the following:

BroadbandReports (*http://www.dslreports.com*)

DNS Park (*http://dnspark.com*)

DynDNS (*http://www.dyndns.com*)

easyDNS (*http://www.easydns.com*)

Namecheap (*http://www.namecheap.com*)

ZoneEdit (*http://zoneedit.com*)

ddclient includes native support for several brands of NAT routers. It stays updated by extracting current IP information from the router's built-in status page. If your router is unsupported, ddclient can be configured to retrieve system IP address information via the Web. This guide provides information on retrieving IP address information via the Web rather than using your router's status page.

Paul Burry originally wrote ddclient and remains one of five developers who maintain the project on SourceForge.net.

RESOURCES

Official ddclient Home Page
http://ddclient.sourceforge.net

REQUIRED

☑ FreeBSD 7.0-RELEASE (see "FreeBSD 7.0" on page 9)

☑ Updated ports collection (see "FreeBSD Ports Collection" on page 23)

☑ Internet connection

☑ Registered domain name

☑ Dynamic DNS update service (see "Summary" on page 65 for a list of providers)

PREPARATION

Become the superuser.

INSTALL

To begin the installation of ddclient, enter the following commands:

```
# cd /usr/ports/dns/ddclient
# make install clean
# rehash
```

CONFIGURE

Once the installation process is complete, it's time to configure ddclient for use on your system.

1. Copy the file *ddclient.conf.sample* to *ddclient.conf*, where you'll configure it for use. Enter the following commands to accomplish this:

```
# cd /usr/local/etc
# cp ddclient.conf.sample ddclient.conf
# ee ddclient.conf
```

2. Scroll down and uncomment the use=web declaration (~51) by removing the hash mark (#) at the beginning of the line. The line should appear as follows:

```
use=web, web=checkip.dyndns.org/, web-skip='IP Address' # ...
```

This line tells ddclient to obtain current IP address information from *http://checkip.dyndns.org*. DynDNS hosts a public service that returns your public IP address when an HTTP request is made to *http://checkip.dyndns.org*. Using this information, ddclient keeps your DNS records current.

3. Scroll down and find your dynamic DNS update provider (~89). Uncomment each appropriate line and provide your login, password, and registered domain name (or names) as shown in bold below. (Remove the hash mark for each line; do not modify lines beginning with two hash marks.) Below is an example of a dyndns.org configuration:

```
##
## dyndns.org custom addresses
##
## (supports variables: wildcard,mx,backupmx)
##
custom=yes,                          \
server=members.dyndns.org,           \
protocol=dyndns2                     \
login=username                       \
password=password                    \
example.com
```

Save and exit.

4. Since *ddclient.conf* contains the password of your dynamic DNS provider, make it readable only to root, like this:

```
# chmod 600 /usr/local/etc/ddclient.conf
```

TESTING

The following basic tests will show whether ddclient performs as expected.

1. To start ddclient automatically at boot time, edit the *rc.conf* file in */etc.* Open *rc.conf*:

```
# ee /etc/rc.conf
```

and add the following startup lines:

```
ddclient_enable="YES"
ddclient_flags="-daemon 600"
```

The ddclient_flags="-daemon 600" statement means that ddclient will check your public IP every 600 seconds (10 minutes), but you may use any value you feel is reasonable. (See "Notes" on page 68 for details on this value.)

2. Save your changes and run the startup script:

```
# /usr/local/etc/rc.d/ddclient.sh start
```

3. Enter this command to confirm that ddclient is running:

```
# ps -ax | grep ddclient

p0  S     0:00.05 ddclient - sleeping for 300 seconds (perl)
```

You may repeat the ps command to check the status of ddclient at any time. After the sleep time expires, ddclient should check your public IP address and make the appropriate changes to your dynamic DNS provider. Status emails will be sent to the root account's email address. (If you set up forwarding of root's email in the */etc/aliases* file, check that email address for status updates.)

CONFIG FILES

/usr/local/etc/ddclient.conf
This is the main configuration file for ddclient.

/usr/local/etc/ddclient.cache
This file saves the last known public IP address of the system so ddclient knows when your dynamic DNS provider needs to be updated. This file is located in */var/tmp*.

LOG FILES

/var/log/messages
ddclient records status messages as well as errors to this file.

NOTES

- Setting the daemon update time to 600 seconds is reasonable. If you set this value too low, it will cause unnecessary traffic from your system. Setting this value too high will delay DNS updates to your dynamic DNS provider.

- When creating an account with a dynamic DNS service provider, avoid using a login and/or password that matches any account on your system. When ddclient updates your public IP address, it may transmit your username and password to your dynamic DNS service provider in the clear (unencrypted). If an attacker analyzed your network traffic, this information could be used to compromise the security of your system. Later versions of ddclient (including version 3.7) support SSL encrypted connections to dynamic DNS providers.

DRUPAL 5.5

HTTP://DRUPAL.ORG

SUMMARY

Drupal is an open source web-based *Content Management System (CMS)*. Content management systems can be used to organize, store, and distribute various kinds of content, including web pages, images, audio, and documents. Modern CMS applications like Drupal make it relatively easy for users to add, remove, and modify content. This provides a viable platform for company intranet sites and even personal blogs. Drupal is written in PHP and stores content in a MySQL (or PostgreSQL) database.

Some of Drupal's features include role-based permissions, a template/theme system, version control, and built-in site analytics. It also has a powerful module/plug-in system that allows third-party developers to extend the default feature set. If you need functionality that isn't included with Drupal's default feature set, it is probably available as a module.

Early Drupal development began in 2000 when Dries Buytaert, a student at the University of Antwerp, built a web-based bulletin board system that he and his friends used to share notes. After graduation, Buytaert continued to add features, and in 2001, he released Drupal as an open source project. Drupal's popularity has increased steadily over the years; it is now deployed on many sites, such as those for *The Onion*, *Forbes* magazine, and the Electronic Frontier Foundation. In 2006, Drupal's developers numbered over 400, with Buytaert serving as the project lead.

RESOURCES

Drupal Handbooks (documentation and video tutorials on using Drupal)
http://drupal.org/handbooks

REQUIRED

- ☑ FreeBSD 7.0-RELEASE (see "FreeBSD 7.0" on page 9)
- ☑ Updated ports collection (see "FreeBSD Ports Collection" on page 23)
- ☑ Apache HTTP server (see "Apache HTTP Server 2.2.8" on page 33)
- ☑ PHP 5 (see "PHP 5.2.5" on page 145)
- ☑ MySQL 5 (see "MySQL Server 5.0.51" on page 99)

☑   Lynx (see "Lynx 2.8.6" on page 91)

☑   Internet connection

☑   Registered domain name

PREPARATION

1. Become the superuser.

2. Create a database in MySQL named *drupal*. Next, create a user named drupal and assign full privileges to this user:

```
# mysql -u root -p
mysql> create database drupal;
mysql> grant all on drupal.* to
    -> drupal@localhost identified by 'password';
mysql> quit
```

Replace *password* with a password of your choice (the single quotes are required). You'll need this password later.

INSTALL

Enter the following commands to begin the Drupal installation:

```
# cd /usr/ports/www/drupal5
# make config ; make install clean
```

A menu with options for Drupal will appear. We will leave them at their defaults, so press [TAB] to highlight **OK** and then press [ENTER] to start the installation.

CONFIGURE

Once installation is complete, it's time to configure Drupal for use on your system.

1. Create a Drupal-specific Apache configuration file. This file points Apache to the correct location of the Drupal files and makes administration easier by keeping Drupal-specific options separate from the main *httpd.conf* file. By default, Apache searches the */usr/local/etc/apache22/Includes* directory for configuration files. Here's how to create one for Drupal:

```
# ee /usr/local/etc/apache22/Includes/drupal.conf
```

Add the following lines:

```
Alias /drupal "/usr/local/www/drupal5/"

<Directory "/usr/local/www/drupal5/">
Options Indexes FollowSymLinks
AllowOverride All
Order allow,deny
Allow from all
</Directory>
```

NOTE *By default, Drupal is set up as a subdirectory of your web server's root site. This means you would enter* http://host.example.com/drupal *into your web browser. To change this default directory, replace* drupal *(in italics) with a different name.*

Save and exit. Restart Apache to commit the changes:

```
# /usr/local/etc/rc.d/apache22 restart
```

2. A line needs to be added to */etc/crontab* to allow Drupal's maintenance tasks to run automatically. Crontab is a system service that allows automatic execution of scripts or programs according to a schedule specified in the */etc/crontab* file.

```
# ee /etc/crontab
```

Add the following line:

```
45 */4 * * * root /usr/local/bin/lynx http://host.example.com/drupal/cron.php
```

Replace *host.example.com/drupal* with your hostname and Drupal directory. This line will run the Drupal maintenance script every four hours.

NOTE *Make sure Lynx is installed or this won't execute properly.*

Save and exit.

3. Open *http://host.example.com/drupal/install.php* in your favorite web browser, substituting your hostname and directory (if you modified it).

4. Change the database type to **mysqli** then enter the database name, username, and password that you set in "Preparation" on page 70. Click **Save configuration**.

5. You should see a Drupal Installation Complete page. Click the **your new site** link and follow the instructions to complete your Drupal installation.

CONFIG FILES

usr/local/www/drupal5/sites/default/settings.php
Holds the username, password, and database information for Drupal

NOTES

When logging in as the Drupal site administrator for the first time, you may notice *Cron maintenance tasks* in red on the status report page. This indicates a possible misconfiguration. The crontab entry we made in step 2 will eventually run and correct this error condition. You may click the **manually run** link if you wish to execute the script sooner, and thus remove the warning.

LEVEL
5

ISCBIND
FreeBSD port path: /usr/ports/dns/bind94
TCP port used – DNS (53) | UDP port used – DNS (53)

ISC BIND DNS SERVER 9.4.2

HTTP://WWW.ISC.ORG/SW/BIND

SUMMARY

BIND (Berkeley Internet Name Domain) is the most widely used DNS server application on the Internet. Slightly over 79 percent of DNS servers use BIND DNS, according to a survey conducted by the Internet Systems Consortium (ISC) in July 2007. Microsoft came in second at 16 percent.[1] The domain name system is responsible for the conversion of domain names, such as *http://unorthodocs.net*, into routable IP addresses like 69.226.238.99. It is considered one of the most critical components of the Internet.

BIND version 9 was a total rewrite of the BIND package that addressed architectural issues and known security problems in previous versions. New features in BIND 9 include DNS Security (DNSSEC), multiprocessor support, support for IPv6, protocol enhancements, and better portability.

BIND also supports dynamic DNS updates (as per RFC 2136). When coupled with the Internet Systems Consortium's DHCP server, dynamic DNS allows real-time updates to the DNS server's zone files as DHCP clients join the network. This gives DHCP clients the luxury of having a locally or publicly resolvable hostname.

BIND was originally conceived as a graduate student project at the University of California, Berkeley in the early '80s. UC Berkeley worked on BIND in cooperation with Digital Equipment Corporation for a few years. Paul Vixie, of Digital Equipment Corporation, later became principal programmer of the BIND project. BIND was passed on to the Internet Systems Consortium (ISC), a nonprofit corporation led by Vixie, who now continues to develop the BIND system independently.

We'll be building a local master authoritative name server for your domain name. This will also provide the benefits of a caching name server. A *caching name server* is basically a DNS relay: It has no zone files of its own and must get DNS information from other DNS servers (also called *forwarders*). Both authoritative and caching name servers store DNS queries in a cache to make subsequent requests faster.

A master authoritative name server also has a zone file (a list of known IP addresses) for your domain. When a DNS query is received for your domain, BIND looks at your zone file and returns the requested information. If the query is for a domain other than yours, the query is forwarded to other DNS servers specified in your forwarder's configuration.

---

[1] See the results of the Internet Systems Consortium's ongoing survey at *http://www.isc.org/ds*.

ISCBIND
FreeBSD port path: /usr/ports/dns/bind94
TCP port used – DNS (53) | UDP port used – DNS (53)

RESOURCES

BIND 9 Administrator Reference Manual
http://www.isc.org/sw/bind/arm94

RFC 1034 – Domain Names: Concepts and Facilities
http://tools.ietf.org/html/rfc1034

RFC 1035 – Domain Names: Implementation and Specification
http://tools.ietf.org/html/rfc1035

The FreeBSD Handbook
http://www.freebsd.org/doc/en_US.ISO8859-1/books/handbook/network-dns.html

REQUIRED

- ☑ FreeBSD 7.0-RELEASE (see "FreeBSD 7.0" on page 9)
- ☑ Updated ports collection (see "FreeBSD Ports Collection" on page 23)
- ☑ Internet connection
- ☑ Registered domain name
- ☑ Public or private static IP address
- ☑ Your ISP's DNS server addresses

OPTIONAL

- ☑ DHCP server (see "ISC DHCP Server 3.0.5" on page 85)

PREPARATION

1. Become the superuser.

2. BIND 9.4.2 is part of the standard FreeBSD 7.0 distribution. Check the current version of BIND available in the ports collection with the command:

```
# cat /usr/ports/dns/bind94/Makefile | grep PORTVERSION
```

If this version supersedes 9.4.2, proceed to the "Install" section below. If it is equal to 9.4.2, skip to "Configure."

INSTALL

To overwrite the base installation of BIND with the version available in the ports collection, use the following commands:

```
# cd /usr/ports/dns/bind94
# make config ; make install clean
```

ISCBIND
FreeBSD port path: /usr/ports/dns/bind94
TCP port used – DNS (53) | UDP port used – DNS (53)

A menu should appear displaying options for bind94. Press [SPACEBAR] to select the **REPLACE_BASE** option; leave other options at their default. Press [TAB] to select **OK** and then press [ENTER] to continue the installation process.

CONFIGURE

Once the installation process is complete, it's time to configure BIND for use on your system.

1. Add the statement "NO_BIND = YES" to the *make.conf* file located in */etc*. The following commands will append this statement to *make.conf* or create the file if it does not exist:

```
# cp /etc/make.conf /etc/make.conf.old
# echo "NO_BIND = YES" >> /etc/make.conf
```

This tells the make command not to build the base version of BIND if you rebuild FreeBSD from source, preventing the system from downgrading BIND to that older version.

2. We need to edit the *named.conf* file in */var/named/etc/namedb*. Open the file:

```
# ee /var/named/etc/namedb/named.conf
```

3. Scroll down and comment the listen-on declaration with two forward slashes (//). This allows BIND's named daemon to answer both external and local DNS queries; the default behavior is to answer only local queries. This line (~21) should appear as follows:

```
//      listen-on       { 127.0.0.1; };
```

4. Scroll down and remove the forward slash and asterisk (/*) on the line above the forwarders declaration. Replace *127.0.0.1* with your ISP's nameservers. Separate nameserver entries with a semicolon (;). Also remove the asterisk and forward slash (*/) following the forwarders declaration. The forwarders declaration (~43–47) should look like this (of course, your IP addresses will be different):

```
forwarders {
        202.13.68.62;68.103.31.52;
};
```

5. Scroll down to the bottom of *named.conf* and add the following lines to add your forward lookup zone (substitute your domain name for *example.com*):

```
zone "example.com" {
    type master;
    file "master/example.com";
    allow-transfer { localhost; };
    allow-update { key rndc-key; };
};
```

ISCBIND
FreeBSD port path: /usr/ports/dns/bind94
TCP port used – DNS (53) | **UDP port used – DNS (53)**

NOTE *A feature of BIND called* dynamic DNS updates *allows BIND and the ISC DHCP server to work together and add/remove entries to your zone files automatically as clients join and leave your local network. If you want to enable dynamic DNS updates with ISC DHCP, then change the italicized* master *(in the* file *line of the preceding code) to* dynamic. *Refer to "ISC DHCP Server 3.0.5" on page 85 for details on the ISC DHCP server.*

6. If you are connected directly to the Internet (no NAT router) and have a dynamic public IP address, then skip to step 8. If you are connected directly to the Internet with a static IP address or have a static local IP address behind a NAT router, add the following lines below the forward lookup zone you specified in step 5. This will define your reverse lookup zone.

```
zone "1.168.192.in-addr.arpa" {
    type master;
    file "master/example.com.rev";
    allow-transfer { localhost; };
    allow-update { key rndc-key; };
};
```

Substitute the first three octets of your server's static IP address in reverse order for *1.168.192*. The above example is correct if your local network uses the IP subnet 192.168.1.*XXX*. Substitute your domain name for *example.com*.

NOTE *If you plan to enable dynamic DNS updates (ISC DHCP required), change the italicized* master *(in the* file *line of the above code) to* dynamic.

7. Write down the reverse zone's name (1.168.192.in-addr.arpa, in this example). You will need it later when you create the reverse zone file. Save and exit.

8. Create the *rndc.key* file and append its contents to the bottom of the *named.conf* file. The *rndc.key* file is an encryption key that the rndc utility needs in order to function; it is also used to authenticate the DHCP server to BIND when communicating dynamic DNS updates. The following commands will create the key and append it to *named.conf*:

```
# rndc-confgen -a
# cd /var/named/etc/namedb
# cp named.conf named.conf.old
# cat rndc.key >> named.conf
```

9. Create the master forward lookup zone file. Replace *example.com* with your domain name; it must match the domain name you specified in step 5.

```
# cd /var/named/etc/namedb/master
# ee example.com
```

ISCBIND
FreeBSD port path: /usr/ports/dns/bind94
TCP port used – DNS (53) | UDP port used – DNS (53)

This is the *example.com* forward lookup zone file, followed by explanations of each line:

```
$TTL    3600

example.com.   IN    SOA   host.example.com.   root.example.com. (

                            1       ;     Serial
                            10800   ;     Refresh
                            3600    ;     Retry
                            604800  ;     Expire
                            86400 ) ;     Minimum TTL
;DNS Servers
example.com.        IN    NS              host.example.com.

;Machine Names
host.example.com.   IN    A               192.168.1.11

;Aliases
www                 IN    CNAME           host.example.com.

;MX Record
example.com.        IN    MX      10      host.example.com.
```

NOTE *Any line preceded by a semicolon (;) is ignored by BIND.*

```
$TTL    3600
```

TTL (or Time To Live) is 3,600 seconds. This is the amount of time for which other DNS servers should cache information from this zone.

```
example.com.   IN    SOA     host.example.com. root.example.com. (
```

example.com. is the forward zone name.

IN is a data type that means *Internet data.*

SOA stands for *start of authority.*

host.example.com. is the hostname of computer that holds this zone file.

root.example.com. is the email address of the person responsible for the zone (in zone files, the @ symbol is used to represent the zone name, so the period is used to separate the username from the domain name in the email address).

```
(    The left parenthesis indicates the start of the SOA record.

    1    ;    Serial
```

The serial number is a number you can choose; it is usually increased by one every time you make a change to the zone file. You may use a date (in the format YYYYMMDD) instead.

ISCBIND
FreeBSD port path: /usr/ports/dns/bind94
TCP port used – DNS (53) | UDP port used – DNS (53)

```
    10800    ;        Refresh
```

If there is a slave server configured, this is the number of seconds it waits before contacting this master server for an update.

```
    3600     ;        Retry
```

This is the number of seconds a slave server would wait before retrying a connection to the master server if it ever loses contact.

```
    604800   ;        Expire
```

If the slave server cannot contact the master server within this time, in seconds, it will stop answering DNS queries.

```
    86400  ) ;        Minimum TTL
```

This is the amount of time in seconds that a negative answer is cached. If a client tries to resolve a host that does not exist, the server will answer negatively until this time runs out before actually trying to resolve the address again.

```
    ;DNS Servers
    example.com.    IN      NS              host.example.com.
```

example.com. is the forward zone's name or domain name.

NS is a record type meaning *nameserver.*

host.example.com. is the fully qualified domain name of the nameserver. (The period at the end means the FQDN is absolute; without it, named would automatically append *example.com* to it—so don't forget the period.)

```
    ;Machine Names
    host.example.com.    IN      A          192.168.1.11
```

host.example.com. is the FQDN of a host on the domain.

A is a record type meaning a *host address.*

192.168.1.11 is the IP address of the host (IP addresses don't need terminating periods; they are considered absolute).

```
    ;Aliases
    www                  IN      CNAME      host.example.com.
```

www is the FQDN of the aliased host on the domain. (Notice that there is no period after www; named will automatically append the domain *example.com.* If this is confusing, you may simply type *www.example.com.* here instead.)

CNAME is a record type meaning *canonical name* for an alias.

host.example.com. is the actual hostname of the alias.

ISCBIND
FreeBSD port path: /usr/ports/dns/bind94
TCP port used – DNS (53) | UDP port used – DNS (53)

```
;MX Record
example.com.          IN      MX      10      host.example.com.
```

example.com. is the MX's domain name.

MX is a record type meaning *mail exchanger.*

10 is the priority of the specified mail server. (Email destined for your domain will be directed to the highest priority mail server, then lower priority mail servers; the lower number is the higher priority.)

host.example.com. is the FQDN of mail server (no IP addresses).

NOTE   *Be sure to double-check the spelling, punctuation marks, and syntax of your forward lookup zone file. BIND will not function correctly if the zone file contains errors.*

10. When you finish creating your forward lookup zone file, save and exit.

11. We will construct the reverse lookup zone file called *example.com.rev.* If you did not specify one in *named.conf* (step 6), skip to "Testing" on page 80. This file contains the same basic information as the forward lookup zone file. All A and CNAME record types now become PTR records. Replace *example.com* with your domain name; it must match the domain name you specified in step 5.

```
# ee example.com.rev
```

This is the *example.com.rev* reverse lookup zone file in the */var/named/etc/ namedb/master* directory, followed by explanations of items not previously covered:

```
$TTL    3600

1.168.192.in-addr.arpa. IN  SOA host.example.com.  root.example.com.   (

                              1       ;       Serial
                              10800   ;       Refresh
                              3600    ;       Retry
                              604800  ;       Expire
                              86400 ) ;       Minimum TTL
;DNS Servers
1.168.192.in-addr.arpa.   IN      NS              host.example.com.

;Machine IPs
11                        IN      PTR             host.example.com.
11                        IN      PTR             www.example.com.
```

The elements in this file are explained in detail below.

```
      1.168.192.in-addr.arpa. IN  SOA host.example.com.  root.example.com.
```

1.168.192.in-addr.arpa. is the reverse zone's name. It should match what you entered in the *named.conf* file (refer to step 7 on page 76).

ISCBIND
FreeBSD port path: /usr/ports/dns/bind94
TCP port used – DNS (53) | UDP port used – DNS (53)

```
;DNS Servers
1.168.192.in-addr.arpa.   IN    NS           host.example.com.
```

The DNS server NS record should point to the reverse zone's name. An @ symbol here would work too. In the context of DNS zone files, the @ symbol represents the zone's name.

```
;Machine IPs
11              IN    PTR           host.example.com.
```

11 is the last octet of *host.example.com*'s IP address.

PTR is a record type meaning *pointer.*

Notice the 11 above does not end with a period. It will be automatically prefixed to this file's zone name (1.168.192.in-addr.arpa.). The result will point *host.example.com* to a reverse IP of 11.1.168.192.in-addr.arpa.. When your reverse zone file is complete, save and exit.

12. If you will not be enabling dynamic DNS updates, skip to "Testing." BIND will expect the forward and reverse zone files to be stored in the */var/named/ etc/namedb/dynamic* directory. Copy these two zone files to the */var/named/etc/ namedb/dynamic* directory like this:

```
# cd /var/named/etc/namedb/master
# cp example.com ../dynamic
# cp example.com.rev ../dynamic
# chown -R bind /var/named/etc/namedb/dynamic
```

Be sure to substitute your domain name for *example.com*.

TESTING

In this section, we'll perform some basic tests to confirm that BIND answers DNS requests properly.

1. Modify the first nameserver entry in the *resolv.conf* file to point to the loopback or localhost address (127.0.0.1). This will force the system to query the local DNS server before attempting to query other DNS servers.

```
# ee /etc/resolv.conf

domain example.com
nameserver 127.0.0.1
nameserver 61.32.24.84
nameserver 206.13.22.96
```

NOTE   *You may specify a maximum of three nameservers.*

Save and exit.

ISCBIND
FreeBSD port path: /usr/ports/dns/bind94
TCP port used – DNS (53) | UDP port used – DNS (53)

2. Configure named to start automatically at boot time. To start named automatically at boot time, open the *rc.conf* file in */etc*:

```
# ee /etc/rc.conf
```

and add the following line:

```
named_enable="YES"
```

Save and exit.

3. Start the named daemon and conduct DNS query tests.

```
# /etc/rc.d/named start
```

4. Perform a basic DNS query for *google.com*:

```
# dig google.com

; <<>> DiG 9.4.1 <<>> google.com.
;; global options:  printcmd
;; Got answer:
;; ->>HEADER<<- opcode: QUERY, status: NOERROR, id: 31313
;; flags: qr rd ra; QUERY: 1, ANSWER: 3, AUTHORITY: 4, ADDITIONAL: 4

;; QUESTION SECTION:
;google.com.                    IN      A

;; ANSWER SECTION:
google.com.             246     IN      A       72.14.207.99
google.com.             246     IN      A       64.233.167.99
google.com.             246     IN      A       64.233.187.99

;; AUTHORITY SECTION:
google.com.             339294  IN      NS      ns2.google.com.
google.com.             339294  IN      NS      ns3.google.com.
google.com.             339294  IN      NS      ns1.google.com.
google.com.             339294  IN      NS      ns4.google.com.

;; ADDITIONAL SECTION:
ns4.google.com.         87732   IN      A       216.239.38.10
ns1.google.com.         86787   IN      A       216.239.32.10
ns2.google.com.         88494   IN      A       216.239.34.10
ns3.google.com.         344254  IN      A       216.239.36.10

;; Query time: 1 msec
;; SERVER: 127.0.0.1#53(127.0.0.1)
;; WHEN: Sat Jun  7 01:43:03 2008
;; MSG SIZE  rcvd: 212
```

The line in bold toward the end of the output confirms that this DNS query was answered by the local DNS server.

ISCBIND
FreeBSD port path: /usr/ports/dns/bind94
TCP port used – DNS (53) | UDP port used – DNS (53)

5. The next command initiates a DNS query known as a zone transfer; this will test the forward lookup zone file (substitute your domain name):

```
# dig example.com axfr

; <<>> DiG 9.4.1 <<>> example.com axfr
;; global options:  printcmd
example.com.          3600    IN      SOA     host.example.com.
example.com.          3600    IN      MX      10 host.example.com.
example.com.          3600    IN      NS      host.example.com.
host.example.com.     3600    IN      A       192.168.1.11
www.example.com.      3600    IN      CNAME   host.example.com.
example.com.          3600    IN      SOA     host.example.com.
;; Query time: 1 msec
;; SERVER: 127.0.0.1#53(127.0.0.1)
;; WHEN: Sat Jun  7 09:58:01 2008
;; XFR size: 6 records (messages 1, bytes 189)
```

Although your results will be different, examine this output to verify whether your DNS server returns the correct information. If you run into trouble, check */var/log/messages* with a text editor for named-related messages and/or errors. Most problems are zone file syntax errors.

UTILITIES

Following is brief information on the rndc program, which is used to control the named daemon.

rndc

This utility controls the operation of the nameserver (named).

Command   rndc

Syntax   rndc *option*

Options

flush   Flushes the DNS server's cache

reload   Reloads the configuration file and zones

stop   Saves updates to zone files and stops the server

status   Displays the status of the server

Example

To flush the DNS server's cache:

```
# rndc flush
```

ISCBIND
FreeBSD port path: /usr/ports/dns/bind94
TCP port used – DNS (53) | UDP port used – DNS (53)

CONFIG FILES

/var/named/etc/namedb/named.conf
> The main configuration file for named

/var/named/etc/namedb/rndc.key
> Contains the encryption key used by the rndc utility to issue commands to named; also used for authenticating ISC's DHCP server when applying dynamic DNS updates

LOG FILES

/var/log/messages
> Contains error and status messages produced by the named daemon

NOTES

- If you intend to run your own public authoritative Internet DNS server, you will need a public static IP address from your Internet provider (which costs more). Your domain registrar will need this static IP address to forward your zone's DNS queries to your DNS server. If you can't or choose not to get a public static IP address, you will need to use the services of your domain name registrar or a third party to host a zone file for your domain name. You may still run your DNS server to be authoritative locally (within your private network) without a public static IP address.

- If you are going to be running a locally authoritative DNS server and you utilize DHCP to configure your network clients, be sure to modify your DHCP server's configuration to point clients to your server's IP for DNS resolution. This will ensure that clients on your local domain benefit from your DNS server's cache and zone information. If you are behind a NAT router and don't intend to use your DNS server authoritatively on the Internet, keep port 53 closed in your router's configuration (this should already be the default).

LEVEL 4

ISCDHCP
FreeBSD port path: /usr/ports/net/isc-dhcp3-server
TCP port used – DHCP (67) | UDP port used – DHCP (67)

ISC DHCP SERVER 3.0.5

HTTP://WWW.ISC.ORG/SW/DHCP

SUMMARY

DHCP (Dynamic Host Configuration Protocol) provides network clients with an automated method of obtaining the configuration parameters necessary to communicate with other systems in an IP (Internet Protocol) based network. The parameters a DHCP server commonly provides to clients include IP address assignments, DNS server addresses, and default routers or gateway addresses.

When a client system first joins a network using DHCP, it broadcasts a request to the local network for configuration information. The DHCP server then answers this request with the parameters set in the DHCP server configuration file. The client system applies this assigned configuration to its network interface in order to communicate with the network.

DHCP servers generally assign IP addresses in one of two ways: statically or dynamically. The *static* method allocates an IP address to a client based on the client's hardware MAC (Media Access Control) address. This IP address will not change. A *dynamic* IP address assignment is a leased address. The DHCP server assigns these addresses from a pool or range set by the administrator. Dynamic IP addresses are returned to the pool when a client disconnects from the network. If the same client rejoins the network, it may be assigned a different IP address if the previously assigned address is unavailable.

DHCP first appeared in October 1993 as a replacement for BOOTP (Bootstrap Protocol). Version 1 of ISC's DHCP server was released by Ted Lemon in December 1997. ISC's DHCP implementation remains one of the most popular and robust open source DHCP solutions.

RESOURCES

Ted Lemon's Paper on the ISC DHCP Distribution (dated 1998)
http://www.isc.org/sw/dhcp/dhcp-freenix.php

ISC DHCP Version 3 README
http://www.isc.org/sw/dhcp/dhcpv3-README.php

RFC 1541 – Dynamic Host Configuration Protocol
http://tools.ietf.org/html/rfc1541

The FreeBSD Handbook
http://www.freebsd.org/doc/en_US.ISO8859-1/books/handbook/
network-dhcp.html

ISCDHCP
FreeBSD port path: /usr/ports/net/isc-dhcp3-server
TCP port used – DHCP (67) | UDP port used – DHCP (67)

REQUIRED

☑ FreeBSD 7.0-RELEASE (see "FreeBSD 7.0" on page 9)

☑ Updated ports collection (see "FreeBSD Ports Collection" on page 23)

☑ Internet connection

☑ Your ISP's DNS server addresses

☑ IP address of your router or default gateway; to find this information:

```
# netstat -rn | grep default
```

OPTIONAL

☑ Authoritative BIND DNS server, if you wish to enable dynamic DNS updates (see "ISC BIND DNS Server 9.4.2" on page 73)

PREPARATION

If you plan on running your own DNS server, install and configure it prior to starting this guide. Become the superuser.

INSTALL

To begin the ISC DHCP server installation process, enter the following commands:

```
# cd /usr/ports/net/isc-dhcp3-server
# make config ; make install clean
# rehash
```

A menu of options will appear. Leave these options at their defaults (unless you have a specific need to change them), press [TAB] to highlight **OK**, and then press [ENTER].

CONFIGURE

Once the installation process is complete, it's time to configure DHCP for use on your system.

1. We need to copy the default configuration file *dhcpd.conf.sample* to a new file named *dhcpd.conf*. Then we'll open it and customize the DHCP server's configuration. Enter the following commands to make the copy and open the file for editing:

```
# cd /usr/local/etc
# cp dhcpd.conf.sample dhcpd.conf
# ee dhcpd.conf
```

ISCDHCP
FreeBSD port path: /usr/ports/net/isc-dhcp3-server
TCP port used – DHCP (67) | UDP port used – DHCP (67)

2. Scroll down to the `domain-name` option and replace *example.org* with your domain name. Replace *ns1.example.org* and *ns2.example.org* with the IP addresses of the DNS servers you'd like the DHCP server to assign to clients. You may use your own DNS server IPs here, or those of your ISP. The two lines (~7) would appear as follows if your domain name was *example.com* and your DNS server IPs were *192.168.1.11* and *61.32.24.84*:

```
option domain-name "example.com";
option domain-name-servers 192.168.1.11, 61.32.24.84;
```

3. Scroll down and uncomment the `authoritative` directive by removing the leading hash mark (#) to make the DHCP server authoritative. The line (~15) should look like this:

```
authoritative;
```

NOTE *Make sure no other DHCP server is on the network. Most routers have a built-in DHCP server; disable it before starting "Testing" on page 89.*

4. Scroll down to the `ddns-update-style` option and change `ad-hoc` to `none` to disable dynamic DNS updates. To enable dynamic DNS updates, change this to `interim` (you must have a local BIND DNS server with dynamic DNS updates configured for this to work). The line (~18) should look like this if dynamic DNS updates are enabled:

```
ddns-update-style interim;
```

5. Scroll down to the second subnet declaration (~32). You should see the following:

```
subnet 10.254.239.0 netmask 255.255.255.224 {
range 10.254.239.10 10.254.239.20;
option routers rtr-239-0-1.example.org, rtr-239-0-2.example.org;
}
```

These lines specify the IP address subnet, netmask, range, and routers that will be assigned to DHCP clients. Modify these lines to fit your desired network setup. As an example, we will use the subnet *192.168.1.0* and netmask *255.255.255.0*. We'll set the DHCP IP range from *192.168.1.12* to *192.168.1.62*. We will assume the router's (default gateway) IP address is *192.168.1.1*. After modifying the lines above, we now have the following:

```
subnet 192.168.1.0 netmask 255.255.255.0 {
range 192.168.1.12 192.168.1.62;
option routers 192.168.1.1;
}
```

6. By default, the *dhcpd.conf* file contains numerous lines of examples that should be commented out or removed. For simplicity, remove all subsequent lines following the subnet declaration mentioned above.

ISCDHCP
FreeBSD port path: /usr/ports/net/isc-dhcp3-server
TCP port used – DHCP (67) | UDP port used – DHCP (67)

7. The next two sections are optional. The first explains how to set static IP addresses so certain DHCP clients will always receive the same IP address; the second enables dynamic DNS updates. In order for the latter to work, ensure the BIND DNS server is configured for dynamic DNS updates. See "ISC BIND DNS Server 9.4.2" on page 73 for details. You may skip to the appropriate section or save, exit, and proceed to "Testing" on page 89 if you do not wish to configure either of these options.

Static IP Assignments

This section shows how to assign a static IP address to a DHCP client. This is useful for devices like network-attached printers.

1. To assign a static (or fixed) IP address assignment to a host (computer) via DHCP, obtain its hardware MAC address. The MAC address can be obtained a number of different ways. On FreeBSD and Macintosh OS X systems, use the `ifconfig` command (on Macintosh, launch the Terminal program and type `ifconfig` at the prompt). The MAC address of each interface will follow the `ether` statement. On a Windows system, use the command `ipconfig /all` at the command prompt; the MAC address of each respective interface will be listed following `Physical Address`.

2. Add the following lines to the end of the *dhcpd.conf* file. Replace *desktop01.example.com* with the target system's hostname, its MAC address, and the IP address you wish to assign. The static IP declaration should appear like this:

```
host desktop01.example.com {
    hardware ethernet 08:00:07:26:c0:a5;
    fixed-address 192.168.1.10;}
```

NOTE *The fixed-address can also be an FQDN if you have an authoritative DNS server with an appropriate entry in the zone's DNS lookup file. Do not assign IP addresses that fall within the range of IPs used for dynamically assigned IPs. In the sample configuration above, the declared range is from 192.168.1.12 to 192.168.1.62; thus 192.168.1.10 would be acceptable while 192.168.1.13 would not.*

You may add multiple static IP address assignments using the same format as above. To enable dynamic DNS updates, proceed to the next section; otherwise save, exit, and skip to "Testing" on page 89.

Dynamic DNS Updates

This section shows how to enable dynamic DNS updates with the ISC BIND DNS server.

1. Copy the contents of the *rndc.key* file into the *dhcpd.conf* file. This will allow the DHCP daemon to encrypt communications with the DNS server when

ISCDHCP
FreeBSD port path: /usr/ports/net/isc-dhcp3-server
TCP port used – DHCP (67) | UDP port used – DHCP (67)

updates are necessary. The following commands will append the contents of *rndc.key* to *dhcpd.conf*, assuming the *rndc.key* file is in its default location:

```
# cd /usr/local/etc
# cp dhcpd.conf dhcpd.conf.old
# cat /var/named/etc/namedb/rndc.key >> dhcpd.conf
```

2. Add two zone declarations to the bottom of the *dhcpd.conf* file. If *dhcpd.conf* isn't already open, type:

```
# ee /usr/local/etc/dhcpd.conf
```

Scroll down to the bottom of the *dhcpd.conf* file using [CTRL-U] and add the following lines:

```
zone example.com. {
     primary 192.168.1.11;
     key rndc-key;
}
zone 1.168.192.in-addr.arpa. {
     primary 192.168.1.11;
     key rndc-key;
}
```

Replace *example.com.* and *1.168.192.in-addr.arpa.* with the names of your forward and reverse lookup zone files. The IP addresses above should point to your BIND DNS server (you may use 127.0.0.1 if your DNS server exists on the same computer). If you did not create a reverse lookup zone file, then simply omit the reverse zone declaration.

3. Add the following line to *dhcpd.conf* if you set up any static IP assignments. This will allow DHCP to update DNS with static assignments.

```
update-static-leases on;
```

Save and exit.

TESTING

In this section, we'll perform some basic tests to confirm that the DHCP server answers DHCP requests properly.

1. If you have an existing DHCP server on your network, disable it before proceeding. Most consumer NAT routers have one built in and turned on by default. The following command will start the DHCP server in debug mode; this allows you to see DHCP messages in real time.

```
# dhcpd -f -d
```

Power on and connect a client system to the network and watch for a DHCPREQUEST followed by a DHCPPACK. You should see real-time DHCP requests and

ISCDHCP
FreeBSD port path: /usr/ports/net/isc-dhcp3-server
TCP port used – DHCP (67) | UDP port used – DHCP (67)

acknowledgments. If a client system is already running, you can force a DHCP renewal by rebooting.

Because the DHCPREQUEST and DHCPACK responses contain both assigned IPs and MAC addresses, you should be able to verify static IP assignments, if you configured any. To quit this mode, press [CTRL-C].

2. If you enabled dynamic DNS updates, try using the host command to resolve client IP addresses with their hostnames. Assuming a computer named *desktop01* is not declared in a DNS zone file previously, you could use the following command to resolve its IP address:

```
# host desktop01.example.com

desktop01.example.com has address 192.168.1.13
```

If you get a host not found message, verify you have renewed that computer's DHCP lease by rebooting it or forcing a renewal with the operating system specific utility. Also, check the messages log file (located in */var/log*) for errors from named or dhcpd when troubleshooting.

3. Configure the DHCP server to start automatically at boot time. To do this, open the *rc.conf* file in */etc*:

```
# ee /etc/rc.conf
```

and add the following line:

```
dhcpd_enable="YES"
```

Save, exit, and start DHCP with this command:

```
# /usr/local/etc/rc.d/isc-dhcpd start
```

CONFIG FILES

/usr/local/etc/dhcpd.conf
Main configuration file for dhcpd

LOG FILES

/var/db/dhcpd.leases
A database of leases dhcpd has issued

/var/log/messages
Contains error and status messages from the dhcpd daemon

LYNX 2.8.6
HTTP://LYNX.ISC.ORG

SUMMARY

Lynx is a text-based web browser capable of accessing Internet resources or content on local filesystems. It is distributed as open source software under the GNU General Public License. Lynx supports connections via the http, gopher, ftp, wais, nntp, finger, and telnet protocols. Secure HTTP with SSL is supported.

Highlighting is accomplished with keyboard arrow keys instead of a mouse. Once a hyperlink is highlighted, it may be followed by pressing [ENTER].

Lynx began as a project of the University of Kansas in 1989. The university wanted to create a campus-wide information system. Lynx was developed as an interface to this information-sharing project. Connections to the campus network were made using Unix-based consoles that did not support graphical interfaces. Early versions of Lynx supported a proprietary hypertext format; this feature was subsequently dropped after support for HTML was added.

Lou Montulli, Charles Rezac, and Michael Grobe were the initial designers of Lynx at the University of Kansas. They have since moved on to other pursuits. Lynx was adopted by an international team of volunteers in 1994; they continue Lynx development today.

RESOURCES

Lynx Users Guide
 http://lynx.isc.org/current/lynx2-8-7/lynx_help/Lynx_users_guide.html

REQUIRED

☑ FreeBSD 7.0-RELEASE (see "FreeBSD 7.0" on page 9)

☑ Updated ports collection (see "FreeBSD Ports Collection" on page 23)

☑ Internet connection

PREPARATION

Become the superuser.

INSTALL

To begin the Lynx installation process, enter the following commands:

```
# cd /usr/ports/www/lynx
# make install clean
# rehash
```

CONFIGURE

This section configures Lynx for use with SSL-encrypted HTTP connections. If you do not need or wish to use this feature, you may begin using Lynx by typing:

```
# lynx
```

In order to avoid errors when visiting SSL-encrypted websites, a file named *cert.pem* containing public certificates of Trusted Root Certification Authorities needs to be present in the */usr/local/openssl/certs* directory. This file can be constructed by exporting an existing collection of trusted root certificates from another operating system, namely Microsoft Windows XP or Macintosh OS X.

Microsoft Windows XP

To export trusted root certificates from a Windows XP system:

1. Click the **Start** menu and open the Control Panel.

2. Double-click the Internet Options icon.

3. Click the Content tab then click the **Certificates...** button.

4. Click the Trusted Root Certification Authorities tab.

5. Click the first entry in the list and then scroll down to the end of the list. While holding the [SHIFT] key, click the last entry in the list. This will select all of the listed certificates.

6. Click the **Export** button and then click **Next >** at the wizard Welcome screen.

7. Click the **Browse...** button and save the file as *cert.p7b* in a location of your choice.

8. Click **Next >** when you are returned to the File Name prompt.

9. Click **Finish** to complete the export.

10. Copy the file *cert.p7b* to the */usr/local/openssl/certs* directory on your FreeBSD system using SFTP or a similar file transfer utility (see "OpenSSH Server 4.7p1" on page 121 for details on SFTP).

11. Once the *cert.p7b* file is in the proper location, run the following command to convert it into the required PEM (Privacy Enhanced Mail) format:

```
# cd /usr/local/openssl/certs
# openssl pkcs7 -inform DER -in cert.p7b –print_certs –text -out cert.pem
```

You should now be able to securely connect to websites "trusted" by Microsoft without Lynx SSL errors.

Macintosh OS X

To export trusted root certificates from a Macintosh OS X system:

1. Open the Applications folder.

2. Double-click the Utilites folder and launch Keychain Access.

3. Click **X509Anchors** in the Keychains pane (upper left).

4. Click any certificate entry in the main window. Hold down the [COMMAND] key (⌘) and press **A** to select all certificates.

5. Click the File menu and select **Export…**.

6. Name the file *cert.pem*, specify a location of your choice (be sure the file format is set to **Privacy Enhanced Mail**), and click **Save**.

7. Copy this file to the */usr/local/openssl/certs* directory on your FreeBSD system using SFTP or a similar file-transfer utility (see "OpenSSH Server 4.7p1" on page 121 for details on SFTP).

You should now be able to securely connect to websites "trusted" by Apple without Lynx SSL errors.

UTILITIES

Following is brief information on the Lynx program.

lynx

Lynx is a text-based World Wide Web browser designed to be used at the command line. It is useful for reading HTML-formatted documentation, browsing the Web, or testing.

Command   lynx

Syntax   lynx *target*

Examples

To start Lynx at its default startup page, enter:

```
# lynx
```

To view a local copy of the Lynx user's guide, enter:

```
# lynx /usr/local/share/lynx_help/Lynx_users_guide.html
```

To visit the Google homepage with Lynx, enter:

```
# lynx http://www.google.com
```

To browse *ftp.freebsd.org*, enter:

```
# lynx ftp://ftp.freebsd.org
```

CONFIG FILES

/usr/local/etc/lynx.cfg
 The main configuration file for Lynx

.lynxrc
 The Lynx user-defaults file located in each user's home directory

MEDIAWIKI 1.11.1
HTTP://MEDIAWIKI.ORG

SUMMARY

MediaWiki is an open source wiki implementation written in PHP (PHP: Hypertext Preprocessor). It utilizes a MySQL database to store content. *Wikiwiki* is a Hawaiian word meaning *quick*. In a technology sense, a *wiki* is a collaborative website where content is modified by users. MediaWiki currently powers Wikipedia, the popular free-content encyclopedia written by volunteers.

Wikis allow users the ability to co-author content on pages without the need for HTML skills or administrative privileges. Editing a MediaWiki page is simpler than editing a typical HTML page. This is made possible by the *Wikitext* format, which uses a simplified syntax and an easy-to-understand word processor–like toolbar. When the user submits an edit to a wiki page, MediaWiki saves the change along with the previous version. This allows for manual reversion, which is useful for fighting vandalism and correcting inaccuracies found by other users.

The software now known as MediaWiki was nameless from its creation in January 2002 until its public release in mid-2003. Magnus Manske, a University of Cologne student, wrote it specifically for Wikipedia to replace the Perl-based UseModWiki engine. The program he developed stored content in a relational database (i.e., MySQL) that provided more functionality than the traditional flat filesystem. Lee Daniel Crocker later rewrote the software to address scalability problems. Brion Vibber eventually took over as lead developer, and in mid-2003 the Wikimedia Foundation named the project *MediaWiki* and released the software to the public.

RESOURCES

MediaWiki Documentation
   http://www.mediawiki.org/wiki/Documentation

REQUIRED

☑   FreeBSD 7.0-RELEASE (see "FreeBSD 7.0" on page 9)

☑   Updated ports collection (see "FreeBSD Ports Collection" on page 23)

☑   Apache HTTP server (see "Apache HTTP Server 2.2.8" on page 33)

☑   PHP 5 (see "PHP 5.2.5" on page 145)

☑   MySQL 5 (see "MySQL Server 5.0.51" on page 99)

☑   Internet connection

☑   Registered domain name

PREPARATION

1. Become the superuser.

2. Create a database in MySQL named *mediawiki*. Create a user named mediawiki and assign full privileges to this user like this:

```
# mysql -u root -p
mysql> create database mediawiki;
mysql> grant all on mediawiki.* to
    -> mediawiki@localhost identified by 'password';
mysql> quit
```

Replace *password* with a password of your choice (the single quotes are required). You'll need this password later.

INSTALL

Enter the following commands to launch the MediaWiki installation:

```
# cd /usr/ports/www/mediawiki
# make config ; make install clean
```

A menu will appear with options for mediawiki. We will leave them at their defaults, so press [TAB] to select **OK** and then press [ENTER] to continue.

CONFIGURE

Once the installation process is complete, it's time to configure MediaWiki for use on your system.

1. Create a MediaWiki-specific Apache configuration file. This points Apache to the correct location of the MediaWiki files and makes administration easier by keeping MediaWiki-specific options separate from the main *httpd.conf* file. By default, Apache searches the */usr/local/etc/apache22/Includes* directory for configuration files. Create the configuration file for MediaWiki:

```
# ee /usr/local/etc/apache22/Includes/mediawiki.conf
```

and add the following lines:

```
Alias /mediawiki "/usr/local/www/mediawiki/"

<Directory "/usr/local/www/mediawiki/">
Options Indexes FollowSymLinks
AllowOverride None
```

```
    Order allow,deny
    Allow from all
    </Directory>
```

NOTE *By default, MediaWiki is set up to be a subdirectory of your webserver's root site. This means you would enter* http://host.example.com/mediawiki *into your web browser. If you would like to change the default directory, replace* mediawiki *(in italics, following* Alias *in the code added to the configuration file) with a different name.*

Save and exit. Restart Apache to commit the changes:

```
# /usr/local/etc/rc.d/apache22 restart
```

2. Open *http://host.example.com/mediawiki* in your favorite web browser (substitute your hostname and your directory if you modified it).

3. You should see the MediaWiki logo along with a link titled *set up the wiki.* Click this link to begin the configuration process. The MediaWiki 1.11.1 Installation page will list some details about your server's environment.

4. There are about 20 different configuration options on this page. Most options are explained well. The following options should be entered carefully to ensure proper functionality of the wiki:

Wiki name

Be sure to set a name for your wiki here. Do not use the name *MediaWiki* or your wiki will advertise itself generically as *MediaWiki* instead of something specific.

Admin username

Choose the username and password you wish to assign to the Administrator of the wiki (remember or record this information, as you will need it later to maintain the site).

SQL server host

This should be *localhost* unless your MySQL server resides on another system.

Database name

Set this to *mediawiki.*

DB username

Set this to *mediawiki.*

DB password

Set this to the password you assigned when you created the database (see "Preparation" on page 96).

5. When you are satisfied with the options you have set, click **Install Media Wiki!** at the bottom of the page to continue.

6. You should see comments pertaining to the options you set. The last line should say Installation successful!.

7. Move the *LocalSettings.php* file into the main MediaWiki directory. The correct permissions should be set to avoid exposure of the MySQL database password it contains. We will also remove the *config* directory to eliminate security risks associated with its existence:

```
# cd /usr/local/www/mediawiki
# mv config/LocalSettings.php .
# chmod 640 LocalSettings.php
# rm -r config
```

8. You can access your wiki with a web browser at *http://host.example.com/ mediawiki* (substitute your server's hostname).

ADMINISTRATION

Use this URL to administer your MediaWiki installation (substitute your server's hostname):

> *http://host.example.com/mediawiki*

At the MediaWiki Main Page, click **log in** (in the upper-right corner), and enter your Admin username and password to access the Administrator account.

CONFIG FILES

/usr/local/www/mediawiki/LocalSettings.php
This file contains configuration data recorded during the installation script. It may be modified with a text editor.

NOTES

You can edit the logo in the upper-left corner of the wiki by editing the *LocalSettings.php* file. Add a line to the bottom of the file that contains the following statement (substitute your hostname and image filename):

```
$wgLogo = "http://host.example.com/logo.gif";
```

LEVEL
3

MYSQL
FreeBSD port path: /usr/ports/databases/mysql50-server
TCP port used – MYSQL (3306)

MYSQL SERVER 5.0.51

HTTP://WWW.MYSQL.COM

SUMMARY

MySQL is an open source SQL (Structured Query Language) database management system. SQL is the most popular computer language used to interface with relational database management systems. A *relational database management system (RDBMS)* generally stores data and their relationships in a table using rows and columns. To be considered an RDBMS, the data must also be editable in this format.

MySQL is commonly paired with PHP to create dynamic websites. Some examples include WordPress (personal weblog software), MediaWiki (the foundation of Wikipedia), and phpBB (a web-based bulletin board system).

MySQL is the most widely deployed open source database in the world, with an estimated 11 million installations. According to a July 2004 report in the *SD Times*, MySQL ranked third (with 33 percent market share) behind commercial giants Oracle and Microsoft's SQL Server.[1]

Michael Widenius and David Axmark wrote MySQL in 1995. Along with Allan Larsson, they are the co-founders of MySQL AB. The company sells support contracts and services for MySQL. Commercial licenses for MySQL are sold for applications that don't fall under the GNU GPL.

RESOURCES

MySQL Reference Manual
   http://dev.mysql.com/doc/refman/5.0/en

REQUIRED

☑ FreeBSD 7.0-RELEASE (see "FreeBSD 7.0" on page 9)

☑ Updated ports collection (see "FreeBSD Ports Collection" on page 23)

☑ Internet connection

☑ Registered domain name

---

[1] "Relational Databases Rule the Roost," *SD Times* (2004), *http://www.sdtimes.com/content/article.aspx?ArticleID=27991*.

MYSQL
FreeBSD port path: /usr/ports/databases/mysql50-server
TCP port used – MYSQL (3306)

PREPARATION

1. Become the superuser.

2. Make sure your server's hostname is locally resolvable. This should already be the case if you are running your own DNS server and have it configured properly. If you aren't running your own DNS server, then make sure you have an entry in your */etc/hosts* file that points to your server's IP address. Open the *hosts* file in a text editor:

```
# ee /etc/hosts
```

Your *hosts* file (~14) should look like this (replace *example.com* with your domain name, *host.example.com* with your hostname, and *192.168.1.11* with your IP address):

```
::1             localhost localhost.example.com
127.0.0.1       localhost localhost.example.com
192.168.1.11    host.example.com
```

INSTALL

Enter the following commands to begin installing MySQL Server:

```
# cd /usr/ports/databases/mysql50-server
# make -D BUILD_OPTIMIZED install clean
# rehash
```

CONFIGURE

Once the installation process is complete, it's time to configure MySQL for use on your system.

1. Run the script *mysql_install_db* to set up the grant tables needed by MySQL. *Grant tables* store information about MySQL user permissions and other security settings. Use this command to run the script:

```
# mysql_install_db --user=mysql
```

2. The following commands will start the MySQL daemon and set up the MySQL root password (replace *localpassword* and *remotepassword* with your own passwords and *host.example.com* with your hostname):

```
# mysqld_safe &
# mysqladmin -u root password 'localpassword'
# mysqladmin -u root -h host.example.com password 'remotepassword'
```

MYSQL
FreeBSD port path: /usr/ports/databases/mysql50-server
TCP port used – MYSQL (3306)

NOTE *The single quotes around* localpassword *and* remotepassword *are required. The remote password is used to log in to the MySQL server from a different computer. By default, MySQL encrypts the login information sent over TCP connections. Queries to and from the database after authentication are transmitted "in the clear."*

3. MySQL includes a set of four sample configuration files located in the */usr/local/share/mysql* directory. Each of these *option files* is tailored to a specific system configuration as follows:

my-small.cnf   For systems with up to 64MB of RAM

my-medium.cnf   For systems with up to 128MB of RAM (ideal for web servers)

my-large.cnf   For systems with 512MB of RAM (dedicated MySQL servers)

my-huge.cnf   For systems with 1 to 2GB of RAM (datacenters, etc.)

Decide which option file suits your system's needs, and then copy it to the */var/db/mysql* directory as *my.cnf*. For example, if you decided to use *my-medium.cnf* as your configuration file, you would enter:

```
# cp /usr/local/share/mysql/my-medium.cnf /var/db/mysql/my.cnf
```

Disabling MySQL TCP Networking

If you intend to use MySQL solely for web-based PHP applications, disabling TCP networking can make your MySQL installation a bit more secure.

NOTE *This only applies if your web server and MySQL database are operating on the same computer.*

1. To disable MySQL TCP networking, modify the *my.cnf* configuration file in the */var/db/mysql* directory:

```
# ee /var/db/mysql/my.cnf
```

2. Scroll down and uncomment (remove the preceding hash mark) line 45 (approximately) to appear as follows:

```
skip-networking
```

3. Save and exit.

More information on the *my.cnf* option file can be found at *http://dev.mysql.com/doc/refman/5.0/en/option-files.html*.

MYSQL
FreeBSD port path: /usr/ports/databases/mysql50-server
TCP port used – MYSQL (3306)

TESTING

In this section, we'll perform a basic test to confirm that MySQL functions properly.

1. Configure MySQL to start automatically at system startup. Open the *etc/ rc.conf* file:

```
# ee /etc/rc.conf
```

and add the following line:

```
mysql_enable="YES"
```

Save and exit.

2. To commit changes that were made in the configuration section above, restart MySQL:

```
# /usr/local/etc/rc.d/mysql-server restart
```

3. Issue the following query to display the existing databases on the server:

```
# mysqlshow -p
```

If the MySQL server is working properly, you should see the following output:

```
+--------------------+
|     Databases      |
+--------------------+
| information_schema |
| mysql              |
| test               |
+--------------------+
```

If you get an error about the inability to connect, check the error log in */var/ db/mysql* for error messages. The error log will be named *host.example.com.err* (with your hostname).

Also, check that the permissions of your */tmp* directory are correct. The permissions can be displayed by typing:

```
# ls -ld /tmp
```

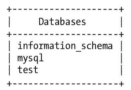

```
drwxrwxrwt   7 root  wheel      512 Feb 17 12:00 /tmp
```

Permissions for the */tmp* directory should be set as shown in italics in the sample output line. If your permissions or ownership are different, the superuser can correct them with the following commands:

```
# chown root:wheel /tmp
# chmod 777 /tmp
# chmod =t /tmp
```

MYSQL
FreeBSD port path: /usr/ports/databases/mysql50-server
TCP port used – MYSQL (3306)

BASICS

This section covers some basic commands for creating, deleting, and adding users to databases with MySQL. To access these commands, log in to the MySQL monitor as root. *MySQL monitor* is a command-line shell used to administer MySQL. You will be prompted to enter the localhost MySQL root password you created in step 2 of "Configure" on page 100.

```
# mysql -u root -p
```

To exit MySQL monitor, enter:

```
mysql> exit;
```

Show Databases

To show a list of databases in MySQL, use the following command at the MySQL prompt:

```
mysql> show databases;
```

NOTE *The semicolon is an important part of MySQL's command line syntax; it signifies the end of a statement.*

Create a Database

Use the following command to create a new database named *testing* (substitute a name of your choice):

```
mysql> create database testing;
```

Add a User to a Database

When you add a user to a database, you can give him full rights, read-only rights, or custom rights.

Full Rights

To add a user and allow full rights to a specific database, use the following command at the MySQL prompt:

```
mysql> grant all on database.* to user@localhost identified by
    -> 'password';
```

Replace *database* with the database name, *user* with the username, and *password* with the password for this user. If you need this database to be accessible externally (using TCP), replace *localhost* with your server's hostname (for locally hosted web-based PHP applications, use localhost).

MYSQL
FreeBSD port path: /usr/ports/databases/mysql50-server
TCP port used – MYSQL (3306)

Read-Only Rights

To add a user with read-only access rights, use the following command at the MySQL prompt:

```
mysql> grant select on database.* to user@localhost identified
    -> by 'password';
```

Replace *database* with the database name, *user* with the username, and *password* with the password for this user. If you need this database to be accessible externally (using TCP), replace *localhost* with your server's hostname (for locally hosted web-based PHP applications, use localhost).

Custom Rights

To add a user with custom access rights, use the following command at the MySQL prompt:

```
mysql> grant options on database.* to user@localhost identified
    -> by 'password';
```

Replace *options* with any or all of the following: select, insert, update, delete, create, or drop (separate multiple items with commas). Replace *database* with the database name, *user* with the username, and *password* with the password for this user. If you need this database to be accessible externally (using TCP), replace *localhost* with your server's hostname (for locally hosted web-based PHP applications, use localhost).

Remove a User from a Database

To remove all privileges to a database for a particular user, use the following command at the MySQL prompt:

```
mysql> revoke all privileges on database.* from user@localhost;
```

Replace *database* with the database name and *user* with the username whose privileges you wish to revoke.

Remove a User from MySQL

To remove a user from MySQL completely, use the following commands at the MySQL prompt:

```
mysql> revoke all privileges, grant option from user@localhost;
mysql> drop user user@localhost;
```

Replace *user* with the username of the user you wish to remove from MySQL.

MYSQL
FreeBSD port path: /usr/ports/databases/mysql50-server
TCP port used – MYSQL (3306)

Delete a Database

To delete a database named *testing* from MySQL, use the following command at the MySQL prompt:

```
mysql> drop database testing;
```

Replace *testing* with the name of the database you wish to delete.

Show User Privileges

To show all of the privileges for a particular user, use the following command at the MySQL prompt:

```
mysql> show grants for user@localhost;
```

Replace *user* with the username you wish to view the privileges for.

Back Up All Databases

To back up all MySQL databases, use the following command (you will be prompted for your localhost root password):

```
# mysqldump -u root -p --all-databases > /path/filename.sql
```

Substitute the path and filename of the backup file.

Back Up a Single Database

To back up a particular MySQL database, use the following command (you will be prompted for your localhost root password):

```
# mysqldump -u root -p --databases dbname > /path/filename.sql
```

Replace *dbname* with the database name and substitute the path and filename of the backup file.

Restore a Database

To restore a MySQL database, use the following command (you will be prompted for your localhost root password):

```
# mysql -u root -p dbname < /path/filename.sql
```

Replace *dbname* with the name of the database you wish to restore and substitute the path and filename of the backup file to import.

MYSQL
FreeBSD port path: /usr/ports/databases/mysql50-server
TCP port used – MYSQL (3306)

CONFIG FILES

/var/db/mysql/my.cnf
   The MySQL configuration file used to specify MySQL options

LOG FILES

/var/db/mysql/host.example.com.err
   Contains MySQL server status messages, errors, and so on

NOTES

A popular administration tool called phpMyAdmin utilizes PHP to create a web interface to handle administration of MySQL. See "phpMyAdmin 2.11.5" on page 157 for more details.

LEVEL
3

NTP
FreeBSD port path: /usr/ports/net/ntp
UDP port used – NTP (123)

NTP SERVER 4.2.2

HTTP://NTP.ISC.ORG

SUMMARY

NTP (Network Time Protocol) is an Internet protocol used for synchronizing the clocks of networked computers. Computer clock accuracy is instrumental in providing a consistent reference for system log files, email timestamps, time-activated scripts, and so on. The NTP system is capable of keeping your computer's clock accurate to within a few milliseconds of an accurate time server. Time servers are usually connected directly to a source of accurate time (e.g., atomic or GPS clocks).

The NTP system consists of a hierarchy, or *strata*, of public and private servers. A *stratum 1* server synchronizes its clock with an accurate external GPS (Global Positioning System) clock, radio clock, or other highly accurate time-keeping device. A *stratum 2* server derives its clock data from one or more stratum 1 servers, a *stratum 3* server derives its clock data from one or more stratum 2 servers, and so on. Servers at the lower stratum levels (numerically speaking) are not necessarily more accurate. The accuracy of the time source, geographic location, and network latency all contribute to the accuracy of a time server.

A server running the NTP daemon periodically synchronizes its clock to one or more established time servers. Over time, the NTP daemon calculates the system-specific clock error. If the system temporarily loses Internet connectivity, the NTP daemon will keep the system clock accurate using this error (or *clock drift*) data until it can re-synchronize with a time server.

David Mills, a professor at the University of Delaware, originally developed NTP in the early '80s. NTP was initially named the Internet Clock Service and was created to provide clock synchronization for the HELLO routing protocol. These early versions of NTP were less accurate than today's because they did not have any frequency correction abilities. Mills, along with a team of volunteers, continues to develop NTP.

RESOURCES

NTP Documentation Index
http://ntp.isc.org/bin/view/Main/DocumentationIndex

RFC 4330 – Network Time Protocol Version 4
http://tools.ietf.org/html/rfc4330

NTP
FreeBSD port path: /usr/ports/net/ntp
UDP port used – NTP (123)

REQUIRED

☑ FreeBSD 7.0-RELEASE (see "FreeBSD 7.0" on page 9)

☑ Updated ports collection (see "FreeBSD Ports Collection" on page 23)

☑ Internet connection

OPTIONAL

☑ Registered domain name

PREPARATION

Become the superuser.

INSTALL

Although NTP 4.2.0 is included in the standard FreeBSD 7.0 distribution, we will install an updated version of NTP from the ports collection. Enter the following commands to begin the installation:

```
# cd /usr/ports/net/ntp
# make config ; make install clean
# rehash
```

CONFIGURE

Once the installation process is complete, it's time to configure NTP for use on your system.

1. Change the default search path. FreeBSD's base version of NTP uses the same filenames as the version we installed from the ports system. If the search path has not been changed from its default, NTP-related commands will run the FreeBSD base version rather than the new version from ports. See "Default Search Path" on page 14 for details on changing the default search path.

2. Create a *drift file* for storing clock correction data. The following command creates this file in the */etc/ntp* directory:

```
# touch /etc/ntp/drift
```

3. Select appropriate time servers for synchronization. Visit *http://ntp.isc.org/bin/view/Servers/StratumTwoTimeServers* for an updated list of public time servers. Select at least three servers from the list. Pick servers that are listed as *OpenAccess* and located in your geographic vicinity.

NOTE *See NTP's web page on Rules of Engagement for recommendations on selecting time servers:* http://support.ntp.org/bin/view/Servers/RulesOfEngagement.

NTP
FreeBSD port path: /usr/ports/net/ntp
UDP port used – NTP (123)

4. Create a new configuration file named *ntp.conf*:

```
# ee /etc/ntp.conf
```

and add the following configuration options:

```
server time.example1.com iburst
server time.example2.com iburst
server time.example3.com iburst
driftfile /etc/ntp/drift
logfile /var/log/ntp.log
```

Replace the hostnames of the servers (in italics) with those you have picked. The iburst modifier allows the NTP daemon to speed up initial synchronization. The driftfile statement tells the NTP daemon where to look for the drift file (created in step 2). The logfile statement directs the NTP daemon to store the log file in the */var/log* directory. Save and exit.

TESTING

In this section, we'll perform some basic tests to confirm that NTP synchronizes time data properly.

1. To start the NTP daemon automatically at boot time, open */etc/rc.conf*:

```
# ee /etc/rc.conf
```

and add the following lines:

```
ntpd_enable="YES"
ntpd_program="/usr/local/bin/ntpd"
```

2. Start the NTP daemon and begin system time synchronization:

```
# /etc/rc.d/ntpd start
```

Wait about 10 minutes, and then execute the following command to check the status of the time synchronization:

```
# ntpq -p localhost
```

You should see results similar to the following:

```
remote           refid      st t when poll reach   delay   offset  jitter
==============================================================================
+gabe.kjsl.com   209.81.9.7  2 u   30   64  377   13.267  1282.65 405.902
+reva.xtremeunix 204.123.2.5 2 u   50   64  377   25.863  1228.18 421.589
*zorac.sf-bay.or 204.123.2.5 2 u   20   64  377   25.283  1017.32 345.212
-time.nist.gov   .INIT.     16 u 159m 1024    0    0.000     0.000 4000.00
```

NOTE *The last line in the above output is an example of a peer that is not reachable or is not working properly. The jitter value will usually be 4000.00 and stratum will be 16, with zeros for delay and offset.*

109

NTP
FreeBSD port path: /usr/ports/net/ntp
UDP port used – NTP (123)

The elements of the above output are described below:

remote   The hostname of the peer (time server). The hostname preceded by an asterisk indicates the server selected for synchronization.

refid   The type of time-keeping device in use by the corresponding peer. Since the time servers above are stratum 2 servers, they list the IP addresses of the servers supplying their time.

st   The stratum of the peer, ranging from 1 to 16.

t   The type of peer (u = unicast, m = multicast).

when   How long ago the peer was heard from in seconds.

poll   The frequency, in seconds, with which the NTP daemon is synchronizing with the peer.

reach   The status, in octal format, of the reachability register. This value will stabilize at 377 if the last 8 attempts to synchronize with each time server were successful (it takes about 10 minutes to reach this value).

delay   The roundtrip packet delay time in milliseconds (smaller is better).

offset   The difference, in milliseconds, between the system time and the remote peer's time. A negative value here indicates that the clock of the local system is behind that of the remote peer's, while a positive value indicates milliseconds ahead.

jitter   The variation, in milliseconds, of the offset (smaller is better).

3. Check to make sure your time server is answering NTP requests properly with this command:

```
# ntpdate -q localhost

server 127.0.0.1, stratum 3, offset 0.000004, delay 0.02579
server ::1, stratum 3, offset 0.000010, delay 0.02583
 6 Jun 20:15:12 ntpdate[2710]: adjust time server 127.0.0.1 offset 0.0004
sec
```

If you are synchronizing with stratum 2 servers your server will indicate stratum 3 as shown.

CONFIG FILES

/etc/ntp.conf
   The main configuration file for ntpd

NTP
FreeBSD port path: /usr/ports/net/ntp
UDP port used – NTP (123)

LOG FILES

/var/log/ntp.log
The NTP daemon records time synchronization messages to this file.

/var/log/messages
The NTP daemon records its status in this file.

/etc/ntp/drift
The NTP daemon stores clock correction values to this file.

NOTES

- The drift file specified in step 2 of "Configure" (page 108) is automatically updated once per hour with the frequency offset (clock error) computed by the NTP daemon. It is important that the empty file be created as outlined in step 2; the NTP daemon will not automatically create the file. If the drift file does not exist, the NTP daemon will assume an error of zero and will take about 15 minutes to complete initial synchronization and enter a stabilized state or *normal mode*.

- If you want to synchronize the clock of your server and deny all client requests to the NTP server, add the following lines to *ntp.conf* in */etc*:

```
restrict default ignore
restrict time.example1.com
restrict time.example2.com
restrict time.example3.com
```

NOTE *Replace the hostnames in italics with the hostnames of the time servers you configured in step 4 of "Configure." You cannot use NTP pool servers here because pool servers assign NTP server addresses dynamically.*

If you wish to allow NTP services to the local network only, add this line to the *ntp.conf* file in */etc*:

```
restrict 192.168.1.0 mask 255.255.255.0 nomodify notrap
```

NOTE *This line is an addition to the four restrict statements above.*

Change the IP address and subnet (in italics) to match your network configuration. The example above would allow systems with an IP address of 192.168.1.*X* to synchronize with your NTP server.

LEVEL
5

OPENLDAP
FreeBSD port path: /usr/ports/net/openldap23-server
TCP ports used – LDAP (389), LDAPS (636)

OPENLDAP SERVER 2.3.38

HTTP://OPENLDAP.ORG

SUMMARY

LDAP (Lightweight Directory Access Protocol) is a TCP-based protocol used to access directory services. *Directory services* provide users with information about other users and resources within a network (usually in the form of address book entries). Entries are stored in a central database and accessed from an LDAP server (OpenLDAP, Windows Server Active Directory, etc.) via an LDAP-capable client (Microsoft Outlook, Mozilla Thunderbird, etc.).

OpenLDAP complies with the X.500 series of directory services standards developed by the ITU-T (the standards division of the International Tele-communication Union). This provides LDAP interoperability between X.500-based applications.

As per the X.500 standard, LDAP entries are stored in a hierarchal format consisting of sets of attributes within directory entries:

```
-DOMAIN COMPONENT (.com)
  -DOMAIN COMPONENT (example)
    -ORGANIZATIONAL UNIT (People)
      -USER ID (jdoe)
        -TELEPHONENUMBER (phone number)
        -GIVENNAME (doe)
```

LDAP was created by Tim Howes, Steve Kille, and Wengyik Yeong in 1992. It started as a project to provide directory services alongside the University of Michigan's email system.

A company named Net Boolean Inc. was formed to provide email services for businesses in early 1998. Available commercial LDAP implementations were too expensive for this young company. Net Boolean created Boolean LDAP from open source LDAP software made available by the University of Michigan. Kurt Zeilenga of Net Boolean later founded the OpenLDAP Foundation and the project in August of 1998. Current OpenLDAP development consists of a core team that includes founder Kurt Zeilenga, Howard Chu, and Pierangelo Masarati.

RESOURCES

OpenLDAP 2.3 Administrator's Guide
http://www.openldap.org/doc/admin23

RFC 4511 – Lightweight Directory Access Protocol
http://tools.ietf.org/html/rfc4511

OPENLDAP
FreeBSD port path: /usr/ports/net/openldap23-server
TCP ports used – LDAP (389), LDAPS (636)

REQUIRED

☑ FreeBSD 7.0-RELEASE (see "FreeBSD 7.0" on page 9)

☑ Updated ports collection (see "FreeBSD Ports Collection" on page 23)

☑ Internet connection

OPTIONAL

☑ OpenSSL with a signed SSL Certificate (see "OpenSSL 0.9.8g" on page 127)

☑ Registered domain name

PREPARATION

Become the superuser.

INSTALL

To begin the OpenLDAP installation process, enter the following commands:

```
# cd /usr/ports/net/openldap23-server
# make config ; make install clean
# rehash
```

A menu should appear displaying options for openldap-server. We will leave the options at their defaults; press [TAB] to select **OK** and then press [ENTER] to continue the installation process.

CONFIGURE

Once the installation process is complete, it's time to configure OpenLDAP for use on your system.

1. Set up an OpenLDAP root password. OpenLDAP stores the LDAP administrator's password in the main configuration file *slapd.conf*. OpenLDAP can read this password either as plaintext or as a hash. A hash obscures the password with an algorithm so it isn't in plain view. The commands below will create an SSHA (Salted Secure Hash Algorithm) hash of your root password for OpenLDAP and insert it into *slapd.conf*.

```
# cd /usr/local/etc/openldap
# sed -I .old 's/rootpw/# rootpw/' slapd.conf
# echo -n "rootpw " >> slapd.conf
# slappasswd >> slapd.conf
```

2. We'll make a few more modifications to the *slapd.conf* file. Open *slapd.conf*:

```
# ee /usr/local/etc/openldap/slapd.conf
```

OPENLDAP
FreeBSD port path: /usr/ports/net/openldap23-server
TCP ports used – LDAP (389), LDAPS (636)

3. Scroll down to the `suffix` declaration (~56). If your domain name is *example.com*, enter `"dc=example,dc=com"`. Proceed to the next entry, `rootdn`, and enter the same information, leaving the `"cn=Manager"` segment alone. The two lines would appear as follows for a domain named example.com:

```
suffix          "dc=example,dc=com"
rootdn          "cn=Manager,dc=example,dc=com"
```

4. Scroll down to the bottom of *slapd.conf* and add the following two lines:

```
include         /usr/local/etc/openldap/schema/cosine.schema
include         /usr/local/etc/openldap/schema/inetorgperson.schema
```

These lines add support for the COSINE schema and the inetOrgPerson object class. COSINE and inetOrgPerson extend the core schema with attributes that are useful to organizations. Examples of additional attributes include employee numbers, room numbers, building names, and so on.

For information on the COSINE schema, see *http://tools.ietf.org/html/rfc4524*.

For information on the inetOrgPerson object class, see *http://tools.ietf.org/html/ rfc2798*.

5. Add a simple access policy to keep the `userPassword` attribute from being displayed to other users. Add these lines to the bottom of *slapd.conf*:

```
access to attrs=userPassword
        by self write
        by anonymous auth
        by * none
```

6. Add another access policy for user information. Users should have write access to their own information and read-only access to other people's information. Anonymous users should have no access. Requests from the localhost should have read access. The lines should appear as follows:

```
access to *
        by self write
        by users read
        by peername.ip=127.0.0.1 read
        by anonymous auth
```

7. If you possess a signed SSL Certificate and wish to enable secure LDAP connections using SSL, continue. Otherwise skip to step 8. The following declarations will tell the slapd program where to find your SSL Certificates.

```
TLSCACertificateFile /usr/local/openssl/certs/example.com-CAcert.pem
TLSCertificateFile /usr/local/openssl/certs/host.example.com-cert.pem
TLSCertificateKeyFile /usr/local/openssl/certs/host.example.com-unencrypted-key.pem
```

OPENLDAP
FreeBSD port path: /usr/ports/net/openldap23-server
TCP ports used – LDAP (389), LDAPS (636)

Remember to change the paths and filenames (in italics) to point to your server certificates and key file. Save and exit.

8. OpenLDAP uses an embedded database called Berkeley DB to store its data. The command below will copy the example database configuration file *DB_CONFIG.example* to OpenLDAP's database path:

```
# cd /usr/local/etc/openldap
# cp DB_CONFIG.example /var/db/openldap-data/DB_CONFIG
```

TESTING

In this section, we'll perform some basic tests to confirm that OpenLDAP answers LDAP requests properly.

1. To start the LDAP server automatically at boot time, add these lines to the *rc.conf* file located in */etc*. Open *rc.conf*:

```
# ee /etc/rc.conf
```

If you did not choose to enable secure LDAP connections with SSL, add the following lines:

```
slapd_enable="YES"
slapd_flags='-h "ldapi://%2fvar%2frun%2fopenldap%2fldapi/ ldap:///"'
slapd_sockets="/var/run/openldap/ldapi"
```

If you chose to enable secure LDAP connections with SSL, add the following lines:

```
slapd_enable="YES"
slapd_flags='-h "ldapi://%2fvar%2frun%2fopenldap%2fldapi/\
 ldap:/// ldaps:///"'
slapd_sockets="/var/run/openldap/ldapi"
slapd_owner="root:ldap"
```

Save and exit, then start the LDAP server:

```
# /usr/local/etc/rc.d/slapd start
```

2. Create data to import into the LDAP database. The first import to the LDAP database will consist of the domain and manager entries. Change to a working directory of your choice. Create a file named *domainmgr.ldif*:

```
# ee domainmgr.ldif
```

OPENLDAP
FreeBSD port path: /usr/ports/net/openldap23-server
TCP ports used – LDAP (389), LDAPS (636)

Enter the following text into the blank file:

```
# Create Domain entry
dn: dc=example,dc=com
objectclass: dcObject
objectclass: organization
o: example.com
dc: example

# Create Manager entry
dn: cn=Manager,dc=example,dc=com
objectclass: organizationalRole
cn: Manager
```

The LDAP abbreviations in use are:

dn   distinguished name

dc   domain component

cn   common name

o   organization

Substitute your domain name appropriately (items in italics must reflect your domain). Do not change any other parts of this file. The ldapadd utility we are going to run next is very specific about the syntax of LDIF (LDAP Data Interchange Format) files. Ensure that there are no extra spaces after the last letter of each line. The single blank line between the domain and manager entries is necessary. Save and exit.

3. Add the entries of *domainmgr.ldif* to the LDAP database (substitute your domain name):

```
# ldapadd -x -D "cn=Manager,dc=example,dc=com" -W -f domainmgr.ldif -c
```

You will be prompted for the LDAP root password you created in step 1 of "Configure" on page 114. If the command completes without any errors, continue; otherwise reopen *domainmgr.ldif*, check spelling and spacing, and run the command again.

4. Create an organizational unit to hold user entries. Create a file named *people.ldif*:

```
# ee people.ldif
```

Enter the following text into the blank file:

```
# Create Organizational Unit (People)
dn: ou=People,dc=example,dc=com
objectclass: top
objectclass: organizationalUnit
ou: People
```

OPENLDAP
FreeBSD port path: /usr/ports/net/openldap23-server
TCP ports used – LDAP (389), LDAPS (636)

Again, substitute your domain name (shown in italics) and be careful with spelling and spacing. Save and exit.

5. Add the entries of *people.ldif* to the LDAP database (substitute your domain name):

```
# ldapadd -x -D "cn=Manager,dc=example,dc=com" -W -f people.ldif
```

6. Add a user to the LDAP database within the organizational unit you created. Create a file named *user.ldif*:

```
# ee user.ldif
```

Enter the following text into the blank file:

```
# Create User Entry
dn: cn=John Doe,ou=People,dc=example,dc=com
objectclass: inetOrgPerson
cn: John Doe
givenname: John
sn: Doe
mail: jdoe@example.com
```

Replace the items shown in italics with the appropriate data. Save and exit.

7. Create a hashed password for this new user and append it to *user.ldif*:

```
# echo -n "userPassword: " >> user.ldif
# slappasswd >> user.ldif
```

8. Add the entries of *user.ldif* to the LDAP database (substitute your domain name):

```
# ldapadd -x -D "cn=Manager,dc=example,dc=com" -W -f user.ldif
```

9. Check that all of the above entries made it into the LDAP database successfully (substitute your domain name):

```
# ldapsearch -W -H ldap://localhost/ -D\
? cn=Manager,dc=example,dc=com -b 'dc=example,dc=com' '(objectclass=*)'
```

You will be prompted for the manager password. Below is a sample of output from the ldapsearch command:

```
# extended LDIF
#
# LDAPv3
# base <dc=turbojets,dc=net> with scope subtree
# filter: (objectclass=*)
# requesting: ALL
#

# example.com
dn: dc=example,dc=com
objectClass: dcObject
```

OPENLDAP
FreeBSD port path: /usr/ports/net/openldap23-server
TCP ports used – LDAP (389), LDAPS (636)

```
objectClass: organization
o: example.com
dc: example

# Manager, example.com
dn: cn=Manager,dc=example,dc=com
objectClass: organizationalRole
cn: Manager

# People, example.com
dn: ou=People,dc=example,dc=com
objectClass: top
objectClass: organizationalUnit
ou: People

# John Doe, People, example.com
dn: cn=John Doe,ou=People,dc=example,dc=com
objectClass: inetOrgPerson
cn: John Doe
givenName: John
sn: Doe
mail: jdoe@example.com
userPassword:: e1NTSEF9MTJTZkh1YkRQelIOZG4wV3hlZUxqRkJFZ2OOUzQOYnQ=
```

NOTE *When logging into the LDAP server from an LDAP client you may need to enter "Base DN," "Bind DN," password, and hostname. Here is what to enter for "Base DN" and "Bind DN" (replace the italicized items appropriately):*

```
Base DN: dc=example,dc=com
Bind DN: cn=John Doe,ou=People,dc=example,dc=com
```

CONFIG FILES

/usr/local/etc/openldap/slapd.conf
    Main configuration file for slapd

LOG FILES

/var/log/debug.log
    Contains slapd logs

NOTES

- Since ldapadd is sensitive to syntax errors, adding entries to the LDAP database manually (as we did in the test section above) can be very inconvenient. Utilities exist that allow you to administer the LDAP database in a more efficient and user-friendly manner. phpLDAPadmin is a web-based LDAP browser designed to manage the LDAP database more intuitively. See "phpLDAPadmin 1.1.0" on page 153 for details.

OPENLDAP
FreeBSD port path: /usr/ports/net/openldap23-server
TCP ports used – LDAP (389), LDAPS (636)

- OpenLDAP 2.3 accepts only LDAPv3 requests by default. Ensure that your LDAP client is set to LDAPv3 if given the option. If LDAPv2 is needed you may add `allow bind_v2` to */usr/local/etc/openldap/slapd.conf*; see the manual page for *slapd.conf* for details (view this by typing `man slapd.conf` at the prompt).

LEVEL
2

OPENSSH
FreeBSD port path: /usr/ports/security/openssh-portable
TCP port used – SSH (22)

OPENSSH SERVER 4.7P1

HTTP://WWW.OPENSSH.COM

SUMMARY

OpenSSH is a set of open source utilities that implement the SSH (Secure Shell) protocol. *SSH* is a secure version of telnet; it's a protocol used to access the console or command line of remote systems. SSH provides administrators and users with access to a remote system as if they were physically at the console.

SSH uses encryption to prevent eavesdropping on connections made between a client and server. The telnet protocol lacks encryption; this gives eavesdroppers the ability to capture usernames and passwords with a packet sniffer. (A *packet sniffer* is a program designed to monitor and capture network traffic.)

OpenSSH commands an overwhelming 87 percent of the SSH market, according to a survey conducted in November 2005.[1] It is included in virtually every distribution of Linux and BSD, as well as Apple's Mac OS X.

The SSH protocol was first developed in 1995 by Tatu Ylönen, a researcher from Helsinki University of Technology. Ylönen founded SSH Communications Security in late 1995 to develop and market SSH. His company currently markets the SSH Tectia Server/Client.

OpenSSH was originally conceived by the OpenBSD team as part of the OpenBSD 2.6 release in December 1999. The team used code from Tatu Ylönen's SSH project, which was originally open source. Bugs were fixed and features were added to the OpenSSH release. Soon after the release of OpenSSH, its developers decided to split into two teams. One group concentrated on the development of OpenSSH for OpenBSD while the other group developed a portable version of OpenSSH for use on other platforms. The portable edition has the letter *P* appended to the version to signify this. OpenSSH is still developed by the OpenBSD team and is led by its founder, Theo de Raadt.

RESOURCES

OpenSSH Manual Pages
http://www.openssh.com/manual.html

RFC 4251 – The Secure Shell (SSH) Protocol Architecture
http://tools.ietf.org/html/rfc4251

---

[1] OpenBSD, "SSH Usage Profiling," *http://www.openssh.com/usage/index.html.*

OPENSSH
FreeBSD port path: /usr/ports/security/openssh-portable
TCP port used – SSH (22)

REQUIRED

☑ FreeBSD 7.0-RELEASE (see "FreeBSD 7.0" on page 9)

☑ Updated ports collection (see "FreeBSD Ports Collection" on page 23)

☑ Internet connection

☑ OpenSSL (see "OpenSSL 0.9.8g" on page 127)

PREPARATION

Become the superuser.

INSTALL

OpenSSH 4.5.p1 is part of the standard FreeBSD 7.0 distribution. In this guide, we will replace the base version with an updated version of OpenSSH from the ports collection.

To begin the OpenSSH installation process, enter:

```
# cd /usr/ports/security/openssh-portable
# make config ; make -D WITH_OVERWRITE_BASE install clean
```

A menu with options for OpenSSH will appear. We will leave them at their defaults, so press [TAB] to highlight **OK** and then press [ENTER] to start the installation.

CONFIGURE

Once the installation process is complete, it's time to configure OpenSSH for use on your system.

1. The line "NO_OPENSSH = YES" must be added to the *make.conf* file in */etc*. This tells make not to build the base version of OpenSSH if you rebuild FreeBSD from source (i.e., this prevents the system from downgrading OpenSSH to the older base version). The following commands will add this line to *make.conf*:

```
# cp /etc/make.conf /etc/make.conf.old
# echo "NO_OPENSSH = YES" >> /etc/make.conf
```

2. OpenSSH's default configuration file has changed slightly from the base version to increase security. We'll replace the base configuration file with this newly installed file.

```
# cd /etc/ssh
# cp sshd_config sshd_config.old
# cp sshd_config-dist sshd_config
# /etc/rc.d/sshd restart
```

NOTE *You may need to re-modify the* sshd_config *file if you previously made any customizations.*

OPENSSH
FreeBSD port path: /usr/ports/security/openssh-portable
TCP port used – SSH (22)

TESTING

In this section, we'll perform some basic tests to confirm that OpenSSH answers SSH requests properly.

1. To start OpenSSH Server automatically at boot time, open *rc.conf*:

```
# ee /etc/rc.conf
```

and add the following line (if it's not already present):

```
sshd_enable="YES"
```

2. Save and exit.

3. To test if OpenSSH is answering properly on port 22, connect via telnet and examine the response. Use the following command:

```
# telnet localhost 22
```

NOTE   *You may replace localhost with the FQDN or IP address of your server if you are testing from a different system.*

The connection should yield the following banner:

```
Trying 127.0.0.1...
Connected to localhost.
Escape character is '^]'.
SSH-2.0-OpenSSH_4.7p1 FreeBSD-openssh-portable-overwrite-base-4.7.p1,1
```

Verify that the correct version appears in the banner (SSH-2.0 and OpenSSH_4.7p1 or later). Press [ENTER] to quit and return to the command prompt. You should now be able to connect with any SSH-capable client and any valid user account other than root.

UTILITIES

OpenSSH includes an SSH client, *SFTP (secure file transfer)* client, and *SCP (secure copy)* client. Each program is designed to operate similarly to the original, but insecure, telnet and FTP protocols. The SSH client enables users to securely log in to remote systems and the SFTP and SCP clients make secure file transfers possible.

SSH Client

This program is used to securely log in to the console of a remote system (i.e., start a terminal session).

Command   ssh

Syntax   ssh -*options user@host*

OPENSSH
FreeBSD port path: /usr/ports/security/openssh-portable
TCP port used – SSH (22)

Options

-p Specify a port in which to connect to the remote host (the OpenSSH server must be configured for the port you specify).

-L localport:host:remoteport Forward a specified local port to a specified host port over the secure connection.

-N Do not execute remote commands (used for port forwarding).

-f Run the SSH client as a background process.

Examples

To log in to a remote host named *host.example.com* as user johnny, enter the following command:

```
# ssh johnny@host.example.com
```

To log in to a remote host named *fluffy.net* as user cat on port 23, enter:

```
# ssh -p 23 cat@fluffy.net
```

To create an SSH tunnel from local port 1234 to remote port 110 on host *host.example.com* as user aeron, enter:

```
# ssh -L 1234:host.example.com:110 -f -N aeron@host.example.com
```

To close this tunnel later, enter:

```
# killall -TERM ssh
```

Secure Copy Client

This utility securely copies files and directories to or from a remote host.

Command scp

Syntax scp *-options filename user@host:path*

Options

-C Enable data compression.

-P Specify a port in which to connect to the remote host (the OpenSSH server must be configured for the port you specify).

-p Preserve the original file's modification times, access times, and file modes.

-r Recursively copy directories.

Examples

To copy a file named *example.doc* from the current working directory to the */usr/home* directory on a remote system *example.com* as user author, enter:

```
# scp example.doc author@example.com:/usr/home
```

OPENSSH
FreeBSD port path: /usr/ports/security/openssh-portable
TCP port used – SSH (22)

To copy everything within the local */usr/samba* directory to */usr/home* on a remote system *example.com* as user author while preserving file modes and enabling data compression, enter:

```
# scp -p -C /usr/samba author@example.com:/usr/home
```

To copy a file named */usr/example.doc* to the */usr* directory on the local system using port 23, using the author account on a host named *server1.example.com*, enter:

```
# scp -P 23 author@server1.example.com:/usr/example.doc /usr
```

Secure File Transfer Client

This program is an interactive and secure file transfer client. It can be used as an alternative to FTP, which is inherently insecure.

Command   sftp

Syntax   sftp *-options user@host*

Options

-o Port=xx   Specify a port in which to connect to the remote host (the OpenSSH server must be configured for the port you specify).

-C   Enable data compression.

Examples

To initiate a connection to a host named *server.example.com* as user test, enter:

```
# sftp test@server.example.com
```

To connect to a host named *example.com* over port 23 as user wilson with compression enabled, enter:

```
# sftp -o Port=23 -C wilson@example.com
```

CONFIG FILES

/etc/ssh/sshd_config
Contains general settings for sshd (SSH server daemon). It is generally safe to leave this file at its defaults.

/etc/ssh/ssh_config
Contains general settings for ssh (SSH client program).

OPENSSH
FreeBSD port path: /usr/ports/security/openssh-portable
TCP port used – SSH (22)

LOG FILES

/var/log/auth.log
    A general log of SSH server activity

NOTES

- By default, all user accounts with shell access on your server will have SSH access (except for root). If you want to limit SSH access to specific users, you will need to add a line to the *sshd_config* file located in */etc/ssh*. Open it like so:

  ```
  # ee /etc/ssh/sshd_config
  ```

  and add the following line:

  ```
  AllowUsers username
  ```

  Replace *username* with the login name of the user you want to allow SSH access. Separate multiple users with spaces. Only users who appear on this line will have access to SSH-based services.

  NOTE *Be aware that this line is case sensitive. Confirm that the usernames are correct, especially if you are making this change from a remote location. You can lock yourself out if this is misconfigured!*

  Save, exit, and restart sshd:

  ```
  # /etc/rc.d/sshd restart
  ```

- Host keys are usually created after the initial FreeBSD installation process, if SSH logins were enabled. If you need to re-create them, it is easiest to remove the old keys and restart the SSH daemon. The SSH daemon will recreate the keys automatically. These commands will accomplish this:

  ```
  # cd /etc/ssh
  # mkdir old_keys
  # mv ssh_host* old_keys
  # /etc/rc.d/sshd restart
  ```

- By default, OpenSSH Server will not allow root logins. If you need root privileges, you will need to log in as a normal user who is a member of the wheel group and then use the su command to become the superuser. See "su" on page 225 for details. To add a user named lucky to the wheel group, log in as root and enter:

  ```
  # pw user mod lucky -G wheel
  ```

OPENSSL 0.9.8G

HTTP://WWW.OPENSSL.ORG

SUMMARY

OpenSSL is an open source toolkit and cryptographic library that implements the SSL (Secure Sockets Layer) and TLS (Transport Layer Security) protocols. OpenSSL is an independent project managed by various volunteers from around the world. In short, OpenSSL provides cryptography tools for securing network connections.

A common SSL implementation is to secure web pages with HTTPS (HyperText Transfer Protocol secured with encryption). An HTTPS handshake consists of the following steps:

1. An HTTP client (web browser) sends a web server an HTTPS request.

2. The server responds by sending the client its SSL Certificate containing its public key, domain name, and issuing certificate authority.

3. The client sends a challenge message encrypted using the server's public SSL key.

4. The server decrypts this message with its private SSL key.

5. The server finally sends the decrypted message back to the client.

6. If the client receives the correct message, the two parties can begin to exchange information securely, assuming the issuing certificate authority is trusted by the client.

OpenSSL provides the tools needed to create certificate signing requests, private server keys, and self-signed certificates. When coupled with a recognized certificate authority, trusted server certificates can be produced for use with TCP protocols like HTTP, SMTP, IMAP, and so on.

OpenSSL is based on the SSLeay library originally developed by Eric A. Young and Tim J. Hudson. SSLeay was an open source implementation of Netscape's Secure Socket Layer protocol, which was used in the Netscape Secure Server and Navigator browser in the mid-1990s.

RESOURCES

OpenSSL Manual Pages
http://www.openssl.org/docs

SSL Certificate Frequently Asked Questions
http://www.verisign.com/ssl/ssl-information-center/faq/ssl-basics.html

RFC 2246 – The TLS Protocol
http://tools.ietf.org/html/rfc2246

REQUIRED

☑ FreeBSD 7.0-RELEASE (see "FreeBSD 7.0" on page 9)

☑ Updated ports collection (see "FreeBSD Ports Collection" on page 23)

☑ Internet connection

☑ Registered domain name

OPTIONAL

☑ Trusted SSL certificate authority (CA) such as GeoTrust, Thawte, Verisign, and so on, if you wish to create industry-trusted SSL Certificates

PREPARATION

Become the superuser. This guide assumes that the default search path for root (the superuser) has been changed as outlined in "FreeBSD 7.0" on page 9. If you didn't make this modification, specify the full path when executing OpenSSL commands (*/usr/local/bin/openssl*).

INSTALL

OpenSSL 0.9.8e is part of the standard FreeBSD 7.0 distribution. In this guide, we will install an updated version of OpenSSL from the ports collection.

```
# cd /usr/ports/security/openssl
# cp Makefile Makefile.old
# echo EXTRACONFIGURE+=no-idea >> Makefile
# make install clean
# rehash
```

NOTE *The second and third commands above prevent the compilation of the license-restricted IDEA encryption algorithm. This is important for the proper functioning of other third-party applications.*

CONFIGURE

Once the installation process is complete, it's time to configure OpenSSL for use on your system.

1. The line `"WITH_OPENSSL_PORT = YES"` needs to be added to the *make.conf* file in */etc*. This will ensure that ports built in the future are linked to the newer version of OpenSSL. The following commands will add the appropriate line to *make.conf*.

```
# cp /etc/make.conf /etc/make.conf.old
# echo "WITH_OPENSSL_PORT=YES" >> /etc/make.conf
```

2. Rename the old *openssl.cnf* file to make it harder to inadvertently use the old version of OpenSSL when creating certificates. Then copy the sample OpenSSL configuration file to a working copy:

```
# mv /etc/ssl/openssl.cnf /etc/ssl/openssl.cnf.old
# cd /usr/local/openssl
# cp openssl.cnf.sample openssl.cnf
```

3. You can modify *openssl.cnf* to fit your needs, but the defaults are usually sufficient. To verify that the new version is functioning, use the following command:

```
# openssl version
OpenSSL 0.9.8g 19 Oct 2007
```

A version later than 0.9.8e signifies that the new version is installed correctly. If the version information still indicates 0.9.8e, you probably haven't modified your default path. This is acceptable as long as you remember to specify the full path to the new version of OpenSSL when using the command-line tool (*/usr/local/bin/openssl*).

SSL CERTIFICATES

In this section, SSL Certificates will be created using the *CA.pl* script (a Perl script) installed by the OpenSSL port.

If you intend to have an official certificate authority sign your SSL Certificate, proceed to "Generate a Certificate Request for CA Submission." If you want to create a self-signed SSL Certificate, skip to "Create a Self-Signed SSL Certificate" on page 131.

Generate a Certificate Request for CA Submission

You can have an official certificate authority sign your SSL Certificate by sending a request. Most certificate authorities charge a fee for this service. See "Notes" on page 134 for more information about the certificate signing process.

1. Certificate authorities will need a certificate request file in order to produce a valid SSL Certificate for your server. We will use the *CA.pl* script included with OpenSSL to create a certificate request. Let's use the */usr/local/openssl/certs* directory as your working directory. The command below will copy the script to the working directory:

```
# cd /usr/local/openssl
# cp misc/CA.pl certs
```

2. Run the script to create the certificate request using the following commands:

```
# cd /usr/local/openssl/certs
# setenv OPENSSL /usr/local/bin/openssl
# ./CA.pl -newreq
```

3. You will be asked to enter a PEM passphrase. Type one of your choosing. Be sure to remember this passphrase because you will need it later. Fill in the rest of the fields as you would like them to be shown when the public views your certificate. Make sure you enter your hostname in the Common Name prompt or the server certificate will not be valid. (If you were creating an SSL Certificate for a server with the hostname *host.example.com*, you would enter the Common Name *host.example.com.*)

NOTE *You may specify wildcard values in the Common Name field. For example, you could enter* *.example.com *as the common name to create an SSL Certificate that would cover any subdomain of* example.com *like* www.example.com, mail.example.com, *and so on. Be aware that if you do specify a wildcard like* *.example.com, *it won't be valid if you're trying to create a certificate for the root domain,* example.com.

After entering an email address, you will be prompted for a challenge password. Just press [ENTER] twice; the challenge password and company name are optional. You will be returned to the command prompt.

4. Running the *CA.pl* script gives you a newly created file named *newkey.pem,* which contains your encrypted private server key. To make identification easier, we'll copy this file to *host.example.com-encrypted-key.pem.* Use the following commands to copy this file (replace *host.example.com* with your actual Common Name):

```
# cp newkey.pem host.example.com-encrypted-key.pem
```

5. You will also have a newly created file named *newreq.pem* that contains your certificate request. You can submit this file to a certificate authority for signing. For clarity, we'll copy this file to *host.example.com-req.pem.* Use the following command to copy this file (replace *host.example.com* with your actual Common Name):

```
# cp newreq.pem host.example.com-req.pem
```

6. The *host.example.com-encrypted-key.pem* file is encrypted with the password you entered earlier. It is important for you to remember this password. You will need to enter it when an SSL application uses it. If this file is going to be used on an unattended server, it may be a good idea to decrypt the file so that daemons are able to load it without user intervention. To remove the encryption and make the unencrypted file readable only to root, use the following commands (replace *host.example.com* with your server's hostname):

```
# openssl rsa -in host.example.com-encrypted-key.pem\
? -out host.example.com-unencrypted-key.pem
# chmod 400 host.example.com-unencrypted-key.pem
```

It is important that the root user be the only user to have access to this file. Lack of strict permissions as set above can jeopardize the security of your server certificate.

7. After the certificate authority signs your certificate request, copy it to the */usr/local/openssl/certs* directory and name it *server.example.com-cert.pem* or whatever you see fit. Some server applications (Apache HTTP Server, Postfix, etc.) need your certificate authority's root certificate file as well. Most root certificate files are downloadable from the certificate authority's website. Save this file in */usr/local/openssl/certs* as *example.com-CAcert.pem*, or using any name you prefer.

Create a Self-Signed SSL Certificate

There are times when an SSL Certificate signed by an official certificate authority is not practical or affordable. In these cases, you may want to create and sign your own SSL Certificates by creating your own certificate authority. The easiest way to accomplish this is by using the included certificate authority script (*CA.pl*) to automate the process as much as possible. Be advised that creating your own certificates will cause an Untrusted Certificate dialog box to appear on client applications (web browsers, email clients, etc.). You can install your server's certificate file on client systems to avoid this warning.

1. Let's use the */usr/local/openssl/certs* directory as your working directory. We'll also extend the default certificate signing length of 365 days to 1,095 days (3 years). The commands below will copy the script to the working directory and set OpenSSL to create certificates that are good for 3 years:

```
# cd /usr/local/openssl
# cp misc/CA.pl certs
# sed -I .old 's/365/1095/' openssl.cnf
```

2. Run the script to create the certificate authority like this:

```
# cd /usr/local/openssl/certs
# setenv OPENSSL /usr/local/bin/openssl
# ./CA.pl -newca
```

3. The first prompt will ask you to enter a CA certificate filename. Since you are creating a new one, just press [ENTER].

4. The second prompt will ask you for a PEM passphrase. Type one of your choosing. Be sure to remember this passphrase because you will need it later. Fill in the rest of the fields as you would like them to be shown when the public views your certificate. The Common Name field can be your company name or something descriptive; it is effectively the name of your certificate. After entering an email address, you will be prompted for a challenge password. Just press [ENTER] twice; the challenge password and company name are optional. Lastly, you will be prompted to enter a passphrase for *./demoCA/private/ cakey.pem.* Enter the PEM passphrase you chose at the beginning of this step.

5. Generate a certificate request with the following command:

```
# ./CA.pl -newreq
```

You will be asked for a passphrase; use the same one you used earlier for simplicity. Enter all of the same information you supplied earlier. Make sure you enter your hostname in the Common Name prompt or the server certificate will not be valid. (If you were creating an SSL Certificate for the website *https://host.example.com,* you would enter the Common Name *host .example.com.*)

NOTE *You may specify wildcard values in the Common Name field as well. For example, you could enter* *.example.com *as the common name to create an SSL Certificate that would cover any subdomain of* example.com *like* www.example.com, server.example.com, *and so on. Be aware that if you do specify a wildcard like* *.example.com, *it won't be valid if you're trying to create a certificate for the root domain* example.com.

After entering an email address, you will be prompted for a challenge password. Just press [ENTER] twice; the challenge password and company name are optional. You will be returned to the command prompt. Don't change the filename of the newly created *newreq.pem* file; the script will be looking for it later.

6. Create the signed certificate from the request and certificate authority files you just created. Use the following command to begin the certificate signing process:

```
# ./CA.pl -signreq
```

Enter the password you chose earlier. Answer **Yes** at the next two prompts to create a signed SSL Certificate. The signed SSL Certificate is in the current working directory and named *newcert.pem.* The private key file is also in the current directory and named *newkey.pem.* The certificate authority and private key certificates reside in the *demoCA* directory and are named *cacert.pem* and *cakey.pem* respectively. To make all of these files easily identifiable we'll make copies of them using the following convention: *commonName-filetype.pem.* The following commands copy all certificates into the */usr/local/openssl/certs* directory (replace `host.example.com` with your server's hostname).

```
# cp newcert.pem host.example.com-cert.pem
# cp newkey.pem host.example.com-encrypted-key.pem
# cp demoCA/cacert.pem ./example.com-CAcert.pem
# cp demoCA/private/cakey.pem ./example.com-encrypted-CAkey.pem
```

The last two lines don't include the server name *host* because the certificate authority files are not specific to any one system; think of a certificate authority as a parent entity.

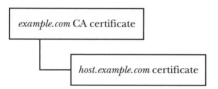

The *host.example.com-encrypted-key.pem* file is encrypted with the password you entered earlier. It is important for you to remember this password. You will need to enter it when an SSL application uses it. If this file is going to be used on an unattended server, it may be a good idea to decrypt this file so that daemons are able to load it without user intervention. To remove the encryption and make the unencrypted file readable only to root, use the following commands, replacing `host.example.com` with your domain name:

```
# openssl rsa -in host.example.com-encrypted-key.pem\
? -out host.example.com-unencrypted-key.pem
# chmod 400 host.example.com-unencrypted-key.pem
```

It is important that the root user be the only user to have access to this file (the commands above accomplish this). Lack of strict permissions as set above can risk the security of your server certificate.

7. It is important to export the CA certificate or *root certificate* (*example.com-CAcert.pem*) that was created in step 2 (page 131) so it can be installed on systems that will utilize your SSL Certificate. This is necessary to eliminate the appearance of Untrusted Root SSL Certificate Warning messages. These messages appear to warn the end user that there is a potential problem with the SSL Certificate. It is more difficult to detect an actual hijacked SSL session if this unnecessary warning isn't eliminated. Most client systems (Windows XP and Mac OS X) recognize SSL Certificate files encoded in DER (Distinguished Encoding Rules) binary format. To convert your PEM (Privacy Enhanced Mail) text based certificate to the DER format, type the following command:

```
# openssl x509 -in example.com-CAcert.pem -inform PEM\
? -out example.com-CAcert.cer -outform DER
```

You can send your DER encoded certificate via email with this command:

```
# uuencode example.com-CAcert.cer example.com-CAcert.cer\
? | mail -s "Subject" user@example.com
```

Substitute your filenames appropriately (the second instance of *example.com-CAcert.cer* can be replaced with a filename you would like the recipient to see) and replace *Subject* with an appropriate email subject line. *user@example.com* can be any valid email address.

CONFIG FILES

/usr/local/openssl/openssl.cnf
    Contains defaults for the OpenSSL command-line tool

NOTES

- Certificate authorities that sign SSL Certificates usually charge a variable fee. Be advised that if you self-sign your SSL Certificate, client programs will display a dialog to users explaining that the certificate is not in the trusted root database. This can confuse users who aren't familiar with the technology. If a small number of known users will be accessing your server with SSL, you can give each user a copy of your server's root certificate to install into their client application to eliminate this warning message (see step 7 on page 133).

- CAcert is a certificate authority that issues free SSL Certificates. If you are new to SSL Certificates, the site is a good place to learn about the SSL Certificate signing process. You can create a certificate signing request as outlined in this guide and have it signed by CAcert. Certificates signed by CAcert have limited support; most web browsers do not include its root certificate in their database of trusted CAs. CAcert's root certificate is, however, included in FreeBSD and several Linux distributions. Visit CAcert on the Web at *http://cacert.org*.

- If you are creating self-signed SSL Certificates and wish to create another one (e.g., if you are adding an additional server to your network), start at step 5 on page 132. (Remember to assign a Common Name consistent with your server's hostname.)

LEVEL 5

OPENVPN
FreeBSD port path: /usr/ports/security/openvpn
UDP port used – OPENVPN (1194)

OPENVPN SERVER 2.0.6

HTTP://OPENVPN.NET

SUMMARY

OpenVPN is an open source VPN implementation that uses the OpenSSL library to encrypt data traveling over a public network. A *VPN (virtual private network)* is a private connection from one point to another that utilizes an existing network as a transport medium. VPNs are popular with businesses because they allow secure communication between sites or employees without the need to lease dedicated WAN (wide area network) lines.

James Yonan began developing OpenVPN in early 2002. Yonan's employer at the time afforded him the freedom to telecommute. As a result, he became interested in telecommunication tools. His examination of the open source VPN community revealed a divide between security-conscious and usability-based software projects. Yonan's OpenVPN has grown into a very popular and complete VPN solution that addresses both security and usability issues. Yonan continues development of OpenVPN as project leader.

There are several VPN implementations, each of which offers various levels of security and functionality.

- PPTP (Point to Point Tunneling Protocol) is used to implement some VPNs. It is considered insecure due to a publicly known security exploit.
- L2TP/IPsec (Layer 2 Tunneling Protocol with Internet Protocol Security) is a reasonably secure VPN solution. However, it has problems traversing many basic NAT routers.
- OpenVPN is a cross-platform VPN solution that has proven to be secure, sustainable across NAT routers, and scalable. OpenVPN does require client software installation to function and can be complicated to set up initially.

OpenVPN supports routed or bridged VPNs. A *routed VPN* creates a virtual subnet for the client and routes traffic over the VPN if addressed to a system on the remote side. A *bridged VPN* connects clients to an existing network subnet. Data is broadcast through the bridge like a virtual Ethernet hub. A bridged VPN tunnel can provide a client with the same network functionality as being connected locally to that network. This guide outlines the setup of a bridged VPN rather than the default routed method.

A bridged VPN joins remote clients to a local network as if they were onsite, with all of the benefits of being on that local network. Also, bridged VPNs can use non-routable protocols (required by Windows file shares, broadcast traffic, LAN games, and so on) that small office and home office users may find useful.

OPENVPN
FreeBSD port path: /usr/ports/security/openvpn
UDP port used – OPENVPN (1194)

RESOURCES

OpenVPN Articles

http://openvpn.net/articles.html

REQUIRED

☑ FreeBSD 7.0-RELEASE (see "FreeBSD 7.0" on page 9)

☑ Updated ports collection (see "FreeBSD Ports Collection" on page 23)

☑ Internet connection

☑ OpenSSL (see "OpenSSL 0.9.8g" on page 127)

OPTIONAL

☑ Local DNS server (see "ISC BIND DNS Server 9.4.2" on page 73) for resolving hostnames of systems on the local network and resolving VPN client DNS queries

PREPARATION

You'll need to determine your local network's default gateway, default DNS servers, and the device name of your server's network interface. The commands shown below will help you obtain these addresses.

1. To display the IP address of the local network's default gateway and the device name, become root and enter:

```
# netstat -rn | grep default

default          192.168.1.1     UGS       0    2144  ed0
```

Here, the default gateway is 192.168.1.1. The device name of the network interface is ed0.

2. To display the DNS servers currently configured for use on your system, enter:

```
# grep nameserver /etc/resolv.conf
```

INSTALL

To begin the OpenVPN installation process, enter the following commands:

```
# cd /usr/ports/security/openvpn
# make config ; make install clean
# rehash
```

A menu should appear with an option for OpenVPN. We will leave this option at its default (off), so press [TAB] to select **OK** and then [ENTER] to continue.

OPENVPN
FreeBSD port path: /usr/ports/security/openvpn
UDP port used – OPENVPN (1194)

CONFIGURE

Once the installation process completes, it is time to configure OpenVPN for use on your system.

1. Create a directory named *openvpn* in */usr/local/etc* and copy the sample configuration file to it with the following commands (we'll edit this file later):

```
# mkdir /usr/local/etc/openvpn
# cd /usr/local/share/doc/openvpn/sample-config-files
# cp server.conf /usr/local/etc/openvpn/openvpn.conf
```

2. Begin creating the SSL Certificates and keys that are necessary for OpenVPN to function. Create a subdirectory of the *openvpn* directory named *keys*, for use as your working directory. The following commands will create the *keys* directory and copy the appropriate OpenSSL and script files to it:

```
# mkdir /usr/local/etc/openvpn/keys
# cd /usr/local/etc/openvpn/keys
# cp /usr/local/openssl/misc/CA.pl .
```

3. Create a CA certificate and key using the *CA.pl* script:

```
# ./CA.pl -newca
```

4. When prompted for a CA certificate filename, simply press [ENTER] to create the file.

5. When asked for a PEM passphrase, enter one, and be sure to remember it. You will need it later.

6. When prompted for Country Name, State, Locality, and so on, enter the appropriate responses. Enter **OpenVPN-CA** for the Common Name.

7. After entering an email address, you will be prompted for a challenge password. Just press [ENTER] twice; the challenge password and company name are optional. You will be returned to the command prompt once you enter the PEM passphrase you created in step 5.

8. Generate a certificate request. Enter the following command to begin this process:

```
# ./CA.pl -newreq
```

9. When asked for a passphrase, enter the same one you used earlier for the sake of simplicity.

10. Enter the same information you entered earlier, but enter **server** for the Common Name.

11. After entering an email address, you will be prompted for a challenge password. Just press [ENTER] twice; the challenge password and company name are optional. You will be returned to the command prompt.

OPENVPN
FreeBSD port path: /usr/ports/security/openvpn
UDP port used – OPENVPN (1194)

12. Create the signed certificate from the request and certificate authority files we produced above. Begin the certificate signing process with:

```
# ./CA.pl -signreq
```

13. Enter the password you assigned earlier.

14. Answer **yes** to the *Sign the certificate* and *commit* prompts to create a signed SSL Certificate.

The signed SSL Certificate is in the current working directory and is named *newcert.pem*. To make it easily identifiable, we'll copy this file to *openvpn-cert.pem* and our private key to *openvpn-encrypted-key.pem* below. The CA certificate and key are in the *demoCA* directory. We will copy them to the current working directory and rename them *openvpn-CAcert.pem* and *openvpn-encrypted-CAkey.pem* respectively.

15. Enter the following commands to organize your SSL Certificates as mentioned above:

```
# cp newcert.pem openvpn-cert.pem
# cp newkey.pem openvpn-encrypted-key.pem
# cp demoCA/cacert.pem ./openvpn-CAcert.pem
# cp demoCA/private/cakey.pem ./openvpn-encrypted-CAkey.pem
```

16. The *openvpn-encrypted-key.pem* file is encrypted with the password you entered earlier. We will remove this encryption so OpenVPN can use the file. The following commands will remove the encryption and make the file readable by the root user:

```
# openssl rsa -in openvpn-encrypted-key.pem -out openvpn-unencrypted-key.pem
# chmod 400 openvpn-unencrypted-key.pem
```

Now we begin producing client certificates with private keys for use with OpenVPN. In this example, we will use the names client01, client02, and so on. (You may use a different naming convention that helps you to identify clients easily.)

17. To create the private key and certificate request for client01, enter the following commands:

```
# openssl req -days 1095 -nodes -new -keyout client01-key.pem\
? -out client01-req.pem
# chmod 400 client01-key.pem
```

18. When prompted for the Country Name, State, Locality, and so on, enter the appropriate responses.

19. You must enter *client01* for the Common Name because each client *must* have a unique Common Name. You may replace *client01* with another name if you used a different naming convention, as long as each new client name is unique.

OPENVPN
FreeBSD port path: /usr/ports/security/openvpn
UDP port used – OPENVPN (1194)

NOTE *You may press* [ENTER] *at the optional challenge password and company name prompts to bypass them; they are not necessary.*

20. Create a signed client certificate using the OpenVPN certificate authority we created earlier:

```
# openssl ca -days 1095 -out client01-cert.pem -in client01-req.pem
```

21. When prompted, enter the password you assigned earlier.

22. Answer **yes** to the *Sign the certificate* and *commit* prompts to continue.

23. To create additional certificates and keys for additional clients, repeat steps 17 through 22 above, substituting client02, client03, and so on for client01. (Be sure to change the Common Name to reflect the iteration of the client you are creating.)

24. Once you have created your client certificates, transfer the appropriate certificate (*client01-cert.pem*) and key (*client01-key.pem*) to your client system using a secure medium (SFTP, removable media, etc.). Do not expose the *client01-key.pem* file to the public!

25. You need to create a Diffie-Hellman parameter in order for OpenVPN to function correctly. To do so, ensure that you are still in the */usr/local/etc/openvpn/keys* working directory, then enter the following command:

```
# openssl dhparam -out dh2048.pem 2048
```

26. Edit the *openvpn.conf* file that you created in step 1. First, open *openvpn.conf*:

```
# ee /usr/local/etc/openvpn/openvpn.conf
```

27. Uncomment the `dev tap` declaration (~52) by removing the semicolon (;) from the beginning of the line. Comment the `dev tun` declaration by inserting a semicolon at the beginning of the line. This tells OpenVPN to use the `tap` device, which is needed for Ethernet bridging. These two lines should now appear like this:

```
dev tap
;dev tun
```

28. Tell OpenVPN where to find the CA certificate, server certificate, and server private key. Scroll down to the `ca` declaration (~78) and replace `ca.crt` with the relative path (relative to the *openvpn* directory) and filename of your CA certificate file. Do the same for the `cert` and `key` declarations. The lines should appear as follows:

```
ca keys/openvpn-CAcert.pem
cert keys/openvpn-cert.pem
key keys/openvpn-unencrypted-key.pem # This file should be kept secret
```

OPENVPN
FreeBSD port path: /usr/ports/security/openvpn
UDP port used – OPENVPN (1194)

29. Tell OpenVPN where the Diffie-Hellman parameter file resides. Modify the dh declaration (~87) to point to *dh2048.pem* in the *openvpn* directory. It should now appear as follows:

```
dh keys/dh2048.pem
```

30. Comment out the server declaration (~96) by inserting a semicolon (;) at the beginning of the line. This line should now appear as follows:

```
;server 10.8.0.0 255.255.255.0
```

31. Uncomment the server-bridge statement (~115) by removing the semicolon from the beginning of the line. Modify the IP addresses on this line to reflect your network: The first IP address should be your local network's default gateway; the second is the netmask of the local network; the third defines the lower limit of the client IP address pool; and the fourth defines the upper limit of the client IP address pool. This line should appear something like this:

```
                   Gateway    Netmask    IP range of VPN clients
                 ┌─────────┐ ┌─────────┐ ┌─────────────────────┐
server-bridge 192.168.1.1 255.255.255.0 192.168.1.61 192.168.1.69
```

NOTE *If you are using a local DHCP server (common in NAT routers) be sure the range you specify here doesn't overlap the range of IP addresses used by the DHCP server. If you are using a DHCP server built into a NAT router, check its configuration interface for this range. For example, if the DHCP server has a starting IP address of 192.168.1.10 with a maximum of 50 users, you would have a range from 192.168.1.10 to 192.168.1.60, and you could safely use a range of 192.168.1.61 to 192.168.1.69 for VPN clients (assuming there are no static IP assignments in this range).*

32. Uncomment the push redirect-gateway declaration (~181). This line should appear as follows:

```
push "redirect-gateway"
```

NOTE *This option changes the default gateway of the VPN client to that of the gateway on the OpenVPN server side network. It is useful when you are on an untrusted remote network (such as those found in hotel rooms, Wi-Fi hotspots, etc.) and want to eliminate the risk of exposing your data to potential attackers. You may leave this line untouched if you do not wish to enable this feature, and skip to step 34 below.*

33. Uncomment the push dhcp-option statement (~187). This option instructs VPN clients to use the specified DNS server for hostname lookups. This line should now appear as follows, with your default DNS server IP substituted for the one shown here in italics.

```
push "dhcp-option DNS 192.168.1.11"
```

OPENVPN
FreeBSD port path: /usr/ports/security/openvpn
UDP port used – OPENVPN (1194)

NOTE *As of this writing the above feature functions on GUI OpenVPN clients running Windows (OpenVPN GUI) or Macintosh (Tunnelblick). If you have clients on other platforms, visit their client software vendor for updates or manually set their DNS server IP after their VPN connection is established.*

34. To enable communication between VPN clients (two users connected simultaneously), uncomment the `client-to-client` declaration (~196). The line should appear as follows:

```
client-to-client
```

35. Uncomment `user nobody` and `group nobody` (~254). This reduces OpenVPN's privileges after initialization. These two lines should appear like this:

```
user nobody
group nobody
```

36. Save and exit.

TESTING

In this section, we'll perform some tests to confirm that OpenVPN answers requests properly. You'll need a computer with an OpenVPN client installed and configured before continuing. (See "Notes" on page 143 for information on client setup.)

1. The kernel modules `if_bridge` and `if_tap` must be loaded in order to allow traffic on a remote client to bridge into the local network. Load these two modules like this:

```
# kldload if_bridge
# kldload if_tap
```

2. Create the virtual bridge and tap network interfaces that will act as a virtual hub between remote clients and the local network, as follows (replace *ed0* with the device name of your network interface):

```
# ifconfig bridge0 create
# ifconfig tap0 create
# ifconfig tap0 up
# ifconfig bridge0 addm ed0 addm tap0
```

3. Start OpenVPN and watch for incoming connections from your OpenVPN client.

```
# cd /usr/local/etc/openvpn
# openvpn openvpn.conf
```

OPENVPN
FreeBSD port path: /usr/ports/security/openvpn
UDP port used – OPENVPN (1194)

You should see output similar to this:

```
Sun Jun 15 17:04:20 2008 OpenVPN 2.0.6 i386-portbld-freebsd7.0 [SSL] [LZO]
Sun Jun 15 17:04:20 2008 Diffie-Hellman initialized with 2048 bit key
Sun Jun 15 17:04:20 2008 TLS-Auth MTU parms [ L:1574 D:138 EF:38 EB:0 ET:0
Sun Jun 15 17:04:20 2008 TUN/TAP device /dev/tap0 opened
Sun Jun 15 17:04:20 2008 Data Channel MTU parms [ L:1574 D:1450 EF:42 EB:135

Sun Jun 15 17:04:20 2008 GID set to nobody
Sun Jun 15 17:04:20 2008 UID set to nobody
Sun Jun 15 17:04:20 2008 UDPv4 link local (bound): [undef]:1194
Sun Jun 15 17:04:20 2008 UDPv4 link remote: [undef]
Sun Jun 15 17:04:20 2008 MULTI: multi_init called, r=256 v=256
Sun Jun 15 17:04:20 2008 IFCONFIG POOL: base=192.168.0.200 size=11
Sun Jun 15 17:04:20 2008 IFCONFIG POOL LIST
Sun Jun 15 17:04:20 2008 client01,192.168.1.61
Sun Jun 15 17:04:20 2008 Initialization Sequence Completed
```

NOTE *If possible, try connecting a client to the server from outside the local network. (Remember to forward UDP port 1194 to the server if it is behind a NAT router.) Once a connection is initiated, you should see status messages scroll by in real time.*

4. When you have completed testing, press [CTRL-C] at the console to shut down OpenVPN. Assuming the test was successful, configure OpenVPN and the necessary bridge and tap interfaces to start automatically at system startup.

5. Enable the if_bridge and if_tap kernel modules at startup by first opening *loader.conf* in */boot* like this:

```
# ee /boot/loader.conf
```

6. Carefully add the following lines and double-check for typos:

```
if_bridge_load="YES"
bridgestp_load="YES"
if_tap_load="YES"
```

7. Save and exit.

8. Add a single line to the *sysctl.conf* file in */etc* to automatically apply the up flag to the tap0 interface when the OpenVPN daemon opens it. To do so, open *sysctl.conf* like so:

```
# ee /etc/sysctl.conf
```

and add the following line:

```
net.link.tap.up_on_open=1
```

Save and exit.

OPENVPN
FreeBSD port path: /usr/ports/security/openvpn
UDP port used – OPENVPN (1194)

9. Add the OpenVPN startup lines and bridge statements to the *rc.conf* file in /etc. Open *rc.conf*:

```
# ee /etc/rc.conf
```

and add the following lines (replace *ed0* with the device name of your network interface):

```
openvpn_enable="YES"
cloned_interfaces="bridge0 tap0"
ifconfig_bridge0="addm ed0 addm tap0"
```

Save, exit, and reboot.

10. Retest OpenVPN by reconnecting with a client system to confirm that it starts properly.

CONFIG FILES

/usr/local/etc/openvpn/openvpn.conf
    Main configuration file

LOG FILES

/var/log/messages
    Contains output from OpenVPN

/usr/local/etc/openvpn/openvpn-status.log
    Shows the status of current connections updated every minute

/usr/local/etc/openvpn/ipp.txt
    Records client virtual IP addresses

NOTES

When you are ready to configure an OpenVPN client, you will need these four files on the client system:

- The OpenVPN public CA certificate file (*openvpn-CAcert.pem*)
- The client certificate (*client01-cert.pem*)
- The client private key (*client01-key.pem*)
- A client OpenVPN configuration file (example below)

You should already have the first three files (we created them earlier). The fourth file is a modification of the *openvpn.conf* file we used to configure the server above.

OPENVPN
FreeBSD port path: /usr/ports/security/openvpn
UDP port used – OPENVPN (1194)

Listed below is a copy of a client version of the *openvpn.conf* that would work with the server configuration in this chapter (change the items shown in italics to match your configuration):

```
client
dev tap
proto udp
remote host.example.com 1194
resolv-retry infinite
persist-key
persist-tun
ca openvpn-CAcert.pem
cert client01-cert.pem
key client01-key.pem
comp-lzo
verb 3
```

You should keep these four files in the same directory on the client system.

See the documentation from your specific client application for additional installation details. The OpenVPN website has a list of popular OpenVPN client GUIs for different platforms at *http://openvpn.net/gui.html*.

PHP 5.2.5
HTTP://PHP.NET

SUMMARY

PHP (PHP: Hypertext Preprocessor) is a server-side scripting language that can be embedded into HTML. It is commonly used to create dynamically generated websites and is the foundation of applications like WordPress (blogging software), MediaWiki (which underlies Wikipedia), and phpBB (a web-based bulletin board system). PHP is also known for its easy integration with relational database management systems. These applications all use a combination of PHP and a relational database system like MySQL.

Unlike JavaScript, which executes functions in a user's web browser, PHP handles functions on the web server. Websites that use JavaScript must send full blocks of code to clients' web browsers, which can eat up bandwidth, especially with large sites. PHP, on the other hand, executes code on the web server and then sends only the necessary HTML to the client to produce the completed page, thus eliminating the need to send lengthy code to web browsers.

PHP began as a small set of Perl scripts written by Rasmus Lerdorf. He used them to monitor traffic to his online resume. In 1995, after adding features, Lerdorf publicly released a tool written in C called PHP/FI (Personal Home Page/Forms Interpreter). In 1997 two Israeli developers, Zeev Suraski and Andi Gutmans, rewrote PHP/FI to accommodate their eCommerce project. This rewrite was released in mid-1998 as PHP 3. That winter, Suraski and Gutmans began another rewrite, this time of PHP's core. The product of this work became the Zend Engine, on which current versions of PHP are based.

RESOURCES

Official PHP Manual
http://us3.php.net/manual/en

REQUIRED

☑   FreeBSD 7.0-RELEASE (see "FreeBSD 7.0" on page 9)

☑   Updated ports collection (see "FreeBSD Ports Collection" on page 23)

☑   Apache HTTP server (see "Apache HTTP Server 2.2.8" on page 33)

☑   Internet connection

OPTIONAL

☑ Lynx (see "Lynx 2.8.6" on page 91) for testing PHP installation from the command line

PREPARATION

Become the superuser.

INSTALL

To begin the PHP installation process, enter the following commands:

```
# cd /usr/ports/lang/php5
# make config ; make install clean
# rehash
```

A menu will appear with options for php5. Scroll to APACHE and press [SPACEBAR] to install the Apache module. Leave the other options at their defaults, then press [TAB] to select **OK** and [ENTER] to begin the install.

CONFIGURE

Once the installation is complete, it's time to configure PHP for use on your system.

1. Edit the *httpd.conf* file to configure Apache to work with the PHP module. Open *httpd.conf*:

```
# ee /usr/local/etc/apache22/httpd.conf
```

2. Scroll down to the DirectoryIndex declaration (~216) and insert **index.php** prior to index.html like this:

```
<IfModule dir_module>
    DirectoryIndex index.php index.html
</IfModule>
```

This setting directs Apache to give priority to *index.php* over *index.html*, if a requested directory contains both files.

3. Scroll down to the bottom of *httpd.conf* and add these lines:

```
AddType application/x-httpd-php .php
AddType application/x-httpd-php-source .phps
```

4. Save and exit.

5. Copy the *php.ini-recommended* file to *php.ini* in */usr/local/etc*. This will set the options in PHP recommended for production server environments.

```
# cd /usr/local/etc
# cp php.ini-recommended php.ini
```

6. Specify the PHP session save path. This directive tells PHP where to store temporary session files and is commented off by default. Uncomment the session.save_path as follows. First, open *php.ini*:

```
# ee /usr/local/etc/php.ini
```

Scroll down to the session.save_path declaration (~1050) and remove its preceding semicolon. It should appear like this after the edit:

```
session.save_path = "/tmp"
```

7. Save, exit, and restart Apache:

```
# /usr/local/etc/rc.d/apache22 restart
```

TESTING

To test your installation of PHP, we'll use the built-in phpinfo() function to display a variety of information about your PHP installation. We will create a file named *phpinfo.php* in your web server's root directory and enter a single line of PHP code.

1. Create *phpinfo.php* in the Apache's default data directory:

```
# ee /usr/local/www/apache22/data/phpinfo.php
```

and add this line:

```
<?php phpinfo(); ?>
```

2. Save and exit.

3. Use a web browser to request *phpinfo.php* from your Apache server. If you have Lynx installed, the command would look like this for a webserver with the hostname *host.example.com*:

```
# lynx http://host.example.com/phpinfo.php
```

You should see several tables of information if PHP is configured properly. If you see a blank page, either PHP is incorrectly installed or there may be a problem with the *phpinfo.php* file. (Check for typos and so on.)

4. Delete the *phpinfo.php* file when testing is complete:

```
# rm /usr/local/www/apache22/data/phpinfo.php
```

UTILITIES

Following is brief information on the PHP command-line interface.

php

The PHP command-line program is useful for testing and development.

Command   php

Syntax   php *-options arguments*

Options

-a   Runs PHP in interactive mode

-f   Parses and executes a file

-c   Specifies a configuration file instead of the default *php.ini*

-v   Displays PHP version

-l   Tests for syntax errors

Examples

To run PHP in interactive mode, enter:

```
# php -a
```

To parse and execute a PHP file named *test.php* in the current working directory using an alternate configuration file named *php-test.ini*, enter:

```
# php -c php-test.ini -f test.php
```

To test a file named *example.php* for syntax errors, enter:

```
# php -l -f example.php
```

CONFIG FILES

/usr/local/etc/php.ini-dist
   Contains options suited for developers

/usr/local/etc/php.ini-recommended
   Contains options better suited for production server environments

NOTE   *The configuration file that you choose to use must be renamed* php.ini *and reside in the* /usr/local/etc *directory.*

PHPBB 3.0.0
HTTP://PHPBB.COM

SUMMARY

phpBB is an open source forum system, or *bulletin board system*, written in PHP. This program uses MySQL to store its data, though it also supports the PostgreSQL, Access, and Microsoft SQL Server database systems. Major features include an unlimited number of forums and posts, multilingual support, private and public forums, a template system for design customization, and a forum search utility.

Web-based bulletin boards have been very popular since the mid-1990s. Many companies use Internet forums to provide technical support to their customers and many enthusiast forums exist where users discuss various subjects.

phpBB is one of the most popular Internet bulletin board systems available. James Atkinson began work on a forum system for his website in the summer of 2000, while he was a college student. He set out to create an open source flat-style message board, of which very few existed at the time. Nathan Codding and John Abela joined the development team, and phpBB 1.0 was released in December 2000. Development of phpBB 2.0 began in February 2001; the source code was rewritten from scratch and released in April 2002. James Atkinson continues to manage and lead the phpBB project with a team of five developers.

RESOURCES

phpBB Userguide
  http://www.phpbb.com/support/documentation/3.0

phpBBHacks.com (large phpBB resource including themes)
  http://www.phpbbhacks.com

REQUIRED

☑ FreeBSD 7.0-RELEASE (see "FreeBSD 7.0" on page 9)

☑ Updated ports collection (see "FreeBSD Ports Collection" on page 23)

☑ Apache HTTP server (see "Apache HTTP Server 2.2.8" on page 33)

☑ PHP 5 (see "PHP 5.2.5" on page 145)

☑ MySQL 5 (see "MySQL Server 5.0.51" on page 99)

☑ Internet connection

☑ Registered domain name

PREPARATION

1. Become the superuser.

2. A MySQL database and user account must be created for phpBB. The commands below create a database named *phpbb* and a user named *phpbb*, and assign full privileges to this user:

```
# mysql -u root -p
mysql> create database phpbb;
mysql> grant all on phpbb.* to
    -> phpbb@localhost identified by 'password';
mysql> quit
```

Replace *password* with a password of your choice and write it down; you'll need it later. (The single quotes around password are required.)

INSTALL

To begin the phpBB installation process, enter the following commands:

```
# cd /usr/ports/www/phpbb3
# make config ; make install clean
```

CONFIGURE

Once the installation process is complete, it's time to configure phpBB for use on your system. We'll create a phpBB-specific Apache configuration file that will point Apache to the correct location of the phpBB files and make administration easier by keeping phpBB-specific options separate from the main *httpd.conf* file.

1. Create a configuration file for phpBB:

```
# ee /usr/local/etc/apache22/Includes/phpbb.conf
```

NOTE *By default, Apache searches the* /usr/local/etc/apache22/Includes *directory for configuration files.*

2. Add the following lines:

```
Alias /phpbb "/usr/local/www/phpBB3/"

<Directory "/usr/local/www/phpBB3/">
Options Indexes FollowSymLinks
AllowOverride None
Order allow,deny
Allow from all
</Directory>
```

NOTE *By default, phpBB is set up as a subdirectory of your web server's root site. This means you would enter* http://host.example.com/phpbb *into your web browser. To change this default directory, replace* phpbb *with a different name.*

3. Save and exit, then restart Apache to commit the changes:

```
# /usr/local/etc/rc.d/apache22 restart
```

4. Open *http://host.example.com/phpbb* in your favorite web browser. (Substitute your hostname and directory if you modified it.)

5. Click the **Install** tab and then click the **Proceed to next step** button at the bottom of the page.

6. The Installation Compatibility page will appear. Scroll to the bottom and click **Start install**.

7. On the database configuration page, select **MySQL with MySQLi Extension**. Enter `localhost` for "Database server hostname or DSN." Enter the database name, username, and password you created earlier and then click **Proceed to next step**.

8. The next page should read *Successful connection*. Click **Proceed to next step**.

9. Enter the appropriate information on the Administrator configuration page. This account will be used to administer phpBB. Click **Proceed to next step**.

10. The next page should read *Tests passed*. Click **Proceed to next step**. phpBB will save the configuration file. Click **Proceed to next step**.

11. The advanced settings page will appear. You may make changes or accept the default settings; then click **Proceed to next step**. phpBB will indicate the creation of the initial database tables. Click **Proceed to next step** to complete installation.

12. The phpBB install directory must be removed to enable normal operation, and the *config.php* file containing your MySQL database password should be set so that it isn't world readable:

```
# rm -rf /usr/local/www/phpBB3/install
# chmod 640 /usr/local/www/phpBB3/config.php
```

ADMINISTRATION

Use this URL to administer your phpBB installation, substituting your server's hostname for *host.example.com*:

http://host.example.com/phpbb/adm

CONFIG FILES

/usr/local/www/phpBB3/config.php
  Holds the username, password, and database information for phpBB

PHPLDAPADMIN 1.1.0

HTTP://PHPLDAPADMIN.SOURCEFORGE.NET

SUMMARY

phpLDAPadmin is an open source web-based LDAP (Lightweight Directory Access Protocol) administration tool written in PHP. Its major features include template-based entry creation; the ability to add, modify, rename, and delete LDAP entries; user password management with hash support; LDIF (LDAP Data Interchange Format) import/export; and an LDAP schema browser.

phpLDAPadmin is popular with LDAP administrators because it is platform independent. As a web-based application, it allows administrators to maintain LDAP databases remotely from virtually any computer with a web browser.

phpLDAPadmin was created by David Smith. Deon George currently maintains the phpLDAPadmin project with the help of various contributors.

RESOURCES

phpLDAPadmin Documentation
   http://wiki.phpldapadmin.info

REQUIRED

☑ FreeBSD 7.0-RELEASE (see "FreeBSD 7.0" on page 9)

☑ Updated ports collection (see "FreeBSD Ports Collection" on page 23)

☑ Apache HTTP server (see "Apache HTTP Server 2.2.8" on page 33)

☑ OpenLDAP (see "OpenLDAP Server 2.3.38" on page 113)

☑ PHP 5 (see "PHP 5.2.5" on page 145)

☑ Internet connection

OPTIONAL

☑ OpenSSL with a signed SSL Certificate (see "OpenSSL 0.9.8g" on page 127)

☑ Registered domain name

PREPARATION

If you will be using phpLDAPadmin from an insecure public network, then begin by ensuring that your Apache HTTP server is correctly configured to accept HTTPS connections with SSL. If your Apache HTTP server lacks SSL support, your LDAP login and password will be transmitted over the network "in the clear" and may be exposed to unauthorized persons.

Become the superuser.

INSTALL

To begin the installation process for phpLDAPadmin, enter:

```
# cd /usr/ports/net/phpldapadmin
# make config ; make install clean
```

CONFIGURE

Once the installation process completes, configure phpLDAPadmin for use on your system.

1. Open the *config.php* file in */usr/local/www/phpldapadmin/config*:

```
# ee /usr/local/www/phpldapadmin/config/config.php
```

2. Scroll down to the $config->custom->session['blowfish'] declaration (~49) and enter an alphanumeric string (letters or numbers) between the single quotes (longer is better). A random alphanumeric string can be found at *https://www.grc.com/passwords.htm*. This encrypts the content of *cookies* (data stored in a web browser that provides identity information to a server) used by phpLDAPadmin. The line should appear as follows (with your alphanumeric string in place of the sample):

```
$config->custom->session['blowfish'] = 'aSD453PAsldiflDSAPOSD';
```

3. Scroll down to the default hashing algorithm setting (~255). Change it from md5 to ssha (which is more secure) and uncomment the line by removing the preceding slashes (//). The line should now look like this:

```
$ldapservers->SetValue($i,'appearance','password_hash','ssha');
```

4. Save and exit.

5. Now we'll create a phpLDAPadmin-specific Apache configuration file. This file will point Apache to the correct location of the phpLDAPadmin files and make administration easier by keeping phpLDAPadmin-specific options separate from the main *httpd.conf* file. By default, Apache searches the */usr/local/etc/apache22/Includes* directory for configuration files. To create a configuration file for phpLDAPadmin, open the file:

```
# ee /usr/local/etc/apache22/Includes/phpldapadmin.conf
```

and add the following lines:

```
Alias /phpldapadmin "/usr/local/www/phpldapadmin/htdocs/"

<Directory "/usr/local/www/phpldapadmin/htdocs/">
Options none
AllowOverride none
Order Deny,Allow
Deny from all
Allow from 127.0.0.1 192.168.1
</Directory>
```

Replace *192.168.1* with the first three octets of your local network to restrict access to the local subnet. If you need access from outside your local network, see "Notes" on page 156 on forcing secure connections to non-local IPs.

NOTE   *By default, phpLDAPadmin is set up as a subdirectory of your web server's root site. This means that in order to reach it you would enter* http://host.example.com/ phpldapadmin *into your web browser. To change this default directory, replace* phpldapadmin *(italicized in the above entry) with a different name.*

6. Save and exit, then restart Apache to commit the changes:

```
# /usr/local/etc/rc.d/apache22 restart
```

To access phpLDAPadmin with a web browser, enter the following URL (using your server's hostname):

```
http://host.example.com/phpldapadmin
```

User John Doe in the organizational unit (ou) People on the domain *example.com* would enter:

```
Login DN:
cn=John Doe,ou=People,dc=example,dc=com
```

ADMINISTRATION

To administer your LDAP server with phpLDAPadmin, enter one of the following URLs, substituting your server's hostname for *host.example.com.*

http://host.example.com/phpldapadmin (for an insecure connection)

https://host.example.com/phpldapadmin (for an SSL encrypted connection)

You will be prompted for your login DN; use the syntax shown below. Replace *example* and *com* with your domain name.

```
Login DN:
cn=Manager,dc=example,dc=com
```

CONFIG FILES

/usr/local/www/phpldapadmin/config/config.php
   Allows for the customization of phpLDAPadmin

NOTES

To ensure the security of logins over the Internet, all communication should be secured by requiring HTTPS connections to phpLDAPadmin. We'll reconstruct our phpLDAPadmin-specific configuration file to ensure this. Apache needs to be configured with SSL support for this to work. Open the existing file:

```
# ee /usr/local/etc/apache22/Includes/phpldapadmin.conf
```

and then modify the file to read as follows:

```
Alias /phpldapadmin "/usr/local/www/phpldapadmin/htdocs/"

<Directory "/usr/local/www/phpldapadmin/htdocs/">
Options none
AllowOverride None
Order Allow,Deny
Allow from All
</Directory>

<IfModule mod_rewrite.c>
RewriteEngine On
RewriteCond %{HTTPS} off
RewriteCond %{REQUEST_URI} /phpldapadmin
RewriteRule (.*) https://host.example.com/phpldapadmin/ [R]
</IfModule>
```

Make the appropriate substitutions for your domain name and then save, exit, and restart Apache:

```
# /usr/local/etc/rc.d/apache22 restart
```

PHPMYADMIN 2.11.5
HTTP://WWW.PHPMYADMIN.NET

SUMMARY

phpMyAdmin is an open source web-based MySQL administration tool written in PHP. Many use phpMyAdmin as a substitute for the command-line tools included with the default installation of MySQL. phpMyAdmin is the recipient of numerous industry awards, and it has garnered much praise from the database administrator community.

Major features include the ability to create and drop databases; create, drop, or alter tables; delete, edit, or add fields; execute any SQL statement; manage keys on fields; manage privileges; and export data into various formats. phpMyAdmin has been translated into more than 50 languages.

Like other web administration utilities, phpMyAdmin allows administrators high flexibility. It is platform independent and management functions can be performed from any Internet-connected computer with virtually any web browser.

Development of phpMyAdmin began in 1998 by IT consultant Tobias Ratschiller. Ratschiller's work was based loosely on a program called MySQL-Webadmin, a product of Peter Kuppelwieser's, who had ceased development at the time. Ratschiller wrote new code for phpMyAdmin, and improved on concepts from Kuppelwieser's project. Ratschiller left the phpMyAdmin project in 2001. A team of eight developers led by Olivier Müller continues development of phpMyAdmin at SourceForge.net (*http://sourceforge.net*).

RESOURCES

phpMyAdmin Documentation
> *http://www.phpmyadmin.net/documentation*

REQUIRED

- ☑ FreeBSD 7.0-RELEASE (see "FreeBSD 7.0" on page 9)
- ☑ Updated ports collection (see "FreeBSD Ports Collection" on page 23)
- ☑ Apache HTTP Server (see "Apache HTTP Server 2.2.8" on page 33)
- ☑ MySQL 5 (see "MySQL Server 5.0.51" on page 99)
- ☑ PHP 5 (see "PHP 5.2.5" on page 145)
- ☑ Internet connection

OPTIONAL

☑ OpenSSL with a signed SSL Certificate (see "OpenSSL 0.9.8g" on page 127)

☑ Registered domain name

PREPARATION

If you plan to use phpMyAdmin from an insecure public network, be sure that your Apache HTTP server is correctly configured to accept HTTPS connections with SSL. If your Apache HTTP server lacks SSL support, your MySQL login and password will be transmitted over the network "in the clear" and may be exposed to unauthorized persons.

Become the superuser.

NOTE *This guide assumes that MySQL and Apache co-exist on the same system.*

INSTALL

To begin the installation process for phpMyAdmin, enter the following commands:

```
# cd /usr/ports/databases/phpmyadmin
# make config ; make install clean
```

A menu of options will appear. Scroll down to **MYSQLI** and press [SPACEBAR] to enable improved MySQL support (which allows access to functionality in MySQL 4.1.*x* and later). Leave the other options at their defaults. Press [TAB] to highlight **OK**, then press [ENTER] to begin installation.

CONFIGURE

Once the installation process is complete, it is time to configure phpMyAdmin for use on your system.

1. Specify configuration options in the *config.inc.php* file located in the */usr/local/www/phpMyAdmin* directory. Open *config.inc.php* like this:

```
# cd /usr/local/www/phpMyAdmin
# ee config.inc.php
```

2. Erase the contents of *config.inc.php* (for easier readability), and then add the lines shown below.

The options shown in italics may need to be modified to fit your specific configuration. Explanations of each line are provided below.

```
<?php
$cfg['blowfish_secret']          = '4fj8Rv15ZFls16Lei23qrn42';
$i                               = 1;
$cfg['Servers'][$i]['connect_type'] = 'socket';
```

```
$cfg['Servers'][$i]['auth_type']    = 'cookie';
$cfg['Servers'][$i]['extension']    = 'mysqli';
?>
```

$cfg[blowfish_secret] = is a random string that the Blowfish algorithm uses to encrypt password information stored in cookies. Enter a string of no more than 46 random characters here.

$i = specifies the array number for the lines below it. If you have multiple MySQL servers, you could specify a specific set (array) of options for each server.

$cfg['Servers'][$i]['connect_type'] = tells phpMyAdmin to contact the MySQL server via either Unix socket or tcp connection. Unix sockets are usually used when Apache and MySQL are running on the same system. TCP connections allow you to administer a MySQL server running on another computer, although MySQL must also be configured to allow incoming TCP connections.

$cfg['Servers'][$i]['auth_type'] = tells phpMyAdmin to use encrypted cookies to store username and password information.

$cfg['Servers'][$i]['extension'] = instructs phpMyAdmin to use the *mysqli* PHP extension, which allows access to added functionality in MySQL 4.1 and later.

3. Save and exit.

NOTE *The next few steps configure the optional* linked-tables infrastructure, *which is a set of phpMyAdmin-specific features, including PDF-generation, bookmarks, and history, among others. If you do not need this functionality, skip to step 8.*

4. Create a MySQL user named pma and grant it select, insert, update, and delete privileges for the *phpmyadmin* database. Here's how to create the user and assign the appropriate privileges:

```
# mysql -u root -p
mysql> grant select, insert, update, delete on phpmyadmin.* to
    -> pma@localhost identified by 'password';
mysql> quit;
```

Substitute *password* above with an arbitrary password, which will be used again later.

5. Use the *create_tables* script included with phpMyAdmin to create the appropriate database and tables. These commands will automatically create the database and tables:

```
# cd /usr/local/www/phpMyAdmin/scripts
# mysql -u root -p < create_tables_mysql_4_1_2+.sql
```

6. Re-edit the *config.inc.php* file in */usr/local/www/phpMyAdmin* to complete the setup. Open the file:

```
# ee /usr/local/www/phpMyAdmin/config.inc.php
```

and add the following lines:

```
<?php
$cfg['Servers'][$i]['pmadb']        = 'phpmyadmin';
$cfg['Servers'][$i]['controluser']  = 'pma';
$cfg['Servers'][$i]['controlpass']  = 'password';
$cfg['Servers'][$i]['table_info']   = 'pma_table_info';
$cfg['Servers'][$i]['pdf_pages']    = 'pma_pdf_pages';
$cfg['Servers'][$i]['history']      = 'pma_history';
$cfg['Servers'][$i]['column_info']  = 'pma_column_info';
$cfg['Servers'][$i]['table_coords'] = 'pma_table_coords';
$cfg['Servers'][$i]['relation']     = 'pma_relation';
$cfg['Servers'][$i]['bookmarktable'] = 'pma_bookmark';
?>
```

Replace *password* with the password you assigned to the pma user in step 4.

7. Save and exit.

8. Create a phpMyAdmin-specific Apache configuration file. This file will point Apache to the correct location of the phpMyAdmin files and make administration easier by keeping phpMyAdmin-specific options separate from the main *httpd.conf* file. By default, Apache searches the */usr/local/etc/apache22/ Includes* directory for configuration files. To create one for phpMyAdmin, open *phpmyadmin.conf*:

```
# ee /usr/local/etc/apache22/Includes/phpmyadmin.conf
```

and add the following lines:

```
Alias /phpmyadmin "/usr/local/www/phpMyAdmin/"

<Directory "/usr/local/www/phpMyAdmin/">
Options none
AllowOverride All
Order Deny,Allow
Deny from all
Allow from 127.0.0.1 192.168.1
</Directory>
```

Replace *192.168.1* with the first three octets of your local network to restrict access to the local subnet. If you need access from outside your local network, see "Notes" on page 161 on forcing secure connections to non-local IPs.

NOTE *By default, phpMyAdmin is set up as a subdirectory of your web server's root site. This means you would enter* http://host.example.com/phpmyadmin *into your web browser in order to access it. To change this default directory, replace* phpmyadmin *(italicized above) with a different name.*

9. Save and exit. Restart Apache to commit the changes:

```
# /usr/local/etc/rc.d/apache22 restart
```

10. You can access phpMyAdmin with a web browser at *http://host.example.com/phpmyadmin* (replace *host.example.com* with your server's hostname).

ADMINISTRATION

To administer your MySQL server with phpMyAdmin, use one of the following URLs, substituting your server's hostname and directory as appropriate:

> *http://host.example.com/phpmyadmin* (for unencrypted communication)

> *https://host.example.com/phpmyadmin* (for encrypted communication)

CONFIG FILES

/usr/local/www/phpMyAdmin/config.inc.php
  phpMyAdmin's main configuration file

NOTE *For details on options, see* /usr/local/www/phpMyAdmin/ Documentation.txt.

NOTES

When allowing logins from the Internet, all communications should be secured by permitting only HTTPS connections to phpMyAdmin. We'll reconstruct our phpMyAdmin-specific configuration file to accommodate this. Apache needs to be configured with SSL support for this to work. Open the existing file:

```
# ee /usr/local/etc/apache22/Includes/phpmyadmin.conf
```

and then modify the file to read as follows:

```
Alias /phpmyadmin "/usr/local/www/phpMyAdmin/"

<Directory "/usr/local/www/phpMyAdmin/">
Options none
AllowOverride All
Order Allow,Deny
Allow from All
</Directory>

<IfModule mod_rewrite.c>
RewriteEngine On
RewriteCond %{HTTPS} off
RewriteCond %{REQUEST_URI} /phpmyadmin
RewriteRule (.*) https://host.example.com/phpmyadmin/ [R]
</IfModule>
```

Make the appropriate substitutions and then save, exit, and restart Apache:

```
# /usr/local/etc/rc.d/apache22 restart
```

LEVEL 5

POSTFIX
FreeBSD port path: /usr/ports/mail/postfix
TCP ports used – SMTP (25), submission (587)

POSTFIX SMTP SERVER 2.5.1
HTTP://WWW.POSTFIX.ORG

SUMMARY

Postfix is an open source mail transfer agent (MTA). An *MTA* is used for routing and delivering email on the Internet. Postfix was originally developed as an alternative to the widely deployed Sendmail MTA. Like Sendmail, Postfix operates using SMTP. An emphasis on security was placed on its development in response to Sendmail's history of security-related problems.

Postfix supports SASL and TLS for secure connections, as well as the Maildir mailbox format (adopted from the Qmail MTA). Postfix is the default MTA for several Linux distributions, NetBSD, and the latest incarnations of Apple's Mac OS X.

Wietse Venema, a computer security specialist and IBM researcher, wrote Postfix in 1998. IBM released Venema's software (then named IBM Secure Mailer) as open source, in hopes that it would become widely adopted to create a faster and more secure email infrastructure. This release helped IBM develop its open source strategy, which was gaining popularity at the time.

RESOURCES

Postfix Documentation
   http://www.postfix.org/documentation.html

RFC 2821 – Simple Mail Transfer Protocol
   http://tools.ietf.org/html/rfc2821

REQUIRED

☑ FreeBSD 7.0-RELEASE (see "FreeBSD 7.0" on page 9)
☑ Updated ports collection (see "FreeBSD Ports Collection" on page 23)
☑ Internet connection
☑ Registered domain name
☑ Administrative access to your domain's DNS MX (DNS Mail Exchanger) records

OPTIONAL

☑ Cyrus SASL2 (see "Cyrus SASL 2.1.22" on page 61)
☑ OpenSSL with a signed SSL Certificate (see "OpenSSL 0.9.8g" on page 127)

POSTFIX
FreeBSD port path: /usr/ports/mail/postfix
TCP ports used – SMTP (25), submission (587)

NOTE *SASL and SSL are used together to create a secure email relay. SASL allows users to relay email if they authenticate successfully. SSL encrypts the authentication transaction and data transfer.*

PREPARATION

To enable TLS/SSL and/or SASL with Postfix, be sure that they are installed before proceeding with the Postfix installation.

NOTE *Write down the FQDN of the outgoing SMTP server for your Internet service provider. It usually looks like* smtp.ispname.com.

Become the superuser.

INSTALL

1. To begin the Postfix installation process, enter the following commands:

```
# cd /usr/ports/mail/postfix
# make config ; make install clean
# rehash
```

A menu will appear asking you to select options for Postfix. If you are planning to use TLS/SSL and/or SASL2, select each by using the arrow keys to highlight the option and press [SPACEBAR] to check the box. Once you have selected the options you wish to install, press the [TAB] key to highlight **OK** and then press [ENTER].

2. During installation, you will be asked to add the user postfix to the group mail. Enter **Y** to accept this and continue installation.

3. When asked if you would like to activate Postfix in */etc/mail/mailer.conf*, enter **Y**. This will create the Postfix-specific *mailer.conf* in */etc/mail.*

CONFIGURE

Once the installation process is complete, it's time to configure Postfix for use on your system.

1. Edit the *main.cf* file located in */usr/local/etc/postfix*. First, open *main.cf* with Easy Editor:

```
# ee /usr/local/etc/postfix/main.cf
```

POSTFIX
FreeBSD port path: /usr/ports/mail/postfix
TCP ports used – SMTP (25), submission (587)

2. Scroll down and uncomment the second of the three mydestination statements (~162) by removing the preceding hash mark. The line should now appear as follows:

```
mydestination = $myhostname, localhost.$mydomain, localhost, $mydomain
```

3. Comment out the mynetworks_style declaration (~247). This will allow relay access to clients without authentication as long as they reside on your local network (subnet). Do not modify this line if your local subnet is untrusted or you wish to enforce authentication of all clients. The line should appear as follows if subnet relay access is allowed:

```
#mynetworks_style = host
```

4. If your ISP blocks port 25, proceed to step 5; if it does not, skip to step 6. (See "Notes" on page 171 for instructions on detecting port 25 blockages.)

5. Scroll down to the relayhost declaration (~311) and specify your ISP's SMTP server. Replace *mailserver.isp.tld* with your ISP's server address and uncomment this line. The line should appear like this:

```
relayhost = [mailserver.isp.tld]
```

6. Uncomment the home_mailbox declaration (~415) to enable mail delivery to Maildir. The line should now appear as follows:

```
home_mailbox = Maildir/
```

If you don't want to set up SASL with SSL encryption, save, exit, and skip to step 12. To enable SASL with SSL encryption, continue.

Enabling SASL with SSL Encryption

7. Scroll down to the bottom of the *main.cf* file (press [CTRL-U] if you're using Easy Editor) and add the following lines to enable Cyrus SASL2:

```
smtp_sasl_auth_enable = yes
smtpd_sasl_auth_enable = yes
smtpd_sasl_security_options = noanonymous
smtpd_sasl_local_domain = $mydomain
broken_sasl_auth_clients = yes
smtp_sasl_password_maps = hash:/usr/local/etc/sasldb2
smtpd_recipient_restrictions =
    permit_sasl_authenticated
    permit_mynetworks
    reject_unauth_destination
```

NOTE *Postfix configuration statements that span multiple lines require preceding whitespace as shown in the last three lines above.*

POSTFIX
FreeBSD port path: /usr/ports/mail/postfix
TCP ports used – SMTP (25), submission (587)

8. Adding the next set of configuration statements to *main.cf* will enable TLS/ SSL encryption. You can separate these lines from the SASL directives with a blank line to make it easier to differentiate SASL2 options from the TLS/SSL options.

NOTE *The naming conventions used here are consistent with the OpenSSL guide in this book. Replace items in italics as appropriate to your system.*

```
smtp_tls_CAfile = /usr/local/openssl/certs/example.com-CAcert.pem
smtp_tls_cert_file = /usr/local/openssl/certs/host.example.com-cert.pem
smtp_tls_key_file =
  /usr/local/openssl/certs/host.example.com-unencrypted-key.pem
smtp_tls_session_cache_database = btree:/var/run/smtp_tls_session_cache
smtp_tls_security_level = may
smtpd_tls_CAfile = /usr/local/openssl/certs/example.com-CAcert.pem
smtpd_tls_cert_file = /usr/local/openssl/certs/host.example.com-cert.pem
smtpd_tls_key_file =
  /usr/local/openssl/certs/host.example.com-unencrypted-key.pem
smtpd_tls_session_cache_database = btree:/var/run/smtpd_tls_session_cache
smtpd_tls_received_header = yes
smtpd_tls_security_level = may
tls_random_source = dev:/dev/urandom
smtpd_tls_auth_only = yes
```

The files used above are:

example.com-CAcert.pem Certificate Authority Root Certificate

host.example.com-cert.pem Server Certificate

host.example.com-unencrypted-key.pem Server Private Key

9. Save and exit.

Assuming all goes well, you've now created a secure means to remotely relay email by enabling SASL with SSL. That said, if your users will be sending email from remote locations, they may be subject to ISP-enforced SMTP port 25 blockages (see "Notes" on page 171) that prevent them from sending outbound mail on the default port. To address this, we'll enable the SMTP submission port 587, via which users can securely submit email to your server.

10. Modify the *master.cf* file located in */usr/local/etc/postfix* to enable the submission port. Open the file:

```
# ee /usr/local/etc/postfix/master.cf
```

and uncomment the following four lines (~12):

```
submission inet n         -         n         -         -         smtpd
  -o smtpd_enforce_tls=yes
  -o smtpd_sasl_auth_enable=yes
  -o smtpd_client_restrictions=permit_sasl_authenticated,reject
```

11. Save and exit.

POSTFIX
FreeBSD port path: /usr/ports/mail/postfix
TCP ports used – SMTP (25), submission (587)

Finishing the Configuration

Whether you enabled SASL with SSL encryption or not, finish the configuration with the following steps.

12. To forward email addressed to the root user, you need to edit a file named *aliases* located in the */etc/mail* directory. Open this file with Easy Editor:

```
# ee /etc/mail/aliases
```

Scroll down (~19), uncomment this line, and enter the email address of the system administrator. The root account's email will be forwarded to this email address. The line should appear as follows, with the correct email address in place of *username@example.com*:

```
root: username@example.com
```

13. Save and exit.

14. To update *aliases.db* with the changes made to the *aliases* file, enter the following command:

```
# newaliases
```

TESTING

In this section, we'll perform some basic tests to confirm that Postfix answers SMTP commands properly.

1. Configure Postfix to start automatically at boot time, rather than the Sendmail MTA, by editing the *rc.conf* file located in */etc*. First, open *rc.conf*:

```
# ee /etc/rc.conf
```

and then add the following lines to automatically start Postfix at boot time:

```
postfix_enable="YES"
sendmail_enable="NO"
sendmail_submit_enable="NO"
sendmail_outbound_enable="NO"
sendmail_msp_queue_enable="NO"
```

2. Save and exit.

3. Create a file named *periodic.conf* in */etc* and add four lines to it. Since Postfix is replacing Sendmail as the MTA, we can remove unnecessary instructions from the daily-run script that pertains to Sendmail. Create and open */etc/periodic.conf*:

```
# ee /etc/periodic.conf
```

POSTFIX
FreeBSD port path: /usr/ports/mail/postfix
TCP ports used – SMTP (25), submission (587)

and then add these lines to the empty file:

```
daily_clean_hoststat_enable="NO"
daily_status_mail_rejects_enable="NO"
daily_status_include_submit_mailq="NO"
daily_submit_queuerun="NO"
```

4. Save and exit.

5. Enter these commands to stop Sendmail and start Postfix for testing:

```
# killall sendmail
# /usr/local/etc/rc.d/postfix start
```

Sending Mail

To check that Postfix is running and handling mail requests, we'll use telnet to send SMTP commands and send a test message.

6. Use the following command to initiate a connection to Postfix using telnet:

```
# telnet localhost 25

Connected to localhost.
Escape character is '^]'.
220 host.example.com ESMTP Postfix
```

Your hostname should appear instead of *host.example.com*.

7. Create the test email message. You can replace *test@example.com* with any email address; it doesn't need to be valid for the purposes of testing.

```
mail from: test@example.com

250 Ok
```

8. Specify the email recipient, replacing *user@example.com* with an external email account that you can access, preferably via webmail. Enter each line as shown below and then end the test message by entering a period (.) on a blank line:

```
rcpt to: user@example.com

250 Ok
data

354 End data with <CR><LF>.<CR><LF>

Subject: test message
This is a test message
.
```

You should see output similar to the following (the italicized ID tag will be different in your output):

```
250 Ok: queued as 1242EC119
```

POSTFIX
FreeBSD port path: /usr/ports/mail/postfix
TCP ports used – SMTP (25), submission (587)

9. Close the connection:

```
quit
```

10. Check the recipient email account to see if the message was successfully sent. If you did not set up SASL and SSL, skip to "Receiving Mail" on page 170.

Testing SASL over SSL

If you configured Postfix with SASL and SSL support, you can initiate an SSL connection and authenticate with SASL.

11. Encode the username and password of the user account that you wish to test into Base-64 format. Enter the following command to encode your username and password, replacing the italic items as appropriate:

```
# perl -MMIME::Base64 -e 'print encode_base64("\0username\0password")'
```

AHVzZXJuYW1lAHBhc3N3b3Jk

Be sure to write this string down exactly as it appears in your output; you will need to enter it in a moment.

12. The next command will start an SSL-encrypted connection to the Postfix SMTP server:

```
# openssl s_client -starttls smtp -crlf -connect localhost:25

CONNECTED(00000003)...
...SSL-Session:
    Protocol  : TLSv1
    Cipher    : DHE-RSA-AES256-SHA
    Session-ID: 3886C410C971913F87CA439B92FA7ED67CFFEE7D3...
    Session-ID-ctx:
    Master-Key: B9F96FB08D2E7C86B2454C7553F0F84D1C2DD3B3...
    Key-Arg   : None
    Start Time: 1196074152
    Timeout   : 300 (sec)
    Verify return code: 19 (self signed certificate in certificate chain)
---
250 DSN
```

13. Authenticate to the server using the encoded username and password that you created previously:

```
AUTH PLAIN AHVzZXJuYW1lAHBhc3N3b3Jk
```

If authentication is successful, you should see this:

```
235 2.0.0 Authentication successful
```

At this point, you can send a test email as shown in "Sending Mail" on page 168.

POSTFIX
FreeBSD port path: /usr/ports/mail/postfix
TCP ports used – SMTP (25), submission (587)

Receiving Mail

Now we'll test the Postfix server's ability to receive email. Be sure your domain's primary DNS MX record points to the IP address of your server (your domain registrar should have details about how to do this). If you have a NAT router, be sure that port 25 is forwarded to your server or this test won't succeed.

14. Send a test message from an external email account (for instance, a Gmail or Yahoo! account) to a valid user account (other than root) on your server.

15. Change to the user's mail directory with the following command (replacing *username* with the username you sent the email to on your server):

```
# cd /usr/home/username/Maildir/new
# more *
```

You should see the contents of your test email.

UTILITIES

Following is brief information on the postfix startup script and the postqueue utility.

postfix

This script is used to control the Postfix daemon.

Command   /usr/local/etc/rc.d/postfix

Syntax   /usr/local/etc/rc.d/postfix *option*

Options

start   Starts the Postfix mail system

stop   Stops the Postfix mail system

reload   Restarts the Postfix mail system and rereads configuration files

Example

To stop the Postfix mail system, enter the following command at the command prompt:

```
# /usr/local/etc/rc.d/postfix stop
```

postqueue

This utility is useful for checking Postfix's mail queue.

Command   postqueue

Syntax   postqueue *-option*

POSTFIX
FreeBSD port path: /usr/ports/mail/postfix
TCP ports used – SMTP (25), submission (587)

Options

-f   Instructs Postfix to flush/deliver mail that is in the queue

-p   Displays the contents of the Postfix queue

Example

To display the contents of the Postfix mail queue, enter the following command at the command prompt:

```
# postqueue -p
```

CONFIG FILES

/usr/local/etc/postfix/main.cf

Contains most of the commonly used configuration options.

/usr/local/etc/postfix/master.cf

Contains the configuration options for the Postfix master process. It also controls how Postfix interacts with other third-party software (filters and so on).

/etc/mail/aliases

A text representation of rules on mail redirections. The newaliases command converts this file into a database file named *aliases.db* for use with Postfix; *aliases.db* is stored in */etc*.

LOG FILES

/var/log/maillog

General log of email activity

NOTES

- **Port 25**   In an attempt to fight spam coming from their users, most major Internet providers block outgoing traffic on port 25 except to their own SMTP server. To see if your ISP blocks port 25, enter the following command:

```
# telnet smtp.stanford.edu 25

Trying 171.67.22.28...
Connected to smtp1.stanford.edu.
Escape character is '^]'.
220 smtp1.stanford.edu ESMTP Postfix
# quit
```

POSTFIX
FreeBSD port path: /usr/ports/mail/postfix
TCP ports used – SMTP (25), submission (587)

If port 25 is not blocked, you should see the output listed above. If you get a message like this:

```
Trying xx.xx.xx.xx...
```

that seems to hang, port 25 is probably blocked. Press [CTRL-C] to abort and return to the prompt.

- Postfix sends email on the Internet using SMTP. Email clients (Outlook, Thunderbird, Apple's Mail, Eudora, and so on) will need another protocol to receive messages from your email server, namely IMAP or POP3. Consult "Courier-IMAP Server 4.3.0" on page 43 for details on installation/ configuration.

- The default size limit for incoming email messages is 10,240,000 bytes (10.2MB). You may change this size limit by adding "message_size_limit = xxx" (replace a numerical value for *xxx* in bytes) to the end of the *main.cf* file in */usr/local/etc/postfix*. The following commands will append this statement to *main.cf* and restart Postfix (replace *xxx* with a numerical value in bytes; for instance, to set a 25MB limit, use 25000000):

```
# cd /usr/local/etc/postfix
# cp main.cf main.cf.old
# echo "message_size_limit = xxx" >> main.cf
# /usr/local/etc/rc.d/postfix reload
```

NOTE   *If you change the message size limit to a value larger than 51200000, you will need to add the* mailbox_size_limit *statement and ensure it is larger than the* message_size_limit *setting. Here's what these two statements would look like if you wanted a message size limit of 100MB:*

```
mailbox_size_limit = 101000000
message_size_limit = 100000000
```

PROCMAIL 3.22
HTTP://WWW.PROCMAIL.ORG

SUMMARY

Procmail is a mail filter, or *Mail Delivery Agent (MDA)*, that is used to process incoming email in accordance with a set of specified rules or actions. These actions can include forwarding email to a different address, routing flagged spam messages into a Junk folder, sending auto-reply messages, and so forth. Processing can be applied to all incoming messages, or limited to messages that contain certain tags or strings.

Setting up Procmail rules can be challenging for new users. The "Resources" section lists sites that host numerous examples and recipes to help with configuration. This guide will provide details on using Procmail to divert flagged spam into a separate Junk folder.

Procmail was originally created by Stephen R. van den Berg in 1990. In 1998, Philip Guenther became Procmail's maintainer; he continues to lead development efforts.

RESOURCES

Procmail Documentation Project
http://pm-doc.sourceforge.net

Procmail FAQ (Era Eriksson)
http://partmaps.org/era/procmail/mini-faq.html

REQUIRED

☑   FreeBSD 7.0-RELEASE (see "FreeBSD 7.0" on page 9)

☑   Updated ports collection (see "FreeBSD Ports Collection" on page 23)

☑   Postfix SMTP server (see "Postfix SMTP Server 2.5.1" on page 163)

☑   SpamAssassin (see "SpamAssassin 3.2.4" on page 197)

☑   Internet connection

PREPARATION

Become the superuser.

INSTALL

To begin the Procmail installation process, enter the following commands:

```
# cd /usr/ports/mail/procmail
# make config ; make install clean
# rehash
```

The installation process will pause to allow you to add directories to the test-lock routines. We'll accept the default, so press [ENTER] to continue.

CONFIGURE

Once the installation is complete, it is time to configure Procmail for use on your system.

1. Create a global configuration file (i.e., one that affects all users) to route email flagged as spam by SpamAssassin to a subfolder of each user's inbox, called Junk:

```
# ee /usr/local/etc/procmailrc
```

Add the following lines:

```
# Environment Variables
MAILDIR=$HOME/Maildir/
DEFAULT=$HOME/Maildir/
DROPPRIVS = yes
LOGFILE=$HOME/proc.log
# Spam to Junk Recipe
:0
*^X-Spam-Status: Yes
.Junk/
```

2. Save and exit.

3. Add a line to Postfix's *main.cf* file to specify Procmail as the Local Mail Delivery Agent. Open *main.cf*:

```
# ee /usr/local/etc/postfix/main.cf
```

Scroll to the bottom of *main.cf* using [CTRL-U] and add this line:

```
mailbox_command = /usr/local/bin/procmail
```

4. Save, exit, and reload Postfix's configuration:

```
# postfix reload
```

TESTING

In this section, we'll perform tests to confirm that Procmail delivers mail to users' mailboxes correctly.

1. Send a test spam message into the mail system. First, open a telnet connection:

```
# telnet localhost 25

Connected to localhost.
Escape character is '^]'.
220 host.example.com ESMTP Postfix
```

NOTE   *Your hostname should appear instead of* host.example.com.

Enter the following (substituting your domain for *example.com*):

```
mail from: test@example.com
250 Ok

rcpt to: spamd@example.com
250 Ok
```

NOTE   *You can specify a different recipient if you like. The spamd account will be present on your system if you used the SpamAssassin guide in this book.*

Next, enter the following lines as shown, pressing [ENTER] after each line.

NOTE   *The long string is known as the* GTUBE *(Generic Test for Unsolicited Bulk Email). It will cause SpamAssassin to flag the message as spam.*

```
data
354 End data with <CR><LF>.<CR><LF>
Subject: This is Spam
XJS*C4JDBQADN1.NSBN3*2IDNEN*GTUBE-STANDARD-ANTI-UBE-TEST-EMAIL*C.34X
.
250 Ok: queued as 1242EC120
```

NOTE   *The italicized ID tag will be different in your output.*

Finally, close the connection:

```
quit
```

2. Give the mail system a minute to process the message, then examine the Procmail log file in the recipient's home directory:

```
# cat /var/spool/spamd/proc.log
```

If Procmail processed the message successfully, you should see output similar to this:

```
From test@example.com Mon Nov 17 13:40:00 2008
  Folder: .Junk/new/1195508418.1125_0.host.example.com      2606
```

CONFIG FILES

/usr/local/etc/procmailrc

The global Procmail configuration file. This file also contains recipes for processing mail messages.

/usr/home/*username*/.procmailrc

User-specific Procmail configuration file. The recipes in this file are processed after processing the recipes in */usr/local/etc/procmailrc*. By default, environment variables from */usr/local/etc/procmailrc* carry over to this file and should not be specified again. All folders are relative to the user's Maildir folder.

LOG FILES

/usr/home/*username*/proc.log

Contains a log of messages processed by Procmail for *username*

/var/log/maillog

General log of email activity

NOTES

For examples of Procmail recipes, see the procmailex manual page:

```
# man procmailex
```

LEVEL
4

PUREFTPD
FreeBSD port path: /usr/ports/ftp/pure-ftpd
TCP port used – FTP (21)

PURE-FTPD SERVER 1.0.21

HTTP://WWW.PUREFTPD.ORG

SUMMARY

FTP (File Transfer Protocol) is used for transferring files between a server and a client system. According to RFC 959,[1] the four objectives of FTP are to promote the sharing of files, encourage use of remote computers, shield users from variations in file storage systems, and transfer data reliably and efficiently.

FTP was first developed in 1971 by the US Department of Defense for use in its network at DARPA. It is regarded as one of the Internet's first protocols.

Pure-FTPd is an open source FTP server that conforms to the original FTP standards with some additional functionality. These include a virtual user system, SSL/TLS encryption support, bandwidth throttling, and upload/download ratios, to name a few. Pure-FTPd supports both virtual users and users that exist on system-level accounts. This guide will exclusively focus on the virtual user scheme as it offers a larger feature set.

Pure-FTPd is based on Troll-FTPd, originally written by Arnt Gulbrandsen in 1995. Active development of Troll-FTPd stagnated in the late '90s, prompting Frank Denis to create the Pure-FTPd project. Denis made some modifications to the Troll-FTPd code, wrote new documentation, and released Pure-FTPd in 2001. A team of nine, led by Denis, continues development of the Pure-FTPd project.

RESOURCES

Pure-FTPd Documentation
   http://www.pureftpd.org/project/pure-ftpd/doc

RFC 959 – File Transfer Protocol
   http://tools.ietf.org/html/rfc959

REQUIRED

☑   FreeBSD 7.0-RELEASE (see "FreeBSD 7.0" on page 9)

☑   Updated ports collection (see "FreeBSD Ports Collection" on page 23)

☑   Internet connection

---

[1] J. Postel and J. Reynolds, "File Transfer Protocol (FTP)," Internet Engineering Task Force, *http://www.ietf.org/rfc/rfc959.txt.*

PUREFTPD
FreeBSD port path: /usr/ports/ftp/pure-ftpd
TCP port used – FTP (21)

OPTIONAL

☑ OpenSSL with a signed SSL Certificate, if you wish to enable encryption of the FTP control channel (see "OpenSSL 0.9.8g" on page 127)

☑ Registered domain name

PREPARATION

Become the superuser.

NOTE *This guide provides instructions for using the virtual user system to manage and control users. This system provides a larger feature set and allows administration of FTP accounts without affecting system accounts.*

INSTALL

To begin the Pure-FTPd installation process, enter the following commands:

```
# cd /usr/ports/ftp/pure-ftpd
# make config ; make install clean
# rehash
```

A menu containing pure-ftpd options will appear. Leave these options at their defaults, then press [TAB] to select **OK** and [ENTER] to continue.

CONFIGURE

Once the installation process is complete, it's time to configure Pure-FTPd for use on your system.

1. Copy the sample configuration file named *pure-ftpd.conf.sample* to *pure-ftpd.conf* in */usr/local/etc*. This file will be used to set configuration options.

```
# cd /usr/local/etc
# cp pure-ftpd.conf.sample pure-ftpd.conf
# ee pure-ftpd.conf
```

2. Specify the location of the virtual users database. Scroll down to the PureDB statement (~126), uncomment it (remove the leading hash mark) and change the path to */usr/local/etc/pureftpd.pdb*. The PureDB statement should appear as follows:

```
PureDB                  /usr/local/etc/pureftpd.pdb
```

3. To make adding new virtual users easier, configure Pure-FTPd to automatically create a user's home directory upon login (if it doesn't already exist). Uncomment the CreateHomeDir statement (~336) to enable this feature.

PUREFTPD
FreeBSD port path: /usr/ports/ftp/pure-ftpd
TCP port used – FTP (21)

The CreateHomeDir statement should look like this:

```
CreateHomeDir       yes
```

4. Pure-FTPd is automatically compiled with SSL/TLS support. It is, however, disabled by default. If you do not wish to enable SSL/TLS encryption, save, exit, and skip to step 8.

Configuring SSL/TLS

An FTP session utilizes a control channel and a data channel. The *control channel* is responsible for handling the initial authentication, commands to the server, and the server's responses. The *data channel* is used to transmit data during file transfers.

Pure-FTPd, if configured with SSL/TLS, can provide encryption for the control channel, although information on the data channel is still transmitted "in the clear." For a higher level of security, look at other solutions like SFTP, which is part of OpenSSH.

5. Uncomment the TLS declaration (~422) and specify 1 or 2. There are two possible SSL/TLS configurations: The first (option 1) allows both unencrypted and encrypted connections to occur, while the second (option 2) allows only encrypted connections. The example below enables both encrypted and unencrypted connections:

```
TLS              1
```

6. Save and exit.

7. Pure-FTPd needs your server certificate and key file combined into a single file to function properly. We will assume your certificates and private key reside in */usr/local/openssl/certs*. The following commands will merge your server's private key file with your server certificate file into a new file that Pure-FTPd can use:

```
# cd /usr/local/openssl/certs
# cp host.example.com-unencrypted-key.pem pure-ftpd.pem
# chmod 400 pure-ftpd.pem
# cat host.example.com-cert.pem >> pure-ftpd.pem
# mkdir /etc/ssl/private
# mv pure-ftpd.pem /etc/ssl/private
```

NOTE *Replace the filenames above to match the naming conventions used when you created your server key and certificate files with OpenSSL (see "OpenSSL 0.9.8g" on page 127).*

host.example.com-unencrypted-key.pem   Your server's unencrypted private key file

host.example.com-cert.pem   Your server's public certificate file

/etc/ssl/private/pure-ftpd.pem   Pure-FTPd looks for the SSL Certificate here

PUREFTPD
FreeBSD port path: /usr/ports/ftp/pure-ftpd
TCP port used – FTP (21)

Importing and Adding Users

8. You may either import users with system-level accounts (those listed in */etc/master.passwd*) en masse or create new users manually. To create users manually, skip to step 9. To import users that already exist on your system into the virtual user database, enter these commands:

```
# pure-pwconvert >> /usr/local/etc/pureftpd.passwd
# chmod 600 /usr/local/etc/pureftpd.passwd
# pure-pw mkdb
```

NOTE *This utility will only import accounts that have shell access. Accounts with their shell set to nologin will need to be added manually.*

9. To add users to the Pure-FTPd virtual user database manually, we need to create a system-level account that will be associated with virtual users. Create a new user named vftp like this:

```
# pw user add vftp -s /sbin/nologin -w no -d /usr/home/vftp\
? -c "Virtual FTP User" -m
```

We are now able to add users to the virtual users database using the commands below. Replace *user* with the username you want to create.

```
# pure-pw useradd user -u vftp -g vftp -d /usr/home/vftp/user
# pure-pw mkdb
```

To add additional users, simply repeat the commands above with a different user.

Configuring Anonymous FTP

We'll configure anonymous FTP access in the next step. If you do not wish to configure anonymous FTP, skip to "Testing" on page 181.

NOTE *Take great care when running an anonymous FTP server. A single ill-configured option can compromise your system's security.*

10. Create a new system-level user named ftp like this:

```
# pw user add ftp -s /sbin/nologin -w no -d /usr/home/ftp\
? -c "Anonymous FTP User" -m
# rm /usr/home/ftp/.??*
```

You may create a directory structure of your choice in */usr/home/ftp*. To create directories that anonymous users can upload to, use a mode of 777 on the directory. For read-only access to files, use a mode of 444. For read-only access to directories, use a mode of 555.

PUREFTPD
FreeBSD port path: /usr/ports/ftp/pure-ftpd
TCP port used – FTP (21)

For example, you could allow upload access to the directory */usr/home/ftp/ upload*. The following commands will make the home directory read only, create the upload directory, and give anonymous users write permissions there:

```
# chmod 555 /usr/home/ftp
# mkdir /usr/home/ftp/upload
# chmod 777 /usr/home/ftp/upload
```

NOTE *Be sure to monitor the files in the* /usr/home/ftp/upload *directory, since you can be held responsible if users place illegal content there. Consult the* pure-ftpd.conf *file in* /usr/local/etc *for anonymous login–related options. Refer to "chown" on page 225 and "chmod" on page 226 for details on setting file ownership and permissions.*

TESTING

In this section we'll perform some basic tests to confirm that Pure-FTPd functions properly.

1. Enter this command to start Pure-FTPd:

```
# /usr/local/etc/rc.d/pure-ftpd onestart
```

2. Initiate an FTP connection with this command (use your system's hostname):

```
# ftp localhost
```

The login message should look like this:

```
Connected to host.example.com.
220---------- Welcome to Pure-FTPd [TLS] ----------
220-You are user number 1 of 50 allowed.
220-Local time is now 15:16. Server port: 21.
220-IPv6 connections are also welcome on this server.
220 You will be disconnected after 15 minutes of inactivity.
Name (host.example.com:user):
```

3. Log in with a user account you created earlier and get a directory listing with the ls command. If the directory listing is successful, the test succeeds. Enter **quit** to exit the FTP session.

NOTE *In order to test TLS/SSL functionality, you'll need a TLS/SSL-capable FTP client like Cyberduck for the Macintosh or FileZilla for Windows.*

4. If the test was successful, configure Pure-FTPd to start automatically at system startup. To do so, open *etc/rc.conf*:

```
# ee /etc/rc.conf
```

and add the following line:

```
pureftpd_enable="YES"
```

PUREFTPD
FreeBSD port path: /usr/ports/ftp/pure-ftpd
TCP port used – FTP (21)

5. Save, exit, and restart Pure-FTPd:

```
# /usr/local/etc/rc.d/pure-ftpd restart
# /usr/local/etc/rc.d/pure-ftpd status
```

UTILITIES

Following is brief information on the pure-pw and pure-ftpwho utilities.

pure-pw

The pure-pw utility adds, deletes, modifies, and displays information about the Pure-FTPd virtual user database.

Command   pure-pw

Syntax   pure-pw *command user -options*

Commands

useradd   Adds a virtual user to *pureftpd.passwd* file

usermod   Modifies a virtual user entry in *pureftpd.passwd* file

userdel   Deletes a virtual user

passwd   Changes a virtual user password

show   Displays details about the specified user

list   Displays a list of users in the *pureftpd.passwd* file

mkdb   Exports the *pureftpd.passwd* file to the *pureftpd.pdb* database file; this command must be run after making any modifications to *pureftpd.passwd*

Options

-u   System user ID

-g   System group ID

-d   Home directory

Examples

To delete a virtual user named jill from the virtual user database, enter:

```
# pure-pw userdel jill
# pure-pw mkdb
```

To change the password of a virtual user named jack, enter:

```
# pure-pw passwd jack
# pure-pw mkdb
```

PUREFTPD
FreeBSD port path: /usr/ports/ftp/pure-ftpd
TCP port used – FTP (21)

pure-ftpwho

The pure-ftpwho utility monitors current FTP client sessions.

Command   pure-ftpwho

Syntax   pure-ftpwho -*options*

Option

-v   Verbose mode (adds local IP address, port, and transfer stats to output)

Example

To display the current FTP client sessions with transfer statistics, enter:

```
# pure-ftpwho -v
```

CONFIG FILES

/usr/local/etc/pure-ftpd.conf
This is the primary configuration file. It contains options that the *pure-config.pl* script passes to the Pure-FTP daemon upon startup.

/usr/local/etc/pureftpd.passwd
This file contains usernames, hashed passwords, and directory information on virtual users.

.banner
This is a text file that is automatically displayed at login when put into a user's home directory.

.message
This text file is automatically displayed when a user enters its parent directory.

LOG FILES

/var/log/xferlog
Stores FTP session information and error messages

/var/log/messages
Records error messages reported by Pure-FTPd

/var/log/debug.log
Stores a log of all client commands if the VerboseLog declaration is set to yes in *pure-ftpd.conf*

PUREFTPD
FreeBSD port path: /usr/ports/ftp/pure-ftpd
TCP port used – FTP (21)

NOTES

- By default all user accounts are *caged*, or restricted, to their respective home directories. If you need to allow access to a specific directory outside a user's home directory, symbolic links may be used. For example, say a webmaster, Michelle (username michelle), needs access to the */usr/local/www/apache22/data* directory to upload web content. You can create a symbolic link to this directory like this:

  ```
  # cd /usr/home/vftp/michelle
  # ln -s /usr/local/www/data-dist www
  ```

  Michelle will have the permissions of the associated userID and groupID you specified when you added her to the *pureftpd.passwd* file. You may need to change her associated userID and/or groupID with the pure-pw utility to allow appropriate read/write/execute access to the newly linked directory. (If so, you might change her user and group IDs to www.) You may also choose to change user or group ownership of files and directories to accommodate her existing userID and groupID.

  NOTE *Be sure you understand file ownership and permissions prior to implementing a scheme like this, as it may have security implications.*

- If your server is behind a firewall (such as a NAT router), problems may arise with clients trying to initiate connections because the Pure-FTP daemon tries to establish data connections on arbitrary ports when in active mode. If you encounter this, configure your FTP client to use passive mode.

- Pure-FTPd contains dozens of other features not documented here. Consult the Pure-FTPd project webpage *http://www.pureftpd.org/project/pure-ftpd* or manual page for details. The following command displays Pure-FTPd's man page:

  ```
  # man pure-ftpd
  ```

LEVEL
4

SAMBA
FreeBSD port path: /usr/ports/net/samba3
TCP ports used – NETBIOS-SSN (139), MICROSOFT-DS (445)

SAMBA 3.0.28

HTTP://WWW.SAMBA.ORG

SUMMARY

Samba is an open source implementation of the *SMB (Server Message Block)* and *CIFS (Common Internet File System)* protocols, which are used for sharing files and printers over a Microsoft network. Samba was created to provide Windows-compatible file and printer sharing services with UNIX-like systems.

SMB was originally developed to run atop the NetBIOS (Network Basic Input/Output System) protocol. However, because NetBIOS was conceived for small networks, it lacked routing capabilities, which limited SMB to local area networks. In 1996, Microsoft modified SMB so that it would not rely on NetBIOS, and renamed it Common Internet File System (CIFS). With the release of Windows 2000, SMB/CIFS was able to run atop TCP/IP.

Samba shares appear just like other shared folders in a Windows network. Access privileges can be cascaded over the normal Unix file permissions, and configurable restrictions based on login may be implemented as well. Unix users may also mount and access shares with the Samba client, which is similar to an FTP client. Samba consists of two daemons, namely smbd and nmbd. The SMB daemon handles file and print services as well as authentication. The NMB daemon handles name resolution and file browsing capability.

Dr. Barry Feigenbaum of IBM developed the SMB protocol in the early '80s as a solution for building small local area networks. Microsoft later built on the original SMB foundation and became the dominant user of the technology. Andrew Tridgell developed Samba in 1992 by reverse-engineering the SMB protocol to fit his needs. The Samba project is now a multi-national team and continues to develop new features.

RESOURCES

Samba Documentation
http://samba.org/samba/docs

The Server Message Block Protocol
http://ubiqx.org/cifs/SMB.html

SAMBA
FreeBSD port path: /usr/ports/net/samba3
UDP ports used – NETBIOS-NS (137), NETBIOS-DGM (138)

REQUIRED

☑ FreeBSD 7.0-RELEASE (see "FreeBSD 7.0" on page 9)

☑ Updated ports collection (see "FreeBSD Ports Collection" on page 23)

☑ Internet connection

OPTIONAL

☑ CUPS, for printer sharing capability (see "CUPS Print Server 1.3.3" on page 51)

PREPARATION

Become the superuser.

System accounts should exist for users you want to allow access to Samba. If they don't exist, add them now with the adduser command. (See Appendix C for details on the adduser command.)

INSTALL

To begin the Samba installation process, enter the following commands:

```
# cd /usr/ports/net/samba3
# make config ; make install clean
# rehash
```

A menu should appear with the available options for samba. Highlight **LDAP** and press [SPACEBAR] to deselect it. Leave the other options at their defaults by pressing [TAB] to select **OK** and then [ENTER] to continue.

CONFIGURE

Once the installation process completes, it is time to configure Samba for use on your system.

1. Change the *smb.conf* file in the */usr/local/etc* directory to suit your system. First, open the file:

```
# ee /usr/local/etc/smb.conf
```

2. Scroll down to the workgroup declaration (~26) and replace MYGROUP with a workgroup name that matches your client systems. This line would appear as follows if you used a workgroup named EXAMPLE:

```
workgroup = EXAMPLE
```

SAMBA
FreeBSD port path: /usr/ports/net/samba3
TCP ports used – NETBIOS-SSN (139), MICROSOFT-DS (445)

NOTE *You can determine the workgroup name of a Windows PC by right-clicking My Computer and then selecting* **Properties.** *The workgroup name will be shown in the Name tab. You can also enter* net config workstation *at the command prompt to retrieve the workgroup name.*

3. Scroll down to the server string declaration (~29) and replace Samba Server with a name you would like to assign the server. The line should appear as follows:

> server string = Example FileServer

4. Scroll down to the hosts allow statement (~41). Samba will allow access to the IP addresses entered here. To allow connections from all clients, leave this line unmodified. To enable SMB connections on the local network, list 192.168.1. (leaving the last octet blank means any addresses from .01 to .255) and 127. (this means any address beginning with 127. is allowed), as shown in the example below. Be sure to uncomment this line by removing the semicolon (;) at the beginning of the line. The line should appear as follows:

> hosts allow = 192.168.1. 127.

NOTE *You may enter full IP addresses here to limit connections to a specific client IP, separating each IP with a space, comma, or tab.*

Configuring Shares

Now we'll create definitions that specify how directories will be shared. There are a variety of different configurations possible, but for now just create a simple share using one of these examples.

Public Shares

The following example is a share that allows all users to log into, read, delete, create, and modify files. This type of share is useful for users who wish to share files without restrictions. To implement this type of share, add the lines below to the end of the *smb.conf* file. (You may substitute a different share name and path.)

```
[public]                             /* name of the share */
comment = Public Files               /* a short description of the share */
path = /usr/home/samba/public        /* path of shared directory */
public = yes                         /* password is not required to connect */
read only = no                       /* users may create, modify, and delete files */
```

Private Shares

With the following configuration, only the users john and jane are allowed access. The files each user creates will have owner permissions of read, write, and execute. The group and world permissions will be read-only by default. This

SAMBA
FreeBSD port path: /usr/ports/net/samba3
UDP ports used – NETBIOS-NS (137), NETBIOS-DGM (138)

type of share is useful for sharing within small groups of people who wish to retain control of their files. To implement this type of share, add the lines below to the end of *smb.conf* (substituting your choice of share name, path, and list of valid users).

```
[private]                           /* name of the share */
comment = Private Files             /* a short description of the share */
path = /usr/home/samba/private      /* path of shared directory */
valid users = john jane             /* users allowed to access this share */
public = no                         /* password required to access this share */
writable = yes                      /* users may create, modify, and delete */
                                    /* files they own */
```

Read-Only Shares

The configuration below allows everyone read-only access to the share without a password. Only users on the write list can create, modify, and delete files they own in the share. This type of share is useful to publish files for public access while giving authors or administrators the ability to retain control of their content. To implement this type of share, add the lines below to the end of *smb.conf*, substituting your choice of share name, path, and list of users with write access.

```
[readonly]                          /* name of share */
comment = Read Only Shares          /* a short description of the share */
path = /usr/home/samba/readonly     /* path of shared directory */
public = yes                        /* password is not required to connect */
write list = bert ernie             /* users allowed write access */
writable = yes                      /* write list users may create, modify, */
                                    /* and delete files they own */
```

Printers

By default, all configured printers in CUPS are shared and available to authenticated users. If you need to apply access restrictions to printers, please see "Notes" on page 194.

Finishing

When you are satisfied with your shares configuration, save and exit.

Test the *smb.conf* file for syntax errors:

```
# testparm
```

Examine the output for any errors and correct them if necessary. Make sure the paths you specified in your share definitions exist. If they don't, create them now.

SAMBA
FreeBSD port path: /usr/ports/net/samba3
TCP ports used – NETBIOS-SSN (139), MICROSOFT-DS (445)

Setting Share Permissions

The sections below correspond to the example share configurations mentioned previously. For example, if you created a public share in the last section, proceed to "Public Share Permissions." When you have completed setting permissions for your configured shares, proceed to "Testing" on page 190.

Public Share Permissions

If you will be hosting a public share, you will need to set the permissions on the public share directory to mode 777 in order to allow all users the ability to create, modify, and delete files. For example, the command below would set the required permissions on the */usr/home/samba/public* directory:

```
# chmod 777 /usr/home/samba/public
```

Private Share Permissions

If you will be hosting a private share, you will need to set the permissions on the private share directory to mode 770. This will allow root and the members of the group full access to the directory (we will also create the group).

Because we want only the users we specify to access this directory, we need to create a new group and add them as members. As an example, we'll create a group called smbprivate with the users john and jane as members.

The following commands will create the group smbprivate, change the */usr/home/samba/private* directory's ownership to this new group, and set the correct permissions. (You can use any group name you like.)

```
# pw groupadd smbprivate -M john,jane
# chgrp smbprivate /usr/home/samba/private
# chmod 770 /usr/home/samba/private
```

Substitute your own usernames, group name, and path as appropriate.

Read-Only Share Permissions

If you will be hosting a read-only share, you will need to set the permissions on the read-only share directory to mode 770. This will allow root and the members of the group full access to the directory.

Because we want only the users we specified in the write list to access this directory, we need to create a new group and add these users as members. As an example, we will create a new group called smbreadonly with users bert and ernie as members.

SAMBA
FreeBSD port path: /usr/ports/net/samba3
UDP ports used – NETBIOS-NS (137), NETBIOS-DGM (138)

The following commands will create the group, change the */usr/home/samba/ private* directory's ownership to this new group, and set the correct permissions.

```
# pw groupadd smbreadonly -M bert,ernie
# chgrp smbreadonly /usr/home/samba/readonly
# chmod 770 /usr/home/samba/readonly
```

Substitute your own usernames, group name, and path as appropriate.

Adding Users

Create Samba user accounts and passwords for the users you wish to allow Samba access. The usernames you specify should match those of their existing system accounts. To set up a new user, use the smbpasswd command (replacing *username* with the username you wish to create):

```
# smbpasswd -a username
```

After entering a password, you should see:

```
Added user username
```

Repeat this for any other users you'd like to add.

TESTING

In this section, we'll perform some basic tests to confirm that Samba answers SMB/CIFS requests properly.

1. Enter this command to start the SMB daemon for testing:

```
# /usr/local/etc/rc.d/samba onestart
```

2. To list the available shares Samba is hosting, use the following command:

```
# smbclient -U username -L localhost
```

Replace *username* with a valid Samba user. After entering the user's password, you should see the list of shares you configured earlier.

3. To log in and browse a share, enter:

```
# smbclient -U username //localhost/sharename
```

Once login is complete, you should see an smb: \> prompt. You may then navigate the share with common Unix commands, such as cd and ls. Enter **quit** to exit.

SAMBA
FreeBSD port path: /usr/ports/net/samba3
TCP ports used – NETBIOS-SSN (139), MICROSOFT-DS (445)

4. If the tests were successful, configure the Samba server to start automatically at boot time. Open */etc/rc.conf*:

```
# ee /etc/rc.conf
```

and then add the following line:

```
samba_enable="YES"
```

5. Save, exit, and restart Samba:

```
# /usr/local/etc/rc.d/samba restart
# /usr/local/etc/rc.d/samba status
```

NOTE *You can run the status command for confirmation that the Samba service started.*

UTILITIES

Following is brief information on the smbpasswd and pdbedit utilities, which are used to maintain user passwords and policies. This section also covers SWAT, an alternative interface for Samba administration.

smbpasswd

This utility manages users' Samba passwords.

Command   smbpasswd

Syntax   smbpasswd *-options username*

Options

-a   Adds a user to the Samba password file

-x   Deletes a user from the Samba password file

-d   Disables a user

-e   Enables a user if previously disabled

Examples

To add the user jake to the Samba password file, enter:

```
# smbpasswd -a jake
```

To disable the user webster, enter:

```
# smbpasswd -d webster
```

NOTE *If a user has shell access to your server, he may change his password by entering smbpasswd with no arguments.*

SAMBA
FreeBSD port path: /usr/ports/net/samba3
UDP ports used – NETBIOS-NS (137), NETBIOS-DGM (138)

pdbedit

This utility manages users in the Samba user database. It is usable by root only.

Command   pdbedit

Syntax   pdbedit *-option argument*

Options

-a   Adds a user

-u   Specifies user to manage

-f   Specifies user's full name

-v   Verbose listing format

-L   Lists all users in the database

-x   Deletes a user

-P   Displays account policy and current value. Valid arguments include:

minimum password age	bad lockout attempt
maximum password age	reset count minutes
min password length	disconnect time
password history	user must logon to change password
lockout duration	refuse machine password change

-C   Changes account policy value

Examples

To add a user John Doe to the Samba database with the username john, enter:

```
# pdbedit -a -u john -f "John Doe"
```

To list all users in the database verbosely, enter:

```
# pdbedit -L -v
```

To display the minimum password length account policy, enter:

```
# pdbedit -P "min password length"
```

To change the minimum password length to 8, enter:

```
# pdbedit -P "min password length" -C 8
```

See pdbedit's man page for more options:

```
# man pdbedit
```

SAMBA
FreeBSD port path: /usr/ports/net/samba3
TCP ports used – NETBIOS-SSN (139), MICROSOFT-DS (445)

Enabling SWAT

SWAT (Samba Web Administration Tool) provides an easy-to-use alternative interface for Samba administration. SWAT is run from FreeBSD's built-in Internet super-server (inetd). To enable SWAT, follow these steps.

1. Open *inetd.conf*:

```
# ee /etc/inetd.conf
```

2. Uncomment the swat declaration (~120). It should appear now as follows:

```
swat  stream  tcp  nowait/400  root  /usr/local/sbin/swat  swat
```

3. Save and exit.

4. Unless you've specifically configured inetd to run at boot time, enter the following to start the service:

```
# /etc/rc.d/inetd onestart
```

To access the SWAT interface, navigate to *http://host.example.com:901* with a web browser (substitute your server's hostname). Log in as root to access the administrative functions.

NOTE *Be aware that your login and password are transmitted in the clear. If you cannot ensure the security of your network, do not use this utility. Use a secure solution like manual configuration via SSH or a browser, like Lynx (see "Lynx 2.8.6" on page 91), on the server console. Do not use this utility from outside your network unless you have taken steps to encrypt the transmission of your root password using something like a secure VPN tunnel.*

Once configuration of Samba with SWAT is complete, you may terminate inetd as follows:

```
# /etc/rc.d/inetd stop
```

To start inetd automatically at boot time, add the following line to */etc/rc.conf*:

```
inetd_enable="YES"
```

CONFIG FILES

/usr/local/etc/smb.conf
> The main configuration file for Samba

/usr/local/etc/samba/smbpasswd
> The Samba encrypted password file; it is created by the smbpasswd utility and contains usernames and hashed passwords for SMB users

SAMBA
FreeBSD port path: /usr/ports/net/samba3
UDP ports used – NETBIOS-NS (137), NETBIOS-DGM (138)

LOG FILES

/var/log/samba

Contains log files for Samba activity and hosts that have connected to a Samba share

NOTES

- If you have CUPS installed and configured without access restrictions, all authenticated Samba users will have permission to print to any installed printer. To restrict printing privileges to specific users, you must modify */etc/smb.conf*. First, open *smb.conf*:

  # ee /usr/local/etc/smb.conf

  Scroll to the bottom of *smb.conf* using [CTRL-U] and add the following lines:

  ```
  [printers]
  valid users = username
  ```

  Replace *username* with the username(s) of the person(s) you want to allow print privileges (separate multiple users with spaces).

  Save, exit, and restart Samba:

  # /usr/local/etc/rc.d/samba restart

- If you configured CUPS printing without access restrictions, consider disabling IPP (Internet Printing Protocol) since you are trying to restrict printing access to specific users. To prevent CUPS from accepting direct IPP print requests, edit the *cupsd.conf* file. First, open *cupsd.conf*:

  # ee /usr/local/etc/cups/cupsd.conf

  Scroll down to the bottom of the *cupsd.conf* file using [CTRL-U] and add the following lines:

  ```
  <Location /printers>
  Order Deny,Allow
  Deny From All
  Allow From 127.0.0.1
  </Location>
  ```

  This directive will cause CUPS to reject all direct IPP printing requests and instead accept only Samba-relayed print jobs.

  Save, exit, and restart CUPS:

  # /usr/local/etc/rc.d/cupsd restart

SAMBA
FreeBSD port path: /usr/ports/net/samba3
TCP ports used – NETBIOS-SSN (139), MICROSOFT-DS (445)

- Windows XP SP2 systems may experience a delay when selecting a Samba printer in some applications or when attempting to access printer properties. This may be resolved by removing Windows registry entries that refer to the Samba hosted printer. The locations of the registry entries are as follows:

  HKEY_CURRENT_USER\Printers\DevModePerUser

  HKEY_CURRENT_USER\Printers\DevModes2

  Delete *samba_server_name**printer_name*.

  NOTE *Use caution when modifying the Windows registry.*

LEVEL
4

SPAMASSASSIN
FreeBSD port path: /usr/ports/mail/p5-Mail-SpamAssassin
TCP port used – UNASSIGNED (783)

SPAMASSASSIN 3.2.4

HTTP://SPAMASSASSIN.APACHE.ORG

SUMMARY

SpamAssassin is a highly effective open source email classifier. It is designed to examine email using a diverse set of tests to determine if a message is spam. Messages are scored using keywords, historical data (e.g., Bayesian filtering), and fingerprinting methods (e.g., Vipul's Razor and DCC databases) to maximize effectiveness by leveraging the benefits of each type of test. SpamAssassin stores the results of these tests in each email's header. Mail Delivery Agents (MDA) like Procmail (see "Procmail 3.22" on page 173) can use these headers to route or perform further processing of the message.

Typically, SpamAssassin is invoked as a daemon or background process. A mail transfer agent like Postfix is configured to pipe email through SpamAssassin for analysis. If a message is determined to be spam, SpamAssassin can be configured to modify the message in a number of ways. By default, spam is re-encoded as an attachment and the body of the message displays the list of tests that triggered the positive result. Spam and *ham* (legitimate email) are then delivered to users' mailboxes.

Many commercially available anti-spam packages incorporate SpamAssassin in their products. These include SpamKiller by McAfee, Kerio MailServer by Kerio, and SmarterMail by SmarterTools.

SpamAssassin was written in 2001 by Justin Mason, an Irish software developer. It is based on filter.plx, a spam filter written in Perl by Mark Jeftovic in 1997. Justin contributed patches to Jeftovic's filter.plx and later decided to rewrite the code (also in Perl) from scratch. This recode became SpamAssassin and is now a project of the Apache Software Foundation. Mason currently directs SpamAssassin development as a vice president of the Apache Software Foundation.

RESOURCES

Official SpamAssassin Documentation
http://spamassassin.apache.org/doc.html

SpamAssassin Test Descriptions and Scores
http://spamassassin.apache.org/tests_3_2_x.html

SpamAssassin Rules Emporium
http://www.rulesemporium.com

SPAMASSASSIN
FreeBSD port path: /usr/ports/mail/p5-Mail-SpamAssassin
TCP port used – UNASSIGNED (783)

REQUIRED

☑ FreeBSD 7.0-RELEASE (see "FreeBSD 7.0" on page 9)

☑ Updated ports collection (see "FreeBSD Ports Collection" on page 23)

☑ Postfix SMTP server (see "Postfix SMTP Server 2.5.1" on page 163)

☑ Internet connection

PREPARATION

Become the superuser.

INSTALL

Install SpamAssassin and support for DCC tests.

NOTE DCC (Distributed Checksum Clearinghouse) *is a method of sharing centralized email fingerprints with a community similar to Vipul's Razor and Pyzor. It is protected by a patent owned by Commtouch Software Ltd. and is free to use for non-commercial applications. If you agree to the terms of the license, you may install DCC as detailed below; if not, omit* -D WITH_DCC *in step 1. The license agreement can be found at* http://www.rhyolite.com/anti-spam/dcc.

1. Enter the following commands to begin the installation of SpamAssassin:

```
# cd /usr/ports/mail/p5-Mail-SpamAssassin
# make config ; make -D WITH_DCC install clean
# rehash
```

A menu with options for p5-Mail-SpamAssassin should appear. Scroll down to DKIM and press [SPACEBAR] to enable DomainKeys support. Continue down to SPF_QUERY and press [SPACEBAR] to enable SPF query support as well. We'll leave the other options at their defaults. Press [TAB] to select **OK** and then press [ENTER] to begin the build process.

2. Enter the following commands to install support for DCC tests:

```
# cd /usr/ports/mail/dcc-dccd
# make config ; make -D WITHOUT_SENDMAIL install clean
# rehash
```

CONFIGURE

Once the installation process completes, it is time to configure SpamAssassin for use on your system.

1. Set up two community-based email fingerprinting tests, Vipul's Razor and DCC. These spam identification systems vary slightly, but both rely on

SPAMASSASSIN
FreeBSD port path: /usr/ports/mail/p5-Mail-SpamAssassin
TCP port used – UNASSIGNED (783)

community input to keep their databases current as spam evolves. Vipul's Razor and DCC employ a web-of-trust scheme to give more weight to clients that accurately report spam.

To set up Vipul's Razor reporting capabilities, create the default configuration file and directory structure and register an identity with the Razor Nomination Servers as follows (substitute your domain name for *example.com*):

```
# razor-admin -home=/var/spool/spamd/.razor -create
# razor-admin -home=/var/spool/spamd/.razor\
? -register -user=postmaster@example.com
# chown -R spamd /var/spool/spamd/.razor
```

2. Create SpamAssassin's primary configuration file, *local.cf*:

```
# cd /usr/local/etc/mail/spamassassin
# ee local.cf
```

3. Add the following lines (replace the italicized items with values that match your network):

```
trusted_networks 192.168.1. 209.85.146.176/29 204.13.250.97
internal_networks 192.168.1.11 204.13.250.97
bayes_file_mode 0770
dns_available yes
razor_config /var/spool/spamd/.razor/razor-agent.conf
add_header all DCC _DCCB_ _DCCR_
add_header ham SCL 1
add_header spam SCL 9
```

trusted_networks specifies an IP or range of IPs for systems that don't relay spam. In other words, you are confident that these computers aren't compromised and the people using them aren't spammers. In the example above you are vouching for your internal network of 192.168.1.*xxx*, 209.85.146.176–182 (Gmail's outbound mail servers), and 204.13.250.97 (this could be the backup mail server/exchanger for your domain). These IPs will be exempt from DNS blacklist checks.

internal_networks specifies an IP or range of IPs for systems that handle mail for your domain. In general, you should specify your domain's mail servers/ exchangers here. In the example above we are saying that 192.168.1.11 and 204.13.250.97 handle mail delivery for our domain. All values of internal_networks must also be present in the trusted_networks statement.

4. Save, exit, and test for configuration file syntax errors:

```
# spamassassin --lint
```

If your configuration file parsed successfully, no message will be displayed.

NOTE *For further information on the* local.cf *file, enter:*

```
# perldoc Mail::SpamAssassin::Conf
```

SPAMASSASSIN
FreeBSD port path: /usr/ports/mail/p5-Mail-SpamAssassin
TCP port used – UNASSIGNED (783)

5. Create a short script to be called by Postfix when new email arrives. This script will send the email to SpamAssassin for analysis and then redirect the result back into the mail system for delivery. Create the script:

```
# cd /usr/local/bin
# touch spamd.sh
# chmod 555 spamd.sh
# ee spamd.sh
```

and add these lines:

```
#! /bin/sh
/usr/local/bin/spamc | /usr/sbin/sendmail -i "$@"
```

6. Configure Postfix to pipe new email messages through the script you just created. First, open the Postfix configuration file, *master.cf*:

```
# ee /usr/local/etc/postfix/master.cf
```

7. Scroll down and find the smtp declaration (~9). Create a new line under the smtp declaration and add a content_filter statement. The smtp declaration should look like this:

```
smtp      inet  n      -      n      -      -      smtpd
  -o content_filter=spamd:
```

NOTE *Be sure to leave at least one space at the beginning of the second line as shown or Postfix will not parse the file correctly.*

8. Add a spamd declaration to tell Postfix to call on the *spamd.sh* script so SpamAssassin can process the message. Scroll to the bottom of *master.cf* and add these two lines:

```
spamd      unix  -      n      n      -      -      pipe
  flags=Rq user=spamd argv=/usr/local/bin/spamd.sh
  -f ${sender} -- ${recipient}
```

NOTE *Again, be sure to leave at least one space at the beginning of the second and third lines so Postfix will parse the file correctly.*

9. Save, exit, and reload the Postfix configuration files:

```
# postfix reload
```

TESTING

In this section, we'll perform some basic tests to confirm that SpamAssassin is being called by Postfix and processing messages correctly.

1. Configure SpamAssassin to start automatically at system startup. Open *rc.conf*:

```
# ee /etc/rc.conf
```

SPAMASSASSIN
FreeBSD port path: /usr/ports/mail/p5-Mail-SpamAssassin
TCP port used – UNASSIGNED (783)

and add the following lines:

```
spamd_enable="YES"
spamd_flags="-u spamd -H /var/spool/spamd"
```

Save and exit.

2. Start the SpamAssassin daemon so it will answer requests submitted by Postfix:

```
# /usr/local/etc/rc.d/sa-spamd start
```

3. Send a test spam message into the mail system. First, open a telnet connection:

```
# telnet localhost 25

Connected to localhost.
Escape character is '^]'.
220 host.example.com ESMTP Postfix
```

NOTE *Your hostname should appear instead of* host.example.com.

Enter the following (substituting your domain for *example.com*):

```
mail from: test@example.com
250 Ok

rcpt to: spamd@example.com
250 Ok
```

Then enter the following lines as shown, pressing [ENTER] after each line.

NOTE *The long string below is known as the* GTUBE (Generic Test for Unsolicited Bulk Email). *It will cause SpamAssassin to flag the message as spam.*

```
data
354 End data with <CR><LF>.<CR><LF>
Subject: This is Spam
XJS*C4JDBQADN1.NSBN3*2IDNEN*GTUBE-STANDARD-ANTI-UBE-TEST-EMAIL*C.34X
.
250 Ok: queued as 1242EC119
```

NOTE *The italicized ID tag will be different in your output.*

Finally, close the connection:

```
quit
```

4. Display the contents of spamd's mailbox:

```
# cd /var/spool/spamd/Maildir/new
# cat * | more
```

SPAMASSASSIN
FreeBSD port path: /usr/ports/mail/p5-Mail-SpamAssassin
TCP port used – UNASSIGNED (783)

If SpamAssassin processed the message successfully, you should see output similar to this:

```
Return-Path: <test@example.com>
X-Original-To: spamd@example.com
Delivered-To: spamd@example.com
Received: by host.example.com (Postfix, from userid 58)
        id 590631171D; Sat, 01 Mar 2008 12:00:04 -0700 (PDT)
Received: from localhost by host.example.com
        with SpamAssassin (version 3.2.4);
        Sat, 01 Mar 2008 12:00:04 -0700
From: test@example.com
To: undisclosed-recipients:;
Subject: This is Spam
Date: Sat, 01 Mar 2008 11:59:37 -0700 (PDT)
Message-Id: <20070630185947.811351171B@host.example.com>
X-Spam-DCC:  host.example.com 1049; Body=many Fuz1=many
X-Spam-Flag: YES
X-Spam-Checker-Version: SpamAssassin 3.2.4 (2008-03-01) on host.example.com
X-Spam-Level: *************************************************
X-Spam-Status: Yes, score=1007.0 required=5.0
tests=ALL_TRUSTED,AWL,DCC_CHECK,
DIGEST_MULTIPLE,DKIM_POLICY_SIGNSOME,DNS_FROM_AHBL_RHSBL,DNS_FROM_RFC_DSN,
DNS_FROM_SECURITYSAGE,GTUBE,RAZOR2_CF_RANGE_51_100,RAZOR2_CF_RANGE_E4_51_100
,
RAZOR2_CHECK autolearn=no version=3.2.4
MIME-Version: 1.0
```

UTILITIES

Following is brief information on the sa-update and sa-learn commands.

sa-update

This utility downloads and installs updates and/or custom rules for SpamAssassin.

Command   sa-update

Syntax   sa-update *options*

Options

--channel   Retrieve rule updates from a specified channel.

--nogpg   Do not use GPG (GNU Privacy Guard) to ensure authenticity.

Examples

To update SpamAssassin's default ruleset:

```
# sa-update
# /usr/local/etc/rc.d/sa-spamd restart
```

SPAMASSASSIN
FreeBSD port path: /usr/ports/mail/p5-Mail-SpamAssassin
TCP port used – UNASSIGNED (783)

To install a ruleset that specializes in catching adult-oriented spam:

```
# sa-update
# sa-update --channel 70_sare_adult.cf.sare.sa-update.dostech.net --nogpg
# /usr/local/etc/rc.d/sa-spamd restart
```

The channel in italics is from:

List of channels
http://wiki.apache.org/spamassassin/SareChannels

Channel information
http://www.rulesemporium.com/rules.htm

sa-learn

This utility helps the Bayesian classifier learn characteristics of spam and ham. Bayesian classification is based on word probabilities and can be highly effective if trained properly.

Command   sa-learn

Syntax   sa-learn *options file*

Options

`--ham`   Learn messages as ham (not spam).

`--spam`   Learn messages as spam.

`--dbpath`   Specify the location of the Bayes database files.

`--progress`   Show progress using a progress bar.

`--dump`   Display contents of the Bayes database.

Examples

To teach SpamAssassin that all messages in the current directory are spam:

```
# sa-learn --spam * --progress --dbpath /var/spool/spamd/.spamassassin
```

To teach SpamAssassin that all messages in the */usr/home/john/Maildir/cur* directory are ham:

```
# sa-learn --ham /usr/home/john/Maildir/cur --progress \
? --dbpath /var/spool/spamd/.spamassassin
```

To show a content summary of the Bayes database:

```
# sa-learn --dump magic --dbpath /var/spool/spamd/.spamassassin
```

SPAMASSASSIN
FreeBSD port path: /usr/ports/mail/p5-Mail-SpamAssassin
TCP port used – UNASSIGNED (783)

CONFIG FILES

Use the following files to customize SpamAssassin's configuration:

/usr/local/etc/mail/spamassassin/local.cf
  SpamAssassin's main configuration file

/usr/local/etc/mail/spamassassin/init.pre
  The plug-in configuration file for 3.0.*x* releases

/usr/local/etc/mail/spamassassin/v310.pre
  The plug-in configuration file for the 3.1.0 release

/usr/local/etc/mail/spamassassin/v312.pre
  The plug-in configuration file for the 3.1.2 release

/usr/local/etc/mail/spamassassin/v320.pre
  The plug-in configuration file for the 3.2.0 release

The plug-in configuration files are loaded when SpamAssassin's spamd daemon is loaded. Each file contains plug-ins that were specifically added at the time of each respective release.

LOG FILE

/var/log/maillog
  Contains a log of activity and status information for SpamAssassin's spamd daemon

NOTES

- **Using a Mail Delivery Agent** SpamAssassin delivers both spam and ham to users' default mailboxes; it cannot apply rules to spam. To set rules for handling email that is flagged as spam, use a tool like Procmail (see "Procmail 3.22" on page 173) to process messages once they have been tagged by SpamAssassin.

- **Whitelisting** If there are certain senders or domains that you want to effectively exempt from SpamAssassin's array of tests, you can add their email addresses or domains to the system whitelist. SpamAssassin will accept whitelist declarations in *local.cf* in */usr/local/etc/mail/spamassassin* or *user_prefs* in */var/spool/spamd/.spamassassin*. Keeping whitelist entries in *user_prefs* is preferable because it keeps them separate from the primary configuration settings.

SPAMASSASSIN
FreeBSD port path: /usr/ports/mail/p5-Mail-SpamAssassin
TCP port used – UNASSIGNED (783)

To demonstrate, we'll add whitelist entries for *vip@example.com* and anyone from *gmail.com* to the *user_prefs* file. Open *user_prefs*:

```
# cd /var/spool/spamd/.spamassassin
# touch user_prefs
# chown spamd:spamd user_prefs
# chmod 440 user_prefs
# ee user_prefs
```

and add the following lines:

```
whitelist_from vip@example.com
whitelist_auth *@gmail.com
```

The `whitelist_from` statement subtracts 100 points from the spam score on all email that claims to be from *vip@example.com*.

The `whitelist_auth` statement subtracts 100 points from the spam score on all email verified by SPF, DomainKeys, or DKIM from any *gmail.com* email address.

If you can confirm that senders employ SPF, DomainKeys, or DKIM on their email systems, use `whitelist_auth` instead of `whitelist_from`.

- **Reporting Spam to Vipul's Razor**   You can report messages to a Razor Nomination Server with the razor-report utility. Reporting spam to the Razor system helps the community better recognize the ever-changing types of spam in circulation. If you have a folder with known spam messages you can submit them to the Razor servers like so (replace the italicized path with a path to your spam directory):

```
# cat /usr/home/john/Maildir/.Junk/cur/* | razor-report \
? -home=/var/spool/spamd/.razor
```

- **Bayesian Classification Tests**   Bayesian classification tests will not run on incoming email until 200 spam and 200 ham messages have been recorded in the database. The Bayes system will automatically learn spam and ham messages over time. If you have an existing collection of spam and ham, use the sa-learn utility to speed up this process. See "sa-learn" on page 203 for examples.

SQUIRRELMAIL 1.4.13
HTTP://WWW.SQUIRRELMAIL.ORG

SUMMARY

SquirrelMail is a web-based email client, or *webmail application*, written in PHP with an emphasis on web standards and widespread compatibility across web browsers. Pages output by SquirrelMail are compliant with HTML 4.0 and don't use any client-side scripting.

SquirrelMail supports IMAP for retrieving and SMTP for sending email. Extensions or plug-ins are also available to add functionality to the SquirrelMail base installation.

Nathan and Luke Ehresman wrote SquirrelMail in 1999. They were active developers on the project until mid-2001. SquirrelMail is currently maintained by a group of 12 programmers who continue development with an eye toward web standards and simplicity.

RESOURCES

SquirrelMail Documentation
   http://www.squirrelmail.org/wiki/SquirrelMail

SquirrelMail on SourceForge.net
   http://sourceforge.net/projects/squirrelmail

REQUIRED

☑ FreeBSD 7.0-RELEASE (see "FreeBSD 7.0" on page 9)

☑ Updated ports collection (see "FreeBSD Ports Collection" on page 23)

☑ Apache HTTP server (see "Apache HTTP Server 2.2.8" on page 33)

☑ PHP 5 (see "PHP 5.2.5" on page 145)

☑ Postfix SMTP server (see "Postfix SMTP Server 2.5.1" on page 163)

☑ Courier-IMAP (see "Courier-IMAP Server 4.3.0" on page 43)

☑ Internet connection

OPTIONAL

☑ OpenSSL with a signed SSL Certificate, if you wish to enable secure HTTP connections (see "OpenSSL 0.9.8g" on page 127)

☑ OpenLDAP for Addressbook lookups (see "OpenLDAP Server 2.3.38" on page 113)

PREPARATION

Become the superuser.

INSTALL

To begin the SquirrelMail installation process, enter the following commands:

```
# cd /usr/ports/mail/squirrelmail
# make config ; make install clean
```

CONFIGURE

Once installation is complete, it's time to configure SquirrelMail for use on your system.

1. PHP has a default file upload limit of 2MB, which effectively limits the size of your email attachments to 2MB. To increase this size limit, you will need to modify the *php.ini* file in the */usr/local/etc* directory as follows. (If 2MB is sufficient for your needs, skip to step 2. See *http://www.squirrelmail.org/wiki/ AttachmentSize* for more details on raising attachment size limits.)

```
# ee /usr/local/etc/php.ini
```

Scroll down to the upload_max_filesize declaration (~606) and change the default of 2M to 8M. The line should now appear as follows:

```
upload_max_filesize = 8M
```

Save and exit.

2. Invoke the SquirrelMail configuration utility:

```
# cd /usr/local/www/squirrelmail
# ./configure
```

Ensure the following configuration options are set correctly:

```
[2] Server Settings
    [1] Domain
```

At the prompt, replace *example.com* with your domain name.

```
[2] Server Settings
    [A] Update IMAP Settings
        [8] Server Software
```

At the prompt, replace *other* with courier.

Type **Q** and then press [ENTER] to quit. Enter **Y** when prompted to save your data.

3. Create a SquirrelMail-specific Apache configuration file. This file points Apache to the correct location of the SquirrelMail files and makes administration easier by keeping SquirrelMail-specific options separate from the main *httpd.conf* file. By default, Apache searches the */usr/local/etc/apache22/ Includes* directory for configuration files. Here's how to create one for SquirrelMail:

```
# ee /usr/local/etc/apache22/Includes/squirrelmail.conf
```

Add the following lines:

```
Alias /squirrelmail "/usr/local/www/squirrelmail/"

<Directory "/usr/local/www/squirrelmail/">
Options None
AllowOverride None
Order allow,deny
Allow from all
</Directory>
```

NOTE *By default, SquirrelMail is set up as a subdirectory of your web server's root site, meaning that you would enter* http://host.example.com/squirrelmail *into your web browser. To change this default directory, replace* squirrelmail *(in italics above) with a different name.*

Save and exit. Restart Apache to commit the changes:

```
# /usr/local/etc/rc.d/apache22 restart
```

TESTING

In this section, we'll test SquirrelMail's configuration.

1. To test your SquirrelMail configuration, point a web browser to the following address: *http://host.example.com/squirrelmail/src/configtest.php.*

Substitute your domain name and directory if applicable.

2. Examine the output for errors. If all went well, you should have a congratulations message at the bottom.

You should now be able to log in to SquirrelMail by clicking the link or entering **http://host.example.com/squirrelmail** into your web browser (again substituting your server's hostname and directory).

CONFIG FILES

/usr/local/www/squirrelmail/configure
This interactive Perl script configures SquirrelMail options with menus.

LOG FILES

/var/log/maillog
General log of email activity

NOTES

- **SSL** In order to protect your users' privacy, it is best to secure all communications by allowing only HTTPS connections to SquirrelMail.

  We'll reconstruct our SquirrelMail-specific configuration to accommodate this. Open the existing file:

  ```
  # ee /usr/local/etc/apache22/Includes/squirrelmail.conf
  ```

  Modify the file to read:

  ```
  Alias /squirrelmail "/usr/local/www/squirrelmail/"

  <Directory "/usr/local/www/squirrelmail/">
  Options None
  AllowOverride None
  Order Allow,Deny
  Allow from All
  </Directory>

  <IfModule mod_rewrite.c>
  RewriteEngine On
  RewriteCond %{HTTPS} off
  RewriteCond %{REQUEST_URI} /squirrelmail
  RewriteRule (.*) https://host.example.com/squirrelmail/ [R]
  </IfModule>
  ```

  Make the appropriate substitutions and then save, exit, and restart Apache:

  ```
  # /usr/local/etc/rc.d/apache22 restart
  ```

- **LDAP**   You can enable LDAP email address lookups in SquirrelMail if you have a functional LDAP server running.

  Ensure you have the php5-ldap shared extension installed using this command:

  ```
  # pkg_info | grep php5-ldap
  ```

  If you don't get any results, rebuild SquirrelMail:

  ```
  # cd /usr/ports/mail/squirrelmail
  # make deinstall
  # make -D WITH_LDAP install clean
  ```

  To set up LDAP lookups:

  ```
  # cd /usr/local/www/squirrelmail
  # ./configure

  [6] Address Books
      [1] Change LDAP Servers
  ```

  These settings should work if you're running an LDAP server on the same system. If you're not, make the appropriate substitutions.

  ```
  [ldap] command (?=help) > +
  hostname: localhost
  base: ou=People,dc=example,dc=com
  port: press [enter]
  charset: press [enter]
  name: LDAP: example.com
  maxrows: press [enter]
  binddn: press [enter]
  protocol: 3
  [ldap] command (?=help) > d
  ```

  Type **Q** and then [ENTER] to quit. Enter **Y** when prompted to save data.

  To perform LDAP lookups in SquirrelMail, click the Compose link and then click the **Addresses** button (not the link) in the Compose window to search or display LDAP records. The Addresses link takes you to your personal address book and is independent of the LDAP directory.

WORDPRESS 2.3.3

HTTP://WORDPRESS.ORG

SUMMARY

WordPress is an open source personal publishing system also referred to as a *blog platform*. Like many other dynamic web applications, WordPress is written in PHP and stores content in a MySQL database.

Major features include trackback/pingback support, third-party plug-in capability, compliance with web standards set by the World Wide Web Consortium (W3C), theme support, static page management, and RSS (Really Simple Syndication) feed support.

Blogs have gained popularity with the advent of tools like WordPress. Justin Hall, a writer and graduate student, is recognized as being one of the first to create a personal blog in 1994. Another notable figure, David Winer, created *ping servers*, which keep records of updates received from blogging applications. Ping servers allow blog readers to quickly check a blog for updated content; *technorati.com* is a popular example of this concept. Winer also created the RSS specification that enables users to see new content on a blog using an RSS-capable client.

WordPress is the successor to the b2/cafelog Content Management System, with development dating back to 2001. Matthew Mullenweg and Mike Little were the original founders of the WordPress project. Mullenweg formed Automattic, Inc. in August 2005 to house a variety of open source projects, including WordPress. WordPress development is led by Mullenweg and Ryan Boren of Automattic, Inc.

RESOURCES

WordPress Documentation
   http://wordpress.org/docs

REQUIRED

- ☑ FreeBSD 7.0-RELEASE (see "FreeBSD 7.0" on page 9)
- ☑ Updated ports collection (see "FreeBSD Ports Collection" on page 23)
- ☑ Apache HTTP server (see "Apache HTTP Server 2.2.8" on page 33)
- ☑ PHP 5 (see "PHP 5.2.5" on page 145)
- ☑ MySQL 5 (see "MySQL Server 5.0.51" on page 99)

☑ Internet connection

☑ Registered domain name

PREPARATION

1. Become the superuser.

2. Create a database in MySQL named *wordpress*. Next, create a user named wordpress and assign full privileges to this user:

```
# mysql -u root -p
mysql> create database wordpress;
mysql> grant all on wordpress.* to
    -> wordpress@localhost identified by 'password';
mysql> quit
```

Replace *password* with a password of your choice (the single quotes are required). You'll need this password later.

INSTALL

Enter the following commands to begin the WordPress installation:

```
# cd /usr/ports/www/wordpress
# make config ; make install clean
```

CONFIGURE

Once installation is complete, it's time to configure WordPress for use on your system.

1. Copy the file *wp-config-sample.php* to *wp-config.php*. The following commands will make the copy, set file permissions, and open *wp-config.php* for modification:

```
# cd /usr/local/www/data/wordpress
# cp wp-config-sample.php wp-config.php
# chmod 640 wp-config.php
# ee wp-config.php
```

2. Modify the DB_NAME, DB_USER, and DB_PASSWORD declarations (~3) to match your MySQL setup. The lines should appear as follows (use the password you assigned earlier):

```
define('DB_NAME', 'wordpress');     // The name of the database
define('DB_USER', 'wordpress');     // Your MySQL username
define('DB_PASSWORD', 'password');  // ...and password
```

Save and exit.

3. Create a WordPress-specific Apache configuration file. This file points Apache to the correct location of the WordPress files and makes administration easier by keeping WordPress-specific options separate from the main *httpd.conf* file. By default, Apache searches the */usr/local/etc/apache22/Includes* directory for configuration files. Here's how to create one for WordPress:

```
# ee /usr/local/etc/apache22/Includes/wordpress.conf
```

Add the following lines:

```
Alias /wordpress "/usr/local/www/data/wordpress/"

<Directory "/usr/local/www/data/wordpress/">
Options Indexes FollowSymLinks
AllowOverride All
Order allow,deny
Allow from all
</Directory>
```

NOTE *By default, WordPress is set up as a subdirectory of your web server's root site. This means you would enter* http://host.example.com/wordpress *into your web browser. To change this default directory, replace* wordpress *(in italics above) with a different name.*

Save and exit. Restart Apache to commit the changes:

```
# /usr/local/etc/rc.d/apache22 restart
```

4. Open *http://host.example.com/wordpress/wp-admin/install.php* in your favorite web browser, substituting your hostname and directory (if you modified it), then follow the instructions to complete the installation.

5. Change your admin password after logging in by clicking the **Users** tab. Click the sub-tab named **Your Profile**, enter a new password (lower-right corner), and click the **Update Profile** button.

ADMINISTRATION

Use this URL to administer your WordPress installation (substituting your server's hostname): *http://host.example.com/wordpress/wp-admin*.

CONFIG FILES

usr/local/www/data/wordpress/wp-config.php
    Holds the username, password, and database information for WordPress

NOTES

You may want to use permalinks on your blog. Here are examples of a permalink and a standard link:

Permalink   *http://host.example.com/wordpress/blog-article*

Standard link   *http://host.example.com/wordpress/?p=123*

The above links would both take you to the same hypothetical blog entry, but the permalink provides a meaningful URL that makes it easier for other sites to reference posts in your blog.

To enable permalinks, open the WordPress web administration interface by pointing your web browser to *http://host.example.com/wordpress/wp-admin*.

Turn on permalinks by going to the **Permalinks** tab nested in the **Options** tab. Click one of the predefined structures, or create your own, and click **Update Permalink Structure**.

View the site by clicking **View site >>** at the top of the page. Click the "Hello, world!" post and confirm that the URL field in the browser's address bar matches the permalink structure you set.

APPENDIX A
COMMANDS

This appendix contains commands that are common to basic FreeBSD system administration, and is meant to provide an abbreviated reference for those unfamiliar with Unix commands. It is organized into the following categories: general, archiving files, and network. The commands are presented in order of relative usage from most used to least. For full documentation on any command, consult its man page. See "Manual Pages" on page 234 for details on man pages.

GENERAL

ls

This command will list the files in the current directory.

Command ls

Syntax ls *-options file*

Options

-a Include all files that start with a dot (hidden files).

-l List the files in long format (permissions, date, time, owner, and group).

-d List directories as plain files (not searched recursively).

-h Use unit suffixes, such as K for kilobyte, M for megabyte, and so on (must be used in conjunction with the -l option).

-F Append symbols after each file or directory type (/ is appended to directories, * to executable files, and @ to symbolic links). The -F option is useful for identifying file types and directories quickly without doing a long listing (-l option).

Below is output from a directory listing in long format using ls -l:

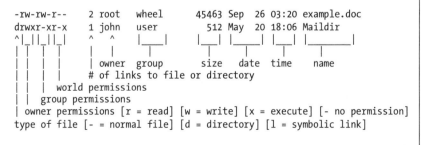

```
-rw-rw-r--   2 root    wheel       45463 Sep  26 03:20 example.doc
drwxr-xr-x   1 john    user          512 May  20 18:06 Maildir
^|_||_||_|   ^    ^     |___|       |__| |___| |__| |_____|
 | | |  |    |    |       |           |    |    |      |
 | | |  |    | owner  group         size date time   name
 | | |  |    # of links to file or directory
 | | |  world permissions
 | |  group permissions
 | owner permissions [r = read] [w = write] [x = execute] [- no permission]
 type of file [- = normal file] [d = directory] [l = symbolic link]
```

Examples

To list all the files in the current directory including those starting with a dot (.) and using long format, type:

```
# ls -al
```

To list only the files and directory names in the root directory starting with *u*, use the * wildcard by typing:

```
# ls -d /u*
```

To list all files and directory names in long format, including those starting with a dot (.), that end in *.txt*, type:

```
# ls -ald *.txt
```

Two useful shortcuts included in the default FreeBSD shell's profile are the commands ll and l (lowercase L). Typing ll is the same as typing ls -alFo and displays just about everything you need to know about the current directory. The command l is equivalent to ls -l.

Notes

For more details and other options for this command, type man ls at the command prompt. Remember that FreeBSD is a case-sensitive operating system. The command ls -l file is entirely different from the command ls -l File. An asterisk (*) can be used as a wildcard, which allows you to specify filtered searches. Think of it as a short way of saying "anything." For example, if you want to search the current directory for all files starting with b, type ls -d b*, which equates to "list files starting with lowercase b followed by anything." The -d tells the system to list directory names starting with b rather than searching for files within directories recursively.

cd

This command will change the working directory to one that you specify.

Command   cd

Syntax   cd *directoryname*

Examples

To change to a directory named *test* in your current working directory, type:

```
# cd test
```

To change to the root directory, type:

```
# cd /
```

To change the current working directory to */usr/local/www*, type:

```
# cd /usr/local/www
```

Notes

In this example, *www* is a subdirectory of */usr/local*, as *local* is a subdirectory of */usr*. If your working directory is */usr/local/www* and you want to navigate to */usr/local*, you can type cd /usr/local or cd .. (the .. is another way of navigating to the parent directory of the current directory). Another shortcut can be executed with the tilde (~) key. Typing cd ~ will place you in the current user's home directory. This location can vary, but is most likely */usr/home/username*, where *username* is the login ID of the current user.

If you need to change to a directory that contains spaces, you will need to use quotation marks to enclose the path. Typing cd "/usr/local/www/webserver" would be correct syntax.

pwd

This command will display the current working directory.

Command   pwd

Syntax   pwd

Example

Type pwd at the command prompt. If you just logged in, you will probably see something like /usr/home/user, where user is your login name. This means that you are in the directory named *user*, which is a child directory of *home*. The parent directory of *home* is *usr*.

cp

This command is used to copy files from one location to another.

Command   cp

Syntax   cp -options sourcefile targetfile

Options

-i   Force cp to prompt the user before copying over a file with an identical filename.

-R   Cause the entire subtree to be copied if the sourcefile is a directory.

-p   Preserve original attributes (modification and access times, file flags, file modes, user and group IDs) of the source file(s) if permissions allow.

Examples

To copy a file named *example.doc* to a new file named *newexample.doc*, type:

```
# cp example.doc newexample.doc
```

To copy the *example.doc* file to the */usr/local/www* directory, type:

```
# cp example.doc /usr/local/www
```

To copy a directory tree named *logs* to a new directory named *archive* while preserving file attributes, type:

```
# cp -R -p logs archive
```

Notes

If you copy a file to a location with an identical filename, cp will overwrite the file if the -i option is not used and permissions allow.

Wildcards can be used to copy multiple files. The command cp *.doc /usr/home/ user would copy all files with the *.doc* extension from the current directory to the directory */usr/home/user.*

mkdir

This command creates directories with the name you specify.

Command   mkdir

Syntax   mkdir *directoryname*

Examples

To create a directory named *documents* in the current working directory, type:

```
# mkdir documents
```

To create a subdirectory named *home* inside the */usr* directory, type:

```
# mkdir /usr/home
```

rm

This command removes files and directories.

Command   rm

Syntax   rm *-options file*

Options

-i   Cause rm to prompt the user for confirmation before removing each file.

-r   Recursively remove all files and directories contained in the specified path.

Examples

To remove the directory *tmp* and all files and directories it contains, type:

```
# rm -r tmp
```

If you want to delete a single file of the name *example.doc* from the current directory, type:

```
# rm example.doc
```

If you want to delete all *.doc* files from the */usr/local/www* directory, with a confirmation for each file, type:

```
# rm -i /usr/local/www/*.doc
```

Notes

A directory can also be removed with the `rmdir` command, provided it is empty. The command `rmdir test` would remove the test directory only if it contained no files.

mv

This command is used to move a file from one location to another.

Command mv

Syntax `mv -options source target`

Options

-i Cause mv to prompt the user before moving a file or directory that would overwrite an existing file or directory.

Examples

To move a file named *example.doc* in the directory */usr/local/www* to the current user's home directory with overwrite confirmation enabled, type:

```
# mv -i /usr/local/www/example.doc ~
```

To rename the file *foobar.conf* to *apache.conf,* type:

```
# mv foobar.conf apache.conf
```

To rename a directory named *www* to *cgi-bin,* type:

```
# mv www cgi-bin
```

ee

Easy Editor is a simple text editing program.

Command ee

Syntax ee *filename*

To start ee, type **ee** at the command prompt.

Press the [ESC] key to access the main menu. At the top, you will see the available commands and their shortcuts. The caret symbol (^) means hold the [CTRL] key followed by the letter associated with the command. At the bottom of the screen, you may see messages and prompts as you execute different commands.

You can open text files with ee by typing:

```
# ee filename
```

Replace *filename* with the actual name of the file.

find

This command is a handy way of finding files nested in a particular directory. You can specify an exact name to search for or use wildcards for a specific set of files.

Command find

Syntax find *startpath -options searchstring*

Options

-name *xxx* Search for the string *xxx*; to search using wildcards such as ? or *, enclose the string in double quotes.

-user *xxx* List files matching the username *xxx*.

-group *xxx* List files matching the group name *xxx*.

Examples

To find all *.doc* files within the */usr* directory, type:

```
# find /usr -name "*.doc"
```

To search all mounted filesystems for the file *example.doc*, type:

```
# find / -name example.doc
```

To search the current directory and its subdirectories for the file *example.doc*, type:

```
# find . -name example.doc
```

To find all files belonging to the user john in the */usr* directory, use the command:

```
# find /usr -user john
```

file

This command will examine files against a pre-compiled list of known file types and return a file type description if it finds a match.

Command file

Syntax file *filename*

Examples

To determine a file type for a file named *example.mov*, type:

```
# file example.mov
```

To display the file types of all files in the current working directory, type:

```
# file *
```

less

This program can be used to display text files and to scroll output from other commands that do not fit on one screen.

Command less

Syntax less *-options file*

Options

-N Display the line number at the beginning of each line.

-M Display the percentage of the file that has been viewed and the line number range currently on screen in the prompt.

Examples

To display the contents of the text file *example.txt*, type:

```
# less example.txt
```

If the file you have chosen to display is longer than the screen, use the arrow keys to scroll up and down through the document. A quick way to find words or letters is to press ?, then type a word or letter to find and press [ENTER]. All instances of the word or letter will be highlighted. Pressing **Q** at any time will quit back to the command prompt.

To display the contents of the text file */etc/services* with line numbers and per-cent into file visible, use the command:

```
# less -NM /etc/services
1 #
2 # Network services, Internet style
3 #
4 # Note that it is presently the policy of IANA to assign a single...
5 # port number for both TCP and UDP; hence, most entries here have...
6 # even if the protocol doesn't support UDP operations.
7 #
8 # The latest IANA port assignments can be gotten from
9 #
10 #      http://www.iana.org/assignments/port-numbers
/etc/services lines 1-10/2114 0%
```

less can also be used to examine output from other commands like ls. By using the pipe symbol (|) you can direct the output of ls to the input of less in order to scroll through the output. For example, to display the contents of the directory */usr/lib* (in long format) with scrolling, type:

```
# ls -l /usr/lib | less
```

grep

This program is used to find strings of text within files or output of other commands. If grep finds the string you specify, it will return the whole line in which the match occurs.

Command   grep

Syntax   grep *pattern file*

Examples

To search the text file named *apache.conf* for the word *server*, type:

```
# grep server apache.conf
```

By using the pipe symbol (|), you can use grep to analyze output from other commands, such as ls. To search the output of a long listing of the root direc-tory for the word *usr*, type:

```
# ls -l / | grep usr
```

You can also search for phrases in files like this:

```
# cat /COPYRIGHT | grep "All rights reserved"
```

su

This utility is used to switch user identities. If a username is not given, root is assumed. Only users that belong to the wheel group are allowed to switch to the root login, unless the sudo command is used to run su as root.

Command   su

Syntax   su *username*

Examples

To switch to the root account from a user who is a member of the wheel group, type:

    # su

chown

Changes the owner and/or group of a specified file or directory. To see the current owner and group associated with a file or directory, list the directory using the long format ls -l.

Command   chown

Syntax   chown *-options owner:group file*

Options

-R   Apply the owner/group change recursively when applied to a directory.

Examples

To change the owner of a file named *example.doc* to john, type the command:

    # chown john example.doc

To change the group ownership of a directory named *Maildir* to user, type:

    # chown :user Maildir

To change the owner and group of a file named *apache.conf* to root and wheel respectively, type:

    # chown root:wheel apache.conf

To change the owner of a directory named *www* to john, including all subdirectories and their files, type:

    # chown -R john www

Notes

Only files you create or own may be modified with this command, unless you are the superuser.

chmod

This command changes the read, write, and execute permissions of a file or directory. Read permission, as it applies to a file, means the ability to read the contents of the file. Read permission, as it applies to a directory, means the ability to list its contents (files or other directories). Write permission, as it applies to both files and directories, means the ability to change or delete its contents. Execute permission, as it applies to a file, means the ability to load and run as a program. Execute permission, as it applies to a directory, means the ability to navigate with the cd command. Much like the chown command, you will need to be the superuser or the owner of the files you intend to modify in order for this command to succeed.

Command   chmod

Syntax   `chmod -options mode file`

Options

-R   Apply the permissions change recursively when applied to a directory.

Examples

Below is a diagram of how to determine the 3-digit file mode for use with chmod.

```
-rwxr-xr--    2 root   wheel     45463 Sep  26 03:20 example.doc
|_||_||_|
 |  |  |
 |  |  r-- [r=4] = 4 = third digit (world/anybody permission)
 |  r-x [r=4]+[x=1] = 5 = second digit (group permission)
rwx [r=4]+[w=2]+[x=1] = 7 = first digit (owner permission)
```

example.doc has a 3-digit mode of 754, since each digit is the sum of the r, w, and x permission values for that user, where r (i.e., *read*) is 4, w (*write*) is 2, and x (*execute*) is 1.

To change the permissions of a file named *example.doc* to have full read, write, and execute permissions for the owner, group, and world, type:

```
# chmod 777 example.doc
```

To change the permissions of a directory named *www* to have read, write, and execute for the owner, read permission for the group, and no permissions for world users, type:

```
# chmod 740 www
```

df

This utility displays the amount of free disk space for all mounted filesystems.

Command df

Syntax df -*options*

Options

-h Produce "human readable" output with suffixes for megabyte, gigabyte, and so on.

-c Display a grand total row on the bottom of output.

Example

To display the free disk space for all mounted filesystems in "human readable" format, type:

```
# df -h
```

du

This utility displays the amount of disk space used by files or directories.

Command du

Syntax du -*options* *filename*

Options

-d *x* List all files and directories *x* directories deep.

-c Display a grand total for listed files and directories.

-h Use unit suffixes like K for kilobyte and M for megabyte.

-a Display all files including hidden ones.

Examples

To display the amount of disk space used for each file and directory in the */usr* directory with unit suffixes, use the command:

```
# du -d 1 -h /usr
```

To display the disk space used for all files in the current directory (including subdirectories) and a grand total, type:

```
# du -ca
```

Notes

Output from this utility may span several pages; use of a text display utility like less may be useful when dealing with long file listings.

mount

The mount command is used to make a disk drive available for use with a computer's filesystem.

Command   mount

Syntax   mount -options device node

Options

-t   Declare the type of filesystem on the device to be mounted; common types include msdos, ufs (default), cd9660, ntfs (limited), udf, and nfs.

NOTE   *A mounted NTFS volume has limited write ability. Files must be nonresident, not contain any spaces, and not contain multibyte characters. Compressed files are also not supported.*

Examples

To mount a data CD (/dev/acd0) to the */mnt* directory, type:

```
# mount -t cd9660 /dev/acd0 /mnt
```

To mount partition *a* of slice *1* of hard disk ad0 (ad0s1a) to the */mnt* node, type:

```
# mount /dev/ad0s1a /mnt
```

umount

The umount command is used to disassociate a disk drive from the computer's filesystem. Removing a removable drive prior to unmounting may cause data corruption or loss.

Command   umount

Syntax   umount *node*

Examples

To unmount a filesystem mounted on the node */mnt*, type:

```
# umount /mnt
```

Notes

Be sure the current working directory is not a directory located within the file-system to be unmounted; if it is, the umount command will return a device busy error.

ARCHIVING FILES

dump

This command has the ability to back up a FreeBSD filesystem.

Command   dump

Syntax   dump -options filesystem

Options

-0   (zero) Specify dump level zero, or full backup.

-a   Auto-size the output until the media returns end-of-media indication.

-L   Tell dump that the filesystem being backed up is "live" (in use) and take a snapshot of the filesystem to maintain consistency. Always include this switch unless the system is in single-user mode.

-f   Tell dump to write its output to a file instead of the default tape drive.

Examples

To back up the */usr* partition to a new file named *usr.dump* in the current working directory outside of */usr*, type:

```
# dump -0 -a -L -f usr.dump /usr
```

To back up the root (/) partition to a new file named *root.dump* in the current working directory, type:

```
# dump -0 -a -L -f root.dump /
```

Notes

It is best to perform backups on a regular basis, and if possible, to store the dump files on a different physical drive or media in case a hardware failure occurs. I cannot stress the importance of this enough: ALWAYS HAVE A BACKUP! Remember to back up each partition you created during the initial FreeBSD installation. If you used the defaults, they are */usr*, */var*, /, and */tmp*. If you are storing your dump files on a different physical drive, note the name of the filesystem where the dump files are stored and keep it with your FreeBSD boot CD. If your primary drive fails, this partition name will be needed to access the dump files when the time comes to restore (you may view partition names with the df command). See Appendix B for details on backup and restore procedures.

tar

This utility is used to manipulate archive files. An archive file may contain a single file or a whole directory tree. Tar archives are commonly used to transfer files or full hierarchies of directories over the Internet, just as Zip files are used on other platforms.

Command tar

Syntax tar -options archive files

Options

-c Create a new archive.

-x Extract from archive to disk.

-t List the archive's contents.

-z Compress the archive using gzip.

-r Append files to an existing archive (must not be compressed).

-f Specify a file to save the archive as, instead of the traditional tape drive.

Examples

To create a compressed archive named *usr.tgz* containing all files and directories within the */usr* directory, type:

```
# tar -c -z -f usr.tgz /usr
```

To extract the gzipped archive named *usr.tgz* to the current directory, type:

```
# tar -x -z -f usr.tgz
```

To append the file *example.xxx* to an existing uncompressed archive named *archive.tar*, type:

```
# tar -r -f archive.tar example.xxx
```

restore

The restore command can restore specific files or a whole filesystem from a dump backup.

Command restore

Syntax restore -options source

Options

-i   Put restore into interactive mode; for restoration of specific files instead of the whole filesystem.

-r   Rebuild the filesystem; used when you are restoring the entire filesystem. (See Appendix B.)

-f   Read input from a file instead of a tape drive.

Examples

To restore a specific file interactively from a dump file named *usr.dump*, type:

```
# restore -i -f usr.dump
```

A prompt will appear; you can navigate through the volume as if it were a live filesystem. To display a list of available options, enter ?.

When you find the file(s) you want to restore, add them to the extraction queue by typing:

```
restore > add filename
```

where *filename* is the name of the file you wish to extract. You can use wildcards here, too.

When you finish adding files to the queue, type the command **extract** to begin the restore. restore will display a message saying you haven't read any tapes yet and asking where to start; press **1** then [ENTER] and press **Y** when it asks you to set the owner/mode. Type **quit** to exit. The file(s) you selected will be nested in their original hierarchy inside the current working directory.

NETWORK

sockstat

The sockstat command lists open Internet ports, or *sockets*. This utility is useful for listing active daemons and their associated ports. Use of the grep command here can help extract information from the output of sockstat.

Command   sockstat

Syntax   sockstat -*options*

Options

-l   Show listening sockets.

-c   Show connected sockets.

-4   Show IPv4 sockets.

-6   Show IPv6 sockets.

Examples

To list all ports listening for service requests, type:

```
# sockstat -l
```

To list all of the ports in use by the HTTP daemon, type:

```
# sockstat | grep httpd
```

To list all processes currently listening on TCP port 443, type:

```
# sockstat | grep 443
```

ifconfig

This utility can be used to check or modify the configuration of a particular network interface. Normally this command executes at boot time from the *rc.conf* file in */etc*. Running ifconfig without any arguments will list all network interfaces and their configurations.

Command   ifconfig

Syntax   ifconfig *interface options*

Options

inet   Set the system's IP address to the specified value.

netmask   Set the system's netmask to the specified value.

Example

To change the IP address of an interface named xl0 to 192.168.0.12 with a netmask of 255.255.255.0, use the following command:

```
# ifconfig xl0 inet 192.168.0.12 netmask 255.255.255.0
```

Notes

There are dozens of options available for this utility; they are beyond the scope of this guide. Refer to the manual page for more details by typing man ifconfig.

ping

The ping utility sends ICMP packets to a specified host and listens for return packets. This is useful for determining if a host is reachable on the network.

Command   ping

Syntax   ping *-options host*

Options

-c Specify the count or number of packets to send before terminating; by default, ping operates until interrupted with [CTRL-C].

Example

To ping a host named *example.com* with five packets, use the command:

```
# ping -c5 example.com
```

netstat

This command displays a variety of information about the network topology.

Command netstat

Syntax netstat *-options*

Options

-f Specify protocol family (inet or unix).

-r Show the contents of all routing tables.

-rs Display routing statistics.

Examples

To display the contents of the routing table, use the command:

```
# netstat -r
```

To display the state of all active Internet connections, use the command:

```
# netstat -f inet
```

dig

dig, short for *domain information groper*, is a utility for interrogating DNS name servers. This tool is useful for troubleshooting DNS problems.

Command dig

Syntax dig *@server name type*

Examples

To query the DNS server *ns2.foo.com* about the domain *example.com*, use the command:

```
# dig @ns2.foo.com example.com
```

To query a DNS server with the IP address of 69.72.158.226 about the mail exchanger (MX) record at the domain *example.com*, use the command:

```
# dig @69.72.158.226 example.com mx
```

traceroute

This utility displays the route taken by data transmitted from the local system to a specified remote host. The traceroute utility is useful for diagnosing route-related network problems.

Command   traceroute

Syntax   traceroute *-options host*

Options

-n   Display IP addresses instead of host names.

Example

To trace a route to the host *www.example.com*, use the following command:

```
# traceroute www.example.com
```

MANUAL PAGES

Manual pages (or *man pages*) constitute a Unix system's online documentation. The FreeBSD man page system is separated into nine categories as follows:

1. General commands
2. System calls and error numbers
3. The C Libraries
4. Devices and device drivers
5. File formats
6. Games
7. Miscellaneous information
8. System maintenance commands
9. Kernel system interfaces

There may be man pages in different categories with the same name. We'll use the subject "tar" as an example. *Tar* is short for *tape archive*. It is also a file format and the name of a utility (program) used to manipulate tar archives. If you want file format information about *tar*, you can look at the categories above and see that that information is found in section 5. To display the file format man page for tar, type `man 5 tar`. To learn more about tar the utility, which is a general command and thus in section 1, type `man 1 tar`.

If you type `man` followed by a subject without the section number, the system will display the first man page it finds (starting from section 1) that matches your query. You will be returned to the command prompt after viewing that man page. To display all man pages from all sections that match your query, use the -a flag, for example: `man -a tar`.

To perform a quick search for a word while viewing a man page, type / followed by the word and [ENTER]. The first match will appear highlighted at the top of the screen; to find the next instance of the word, press **N**.

There may be times when you don't know what command to use for a desired task. The `apropos` and `whatis` commands are useful in these situations. The `apropos` command searches the command database for a specified string. For example, to search all man pages containing the string ftp, type `apropos ftp`. The `whatis` command searches the same command database, but returns only whole-word matches. For example, to search all man pages containing the word ftp, type `whatis ftp`.

Below is an example of output from the `whatis` command:

```
# whatis ftp

ftp(1)         - Internet file transfer program
ftp-proxy(8)   - Internet File Transfer Protocol proxy server
smbclient(1)   - ftp-like client to access SMB/CIFS resources on servers
Net::Cmd(3)    - Network Command class (as used by FTP, SMTP etc)
Net::FTP(3)    - FTP Client class
```

The first column contains the entry's name and its numerical category, and the second a brief description. For more information on the first item, type `man 1 ftp`. To display the man page for the second, type `man 8 ftp-proxy`.

APPENDIX B
BACKUP AND RESTORE

It is very important to back up your system on a regular basis. It is easy to inadvertently "break" the system by accidentally deleting or misconfiguring crucial files. It is also prudent to back up a system before installing any software, to safeguard yourself from frustration if the installation doesn't go as planned. This section provides a basic guide on using the dump and restore commands to make full system backups for disaster recovery.

NOTE *Perform a few experimental backups and restores before putting a server "online." It is important for new users to become familiar with this process rather than fumble with these procedures when time and data are crucial. It is advisable to store backup files on a different physical medium (e.g., a secondary hard disk) in case the primary disk fails. See "Adding a Second Hard Disk" on page 239 for details.*

BACKUP

Backup using the dump utility is a fairly straightforward process. For more detail on the dump command, see "Archiving Files" on page 229. For this example, we will assume that there are two physical hard disks installed. The second hard disk is mounted to the system as /backup. If you do not have a second hard drive on the system, you should consider adding one. A backup hard drive is well worth the investment; see "Adding a Second Hard Disk" on page 239 for instructions.

Before starting the backup, we'll examine the filesystem name for each partition we wish to back up. Normally, the root (/), */var*, and */usr* partitions should be backed up if you chose to partition your drive automatically when you set up FreeBSD.

1. To view a list of mounted filesystems, type:

```
# df

Filesystem    1K-blocks     Used    Avail Capacity  Mounted on
/dev/ad0s1a      253678   119942   113442     51%    /
devfs                 1        1        0    100%    /dev
/dev/ad0s1e     2026030       12  1863936      0%    /tmp
/dev/ad0s1f   24767644  1572648 21213586      7%    /usr
/dev/ad0s1d    1012974    60350   871588      6%    /var
/dev/ad1s1d   37846636  1914068 32904838      5%    /backup
```

The output of the df command shows that the root partition (/) is associated with the filesystem name of ad0s1a, */var* with ad0s1d, and */usr* with ad0s1f. Also be sure to note the backup partition's filesystem; in this case it is ad1s1d.

2. To create a backup of the root, */var*, and */usr* filesystems to the secondary hard drive, type the following commands:

```
# dump -0 -a -L -f /backup/root.ad0s1a.dump /
# dump -0 -a -L -f /backup/var.ad0s1d.dump /var
# dump -0 -a -L -f /backup/usr.ad0s1f.dump /usr
```

Notice that the filenames include both the partition and filesystem names. This will be helpful during the restore process if it ever becomes necessary. The first two commands should complete relatively quickly. The third will take substantially longer depending on the size of your */usr* directory tree. When all three commands are complete, you should have a backup set that is capable of restoring an identical copy of the critical filesystems.

RESTORE

We are going to assume that you have backed up your system to a separate drive using the instructions in the "Backup" section. We will be replacing the contents of the primary drive, so proceed only in a disaster recovery situation or on a test system. You might consider moving the drive containing the backups to a spare computer and practicing the restoration process there.

1. Insert a copy of the FreeBSD distribution CD in the CD-ROM drive and reboot. After booting from the FreeBSD CD, you will be presented with the Sysinstall Main Menu. Scroll down to **configure** with the arrow keys and press [ENTER]. Next, scroll down to **Fdisk** and press [ENTER].

2. A menu will appear asking you to select a drive. You will be restoring the primary drive, so scroll to it (likely ad0 or da0) and press [ENTER].

3. You are now in FDISK Partition Editor, so press **A** to automatically create a slice, press the down arrow until the newly created slice is highlighted (likely named ad0s1), and press **S** to set it as bootable. Press **Q** to exit FDISK.

4. A dialog asking if you want to install a boot manager will appear. Select **standard** and press [ENTER]. You may be returned to the Select Drive(s) menu; if so, press [ESC] to cancel. You will be returned to the FreeBSD Configuration Menu.

5. Scroll down, select **Label**, and press [ENTER]. The FreeBSD Disklabel Editor will appear. Press **A** to automatically create default partitions, then press **W** to write changes (you can do this manually if you wish). A dialog will appear asking "Are you absolutely sure you want to do this now?" Verify the correct disk is displayed in the upper left corner (if you are restoring the primary IDE drive it should be ad0, or da0 for SCSI). If you are ready, select **yes** with the arrow keys and press [ENTER]. After the operation is performed, you will be returned to the FreeBSD Disklabel Editor. Press **Q** to quit back to the configuration menu. Scroll up to **exit** and press [ENTER].

6. Scroll to **fixit** and press [ENTER]. A dialog will appear asking you to choose a fixit option. Choose **CDROM/DVD** and press [ENTER]. You will be taken to the command prompt. First, you'll need to mount the partition that contains your dumpfiles. Then you will change to the appropriate directories and restore each filesystem from the dumpfiles.

7. To begin restoring files, type the following commands (replace the filesystem name in italics with the filesystem name that contains your dumpfiles):

```
# mount /dev/ad1s1d /tmp
# cd /mnt
# restore -r -f /tmp/backup/root.ad0s1a.dump
# cd /mnt/var
# restore -r -f /tmp/backup/var.ad0s1d.dump
# cd /mnt/usr
# restore -r -f /tmp/backup/usr.ad0s1f.dump
```

NOTE *Disregard any messages about "file exists." If you have MySQL installed you may need to reset permissions on the /*tmp *directory after restoration. See "MySQL Server 5.0.51" on page 99 for more details.*

8. After completing the restore, type **exit**. This will take you back to sysinstall. You will be at the fixit menu; choose **exit** and press [ENTER], then select **exit install** and press [ENTER]. You will be asked if you are sure. Select **yes** and press [ENTER]. Remove the FreeBSD CD from the CD-ROM drive. The system is now restored.

ADDING A SECOND HARD DISK

This guide assumes that you have added a Parallel or Serial ATA hard drive to the system. If you'll be using a USB or SCSI hard drive, you may substitute all references to ad with da and proceed normally. We are going to assume that the hardware installation is correct and complete, and that you don't intend to keep any data that may be on the new hard drive. After booting with the new hard drive installed, log in as the superuser.

1. To begin configuring the new drive, type `sysinstall` at the command prompt. You will be taken to the main menu. Scroll down to **Configure** and press [ENTER].

2. Select **Fdisk** and press [ENTER]. A dialog asking you to select the drive will appear. Select the appropriate drive and press [ENTER] (the new drive will probably be the second in the list with a name like ad1 or ad2). A warning message may appear explaining that your drive geometry is incorrect. FreeBSD will automatically adjust this, so press [ENTER] to continue.

3. You are now in the FDISK Partition Editor. Press **A** to automatically partition and then press **W** to write changes. A dialog will appear saying that this should only be performed on an existing installation and asking if you are sure you want to do this now. Confirm that you are modifying the correct physical drive by checking the upper left corner, where the disk name is displayed. If you are ready to erase the drive, select **yes** and press [ENTER]. A dialog asking if you want to install a boot manager will appear. Select **none** and press [ENTER]. The next dialog will say that the operation was successful. Press [ENTER]. Type **Q** to quit FDISK.

4. You will be returned to the Select Drive menu. Select **cancel** to return to the configuration menu. Select exit by pressing **X** and then [ENTER]. You will be at the sysinstall Main Menu; press **X** again to exit (you need to exit sysinstall for the changes to take effect).

5. You will be at the command prompt at this point. Restart sysinstall by typing `sysinstall`. Select **Configure** and press [ENTER]. Select **Label** and press [ENTER]. A dialog asking you to select the drive will appear. Select the appropriate drive and press [ENTER] (this will be the same drive you selected in step 2). The disk label editor will now appear. Press **C** to create a partition. A dialog will appear asking you to specify partition size. To use the whole drive, press [ENTER]. The next menu will ask you what type to create. Choose **fs** and press [ENTER]. The next prompt will ask you for a mount point (directory name). Type one of your choice (*/backup*, for example; don't use the name of a directory that already exists because sysinstall will mount the new partition on top of it) and press [ENTER]. To finalize the changes, press **W**. The same dialog you saw in FDISK will appear. If you are ready, select **yes** and press [ENTER].

6. Write down the partition name(s) and the corresponding mount name(s); you will need this information in the following steps. When you are ready to continue, press **Q** to quit the label editor. You will be returned to the select drive menu. Select **cancel** to return to the configuration menu. Scroll up to **exit** and press [ENTER]. Select **exit install** and press [ENTER]. Your newly configured drive should now be mounted and ready for use.

7. The */etc/fstab* file needs to be modified so that your new hard drive will mount each time the system starts. Open */etc/fstab*:

```
# ee /etc/fstab
```

Add a new line and insert the partition name you wrote down in step 6. You'll need to precede the partition name with */dev/*. You'll also need to insert the mount name you used in step 6 under the mountpoint column. The remaining columns can be set to the values shown below:

```
# Device        Mountpoint    FStype  Options     Dump    Pass#
/dev/ad0s1b     none          swap    sw          0       0
/dev/ad0s1a     /             ufs     rw          1       1
/dev/ad0s1e     /tmp          ufs     rw          2       2
/dev/ad0s1f     /usr          ufs     rw          2       2
/dev/ad0s1d     /var          ufs     rw          2       2
/dev/acd0       /cdrom        cd9660  ro,noauto   0       0
/dev/ad1s1d     /backup       ufs     rw          2       2
```

Save and exit. The new drive should now mount automatically at boot time.

APPENDIX C
MANAGING USER ACCOUNTS

This section is meant to give new administrators a brief look at adding, removing, and modifying users with FreeBSD. For more information, refer to the FreeBSD Handbook, *http://www.freebsd.org/doc/en_US.ISO8859-1/books/handbook/users.html.*

ADDING USERS

FreeBSD includes the adduser command, which calls an interactive script that makes adding users quite easy. We'll create a theoretical user named John Doe and give him shell or command-line access.

1. After typing **adduser** at the command line, you will be prompted for a username. This is the login name; you can use any convention you like, but we are just using the first name in this example. Note that usernames are case sensitive, meaning *john* is not the same as *John.*

```
# adduser
Username: john
```

2. The Full name prompt will appear next. Enter the user's first and last name. This is only a description field in the password database, so spaces are allowed and users don't have to worry about case sensitivity.

```
Full name: John Doe
```

3. The third prompt will ask for Uid. Just press [ENTER] to accept the default user identification number.

```
Uid (Leave empty for default):
```

4. The next prompt will ask for the login group; it will be the username by default. Press [ENTER] to accept the default.

```
Login group [john]:
```

5. You'll be asked if you want to invite the user to another group. If this user needs to be able to become the superuser using the su command, enter **wheel**. Otherwise leave it blank and press [ENTER].

```
Login group is john. Invite john into other groups? []:
```

6. The following prompt will ask for the login class. Press [ENTER] to continue.

```
Login class [default]:
```

7. The next prompt will ask you to choose the user's shell. You can press [ENTER] to accept the default sh shell. If the user plans on using the command line extensively, consider changing the shell to tcsh, which will provide the user with command-line history and tab completion. You may enter nologin here if you don't want to give the user shell (command-line) access.

```
Shell (sh csh tcsh nologin) [sh]:
```

8. The following prompt will allow you to specify the home directory location. Press [ENTER] to accept the default. The actual path will start with */usr*, so it will be */usr/home/john* in this case.

```
Home directory [/home/john]:
```

9. You'll be asked if you want to use password authentication. Press [ENTER] to accept the default of yes.

```
Use password-based authentication? [yes]:
```

10. The next prompt will ask if you want to use an empty password. Press [ENTER] to accept the default of no.

```
Use an empty password? (yes/no) [no]:
```

11. The subsequent prompt will ask if you want to use a random password. Press [ENTER] to enter your own password.

```
Use a random password? (yes/no) [no]:
```

12. The next two prompts will ask you to enter a password. You won't see anything on the screen while you type the password, so be very careful.

```
Enter password:
Enter password again:
```

13. The script will ask if you want the account locked out after creation. Press [ENTER] to accept the default of no.

```
Lock out the account after creation? [no]:
```

14. You will see a summary of the information you entered. If you are happy with the results, type **y** and press [ENTER]. If you want to add another user, answer **yes** to the "Add another user?" prompt.

```
Username   : john
Password   : *****
Full Name  : John Doe
Uid        : 1002
Class      :
Groups     : john
Home       : /home/john
Shell      : /bin/sh
Locked     : no
OK? (yes/no): yes
```

MODIFYING USERS

Modifying a user's shell, personal information, password rules, home directory, and so on can be accomplished using the chpass command. The chpass command will use the default editor set in the current user's environment variables. The root account defaults to the tcsh shell and stores these variables in */root/.cshrc*. By default, other users use the sh shell and store their environment variables in */usr/home/username/.profile*. The default editor is normally set to vi. It is easy to become lost if you aren't familiar with vi, so we'll change the default editor. To determine the current shell, type:

```
# ps | grep sh
```

You should be able to identify your shell by examining the first line of output. To set your default editor to ee when using the csh or tcsh shells, enter:

```
# setenv EDITOR ee
```

If you're using the sh shell, enter:

```
# EDITOR=ee ; export EDITOR
```

NOTE *This change will only be effective for the duration of your login session. Your default editor will change back to the value set in your shell's environment variable file the next time you log in. To make the change permanent, add the above lines to the appropriate shell configuration file (*/root/.cshrc *or* /usr/home/username/ .profile*).*

The following example illustrates what you might see when running chpass as the superuser (root) for a user account named john.

```
# chpass john

#Changing user information for john.
Login: john
Password: $1$/q2SQ1Aa$vxTRAUvIOyvdhPryn7r/L/
Uid [#]: 1002
Gid [# or name]: 1002
Change [month day year]:
Expire [month day year]:
Class:
Home directory: /home/john
Shell: /bin/sh
Full Name: John Doe
Office Location:
Office Phone:
Home Phone:
Other information:
```

You may change any of the fields except for the Password field. The password is hashed and is not editable here. If you wish to disable the account, you may comment the Password field by adding a hash mark (#) to the beginning of the line. The Change field is used to force the user to change his password on the date you specify. The Expire field disables the account on the specified date (the user's home directory will remain intact).

NOTE *If a user other than root executes the* chpass *command, she will be presented with a smaller set of editable fields and will only be able to modify her own information.*

CHANGING PASSWORDS

Changing a user's password can be accomplished with the passwd command. The following example will change the password for a user named john. You will need to become the superuser to execute this command.

```
# passwd john

Changing local password for john
New Password:
Retype New Password:
```

Users may change their own passwords by using the passwd command without specifying a username.

REMOVING USERS

Removing a user from FreeBSD is accomplished with the rmuser command. The following command will remove a user named john (replace *john* with the username you wish to remove):

```
# rmuser john

Matching password entry:

john:*:1002:1002::0:0:John Doe User:/home/john:/bin/sh

Is this the entry you wish to remove?
```

The system will display some details about the account. If you are sure you want to remove the user, type **y** and then press [ENTER].

```
Remove john's home directory (/home/john)? y
Removing user (john): mailspool home passwd.
```

The final prompt will ask if you would like to remove the user's home directory. If you would like to remove this directory, type **y** and then press [ENTER].

HOME DIRECTORY DOT FILES

When users are added to the system, a set of dot files (hidden configuration files) are copied to the new user's home directory. This set of dot files contains defaults for the user's shell settings, among others. You may change the default dot files located in */usr/share/skel* to suit your preferences. For example, let's make a change to one of these dot files, namely the *dot.profile* file. We will change the default text editor from vi to ee since it is much simpler to learn. Open the *dot.profile* file with Easy Editor:

```
# ee /usr/share/skel/dot.profile
```

Change vi to ee (~18):

```
EDITOR=ee;     export EDITOR
```

Save and exit. User accounts added after this modification will use Easy Editor as the default text editor, assuming you assign them the default sh shell.

APPENDIX D
THE PROTOCOLS

This appendix is meant to provide some basic information about common Internet protocols and concepts relevant to a networked server. A clear understanding of network topology will save a lot of time and frustration when malfunctions occur. For a more comprehensive look at Internet protocols, pick up a copy of *The TCP/IP Guide* by Charles M. Kozierok (No Starch Press, 2005).

This appendix is organized using the Department of Defense Networking Model, also known as the TCP/IP suite. The four-layer model was adopted in the early '70s when DARPA began work on the Internetwork Project, which was the beginning of the Internet we know today. The layers can be mapped to their associated protocols as follows:

```
TCP/IP LAYER                PROTOCOLS
(4) Application Layer        DHCP, DNS, FTP, HTTP, IMAP, POP3, SMTP
(3) Host-to-Host Layer       TCP, UDP
(2) Internetwork Layer       ARP, IP, ICMP
(1) Network Access Layer     ETHERNET, WIFI
```

Data is passed through each layer in a linear fashion. For example, HTTP data coming from the Application layer on the sending system is relayed to the Host-to-Host layer where the TCP protocol attaches a header that includes information such as the source port, destination port, and checksum (for error checking). This *packet* is handed over to the Internetwork layer where the IP protocol attaches yet another header with information including the source address, destination address, Time To Live, and header size. The packet is then transferred to the Network Access layer where another header is added; this layer is read by network hardware in order to correctly relay the packet to its intended destination.

The following figure shows some of the information contained in the various headers of a typical HTTP packet.

Ethernet header: *sourceMAC/destinationMAC/EtherType*	Layer 1
IP header: *sourceIP/destinationIP/length/timetolive/checksum*	Layer 2
TCP header: *sourceport/destinationport/sequence/checksum*	Layer 3
HTTP header: *contenttype/server/date/length*	Layer 4
Data	

Below is a closer look at each layer and the important protocols that constitute the TCP/IP suite.

APPLICATION LAYER

This layer includes protocols that are responsible for delivering data to applications (programs) at the user level. These application-level protocols specify the syntax a client must use to interact with a server. For example, an HTTP request from a web browser to a web server might look like GET /index.html. Below are some of the most commonly used Application layer protocols.

DHCP [UDP port 67, 68]   The Dynamic Host Configuration Protocol is responsible for automating the process of connecting devices (e.g., computers and printers) to a network. A DHCP server provides each client with an IP address, default gateway, and DNS server address.

When a client device first connects to the network, it broadcasts a DHCP discover message. The DHCP server is constantly listening for these types of broadcasts and responds with a DHCP offer message that contains various configuration parameters. The client device accepts the parameters and notifies the server with another broadcast message. The server responds with a final acknowledgment message and stores the configuration. The DHCP client applies the configuration to its network interface, thereby enabling access to the network's resources. This entire process is transparent to the user and happens in just a few seconds.

DHCP assigns client IP addresses dynamically using a lease policy. This allows the server to reuse IPs that may no longer be in use when a client leaves the network or fails to renew its IP lease. The DHCP server will specify an expiration time when the initial configuration parameters are sent during DHCP negotiation. Client devices usually renew their lease when half of the expiration time has elapsed.

DNS [UDP port 53]   The domain name system is responsible for distributing DNS data from servers to clients for the purposes of hostname-to-IP-address resolution. It is a distributed system of information that stores domain names like *google.com* with their associated IP addresses. Network-aware applications (web browsers, etc.) use IP addresses as a point of contact when requesting services. DNS allows the use of easily remembered names like *unorthodocs.net* rather than cumbersome IP addresses like 69.227.55.189.

FTP [TCP port 21, 20 (if in active mode)]   The File Transfer Protocol is responsible for transferring files from servers to clients over TCP/IP networks. Once an FTP connection is made, the user (client) may also interactively manipulate files on the server.

FTP is unique among other popular Internet protocols, like HTTP, because it employs multiple TCP/IP connections. The initial connection, or *control channel*, occurs over port 21. This channel is used to send commands to the FTP server. The secondary connection, or *data channel*, is used to transfer data. The data channel can be established in active or passive mode. In active mode, the server tells the client to listen for an incoming connection on a random port above 1023. The server connects to the client to establish the data channel. This can be a problem if the client is behind a firewall because most firewalls block incoming traffic. Here's how an initial FTP connection is made in active mode:

```
FTP Server (port 21) <----control----- FTP Client (port 21)
FTP Server (port 20) ------data------> FTP Client (random port >1023)
```

In passive mode, the initial data connection direction is reversed. The server gives the client a random port that the server listens on. The client then initiates an outbound connection to the server to establish the data channel. If a firewall is in use, the server administrator can open the appropriate ports to allow inbound connections. Here's how an initial FTP connection is made in passive mode:

```
FTP Server (port 21) <----control----- FTP Client (port 21)
FTP Server (random port >1023) <--data-- FTP Client (random port >1023)
```

FTP transmits username and password information in the clear. This may present a security risk because a potential attacker can capture this data quite easily with a network analyzer. With this in mind, FTP should only be used on trusted networks when no alternatives exist. Alternatives to FTP include SFTP (part of OpenSSH) or using a secure tunneling protocol to encapsulate FTP packets (e.g., OpenVPN).

HTTP and HTTPS [TCP port 80, 443 respectively]   The HyperText Transfer Protocol is responsible for transmission of data on the World Wide Web, a link-based system for browsing Internet sites. HTTP is a request/response protocol whereby clients send specific requests to an HTTP server for information. Data transferred is encoded in a format similar to that of MIME (Multipurpose Internet Mail Extensions), which is used in electronic mail. Like MIME-encoded email, HTTP packets include headers that specify the contents of the data being transmitted. Web resources are addressed using a *URL (uniform resource locator)* like *http://www.nostarch.com*.

HTTP can be encrypted to prevent the eavesdropping of data transmitted between server and client. The URL scheme https: tells the web browser to use an SSL (Secure Sockets Layer) connection over the secure HTTP port 443. This is commonly used on sites conducting e-commerce, where financial information needs to be kept private.

IMAP and IMAPS [TCP port 143, 993 respectively]   The Internet Message Access Protocol is responsible for the transport, manipulation, and synchronization of email messages between a mail server and a client application such as Outlook, Thunderbird, or Eudora. IMAP is a request/response protocol that requires authentication to match users to their respective mailboxes. IMAP does not support the sending of email messages; it is designed to retrieve messages only. SMTP is used to send email independently of IMAP.

IMAP differs from the other Internet email retrieval standard, POP3 (Post Office Protocol version 3), as IMAP supports persistent connections. This means that an IMAP connection stays open for as long as the email client program is open, allowing for constant updating of email messages between the server and the client. With POP3, the client must reconnect to the server to check for messages. IMAP stores email messages on the server, which provides a central location in which to access messages. POP3 downloads all messages to the email client and subsequently removes the server copies. This means that messages will only be viewable on the computer that downloaded it. IMAP also supports simultaneous connections to the same mailbox; POP3 does not. Simultaneous connections allow multiple clients to stay synchronized with the same mailbox.

IMAP can be encrypted to prevent the eavesdropping of data transmitted between server and client. Port 993 is standard for SSL encrypted IMAP sessions.

POP3 and POP3S [TCP port 110, 995 respectively]   Post Office Protocol version 3 is responsible for the retrieval of email messages between a mail server and a client application such as Outlook, Thunderbird, or Eudora. POP3 is a request/response protocol that requires authentication to match users to their respective mailboxes.

POP3 is probably the most widely used protocol for the retrieval of Internet email. This is because virtually all Internet service providers support it for customer email accounts. A POP3 connection begins when an email client authenticates with a POP3 server. After authentication, all messages for the user are transferred to the mail application and deleted from the server. The connection is then terminated. POP3 has maintained popularity with Internet providers because the deletion of messages after client retrieval lessens storage demands, in contrast to IMAP, which keeps messages on the server.

The POP3 protocol can be encrypted to prevent the eavesdropping of data transmitted between server and client. Port 995 is standard for SSL encrypted POP3 sessions.

SMTP [TCP port 25]   The Simple Mail Transfer Protocol is responsible for relaying email between SMTP servers. SMTP is an *ASCII (American Standard Code for Information Interchange)* based protocol, meaning it transfers data by using only text characters. MIME was developed to solve the problem of transferring binary data with SMTP mail in order to allow attachments.

The MIME standard defines rules for converting binary data into ASCII (text) characters that can be sent using the text-only SMTP protocol. The recipient's email client decodes the MIME-encoded text back into binary data.

An email message is constructed with an email client such as Outlook, Thunderbird, or Eudora, and then sent to a designated SMTP server. The SMTP server reads the destination information encoded in the SMTP packet and resolves the IP address of the mail server responsible for that destination's domain using a DNS server. The server then connects to the destination SMTP server to deliver the message. SMTP was designed to relay mail from source to destination; it is expected that the client will use POP3 or IMAP to retrieve the message from the SMTP server.

SMTP normally transmits data in the clear and does not include protection against eavesdropping on transmitted data. SMTP servers can be configured to use SSL/TLS to provide encryption services. This allows email clients to transmit messages to an SMTP server securely. Security thereafter, however, cannot be assured because the message is stored on the server in unencrypted form and may pass through other SMTP servers that do not employ encryption. PGP (Pretty Good Privacy), a client program, or S/MIME (Secure/Multipurpose Internet Mail Extensions), a public key infrastructure–based standard, may be used to encrypt email when security is necessary.

HOST-TO-HOST LAYER

This layer includes the TCP protocol, which is responsible for opening, maintaining, and closing connections while maintaining integrity using error-correction. The layer also includes the UDP protocol, which does not provide the error-correction and persistent connection of TCP, but is useful for its efficiency. Application Level protocols are designed specifically to use either TCP or UDP. For example, HTTP uses TCP and DHCP uses UDP.

TCP   The Transmission Control Protocol is used to prepare data received from application level protocols for transmission over computer networks. TCP interoperates with the Internet Protocol (IP), which is responsible for the routing of packets from source to destination. TCP is considered a state-dependent protocol because it requires first that a connection be established before actual data is sent. TCP also terminates the connection when data transmission is complete.

To better illustrate the concept of TCP, think of a data file as a completed jigsaw puzzle. To transmit this completed puzzle across a network, TCP takes it apart, sequentially labels each piece, puts each piece in an envelope (header), sends it to the post office (IP), and buys tracking and insurance for each piece. If any of the pieces are lost, they are simply resent. As pieces of the puzzle start to arrive at the destination system, the TCP protocol on the destination system carefully puts all of the pieces together sequentially, reconstructing the puzzle.

UDP   The User Datagram Protocol is used to prepare data from application level protocols for transmission over computer networks. UDP is responsible for taking streams of data passed from applications and adding minimal header information before passing it quickly to the underlying Internet Protocol, which is responsible for the routing of packets from source to destination. Unlike TCP, UDP does not provide any ordering or reliability measures. Lack of error-correction allows UDP to be faster and more efficient for applications where the overhead of TCP is less desirable, such as voice-over-IP and multimedia streams.

TCP/UDP ports When creating header information, TCP and UDP utilize what is known as a *port* to address data to a specific application. Think of a long hallway lined with hundreds of doors labeled numerically, as in a hotel. Each door represents a port. Since the Apache web server uses HTTP on TCP port 80, data sent to the web server would walk down this hallway to room 80, pass through the open door (port), and be able to communicate to the web server.

The *IANA (Internet Assigned Numbers Authority)*, now run by ICANN (Internet Corporation for Assigned Names and Numbers), has the responsibility for assigning port numbers to protocols and applications. Pairing port numbers with specific protocols allows network-aware applications to communicate with a wide variety of services over a single physical connection. FreeBSD's service name database resides in */etc/services*. This file contains a comprehensive list of protocol names and their IANA assigned port numbers. Visit *http://www.iana.org/assignments/port-numbers* for the latest IANA port assignments.

INTERNETWORK LAYER

This layer includes the *Internet Protocol (IP)*, which is responsible for routing packets of data from source to destination. IP was designed to carry packets prepared by higher-level protocols such as TCP and UDP.

ARP The Address Resolution Protocol is responsible for the resolution of IP addresses to MAC (Media Access Control) addresses on Ethernet networks. A *MAC address* is a hard-coded (permanent) identifier assigned to Ethernet networking devices at the time of manufacture. An example of a MAC address is 00:0d:93:8e:b0:34; the `ifconfig` command is used to view MAC address information on Unix systems.

In contrast to IP addresses used at the Internetwork layer, Ethernet uses a network device's MAC address. For example, let's say computer A attempts to send an IP packet to computer B. If they happen to be on the same subnet, computer A will transmit an ARP broadcast containing the IP address of computer B. Computer B responds with its MAC address and computer A stores this address for future communications. Actual data transmission can occur over Ethernet once this process (called *ARP resolution*) is complete. If computers A and B are on different subnets, it is the job of the router to relay packets between the two subnets. Ethernet switches store ARP tables so they can route traffic to other switches or routers.

ARP is considered an intermediary between the Internetwork and Network Access Layers.

IP   The Internet Protocol is a network layer protocol responsible for routing traffic on the Internet. The IP header, containing information like TTL (Time To Live), source IP address, and destination IP address, is read by routing network hardware that processes or forwards the packet according to configured rules or policies.

A simple way to think of the Internet Protocol is to consider it the "post office" of the network. The protocol dictates the addressing format and size of packets much like a traditional post office does with mail. Think of the router as the mail sorter which uses the addressing information to determine what to do with each packet to send it along its way to the final destination.

IPv4, or version 4 of the Internet Protocol, is widely used on the public Internet. IPv4 uses a 32-bit address system composed of four octets, each representing 8 bits. There are 4,294,967,296 possible unique addresses using this 32-bit address system. Some of these addresses were reserved for private networks and other administrative uses. For example, 192.168.*x.x* and 10.*x.x.x* are reserved for private networks. 127.*x.x.x* are referred to as *localhost addresses*. The slowly diminishing number of unique IP addresses prompted work on IPv6, which is still under development. The popularity of NAT routers has, to some extent, quelled the fear of an IP address shortage. NAT technology corrals several computers together to use a single IP address rather than assigning unique IPs to each.

IP address   An *Internet Protocol address* is a string of digits separated by periods that represent a computer's virtual address on a network. An example of an IP address is 17.254.0.91. A static IP address is an IP address set up to be used by a specific computer when it is reachable on a network. A dynamic IP address is a leased IP address that is typically assigned by a DHCP server. The IP address may change when the lease expires or when the computer is unreachable on a network.

ICMP   The Internet Control Message Protocol is meant to provide feedback about problems in the transmission of packets on IP networks. ICMP packets are IP packets that carry error types and codes in their headers.

For example, let's say that we are transmitting data between two computers over the Internet. Computer A is connected on a high-speed fiber optic network and computer B is connected on a dial-up modem. When computer A sends data to computer B, it sends it faster than computer B's connection can accept it. When computer A begins to overload computer B's router, an ICMP Source Quench message is sent to computer A to request that it cut back the transmission rate to avoid packet loss.

A common network tool, ping, utilizes ICMP echo messages to provide information on network accessibility. Another network tool, traceroute, employs ICMP time exceeded messages to attempt to trace the route of packets between hosts.

For more information on ICMP, see RFC 792: *http://tools.ietf.org/html/rfc792.*

NETWORK ACCESS LAYER

Protocols and technologies in this layer are responsible for the transfer of packets from the physical topology of one network device to another. This layer adds a packet header, typically referred to as a frame, to aid in the journey from one network to another. This extra header information is stripped whenever the packet enters an intermediary router; the router creates a new frame as it transmits the packet onto the next network. This process continues until the packet reaches its final destination.

10BASE-T 10BASE-T is an Ethernet network topology standard used to physically connect devices using 8-wire twisted pair (UTP) cables with RJ-45–type connectors. The *10* in 10BASE-T stands for the transmission speed of 10 Mbps. *BASE* stands for *baseband*, which means only a single Ethernet signal is present per twisted pair. The *T* stands for *twisted pair*, which is a type of wiring that uses windings to minimize electromagnetic interference. 100BASE-T and 1000BASE-T are newer standards with transmission speeds of 100 and 1,000 Mbps, respectively.

Cable/DSL modem These devices are used to modulate (change) data signals transmitted by cable and phone service providers into signals usable by your computer. Broadband Internet access has become possible with the use of these devices. Typical downstream speeds are 1.5 to 6 Mbps with upstream speeds averaging 350 Kbps.

Ethernet This frame-based networking technology is the most widely used local area networking standard. Ethernet is considered a peer-type network that originally implemented the CSMA/CD (Carrier Sense Multiple Access with Collision Detection) protocol to transmit data. This is also known as *half-duplex Ethernet*, and comprises a set of rules that all Ethernet devices obey:

1. If a wire is idle, begin transmitting.

2. If a collision (two devices talking at once) is detected, cease transmission after a specified time to ensure the other transmitter also detects the collision.

3. Wait a random amount of time before retransmitting data.

4. Data is retransmitted.

5. Device exits transmit mode if data is sent successfully.

A second mode of operation, called *full-duplex Ethernet*, bypasses the CSMA/CD protocol by allowing Ethernet devices to transmit and receive simultaneously. This eliminates the collision problem because the send and receive paths are separated. In order to operate at full-duplex, hosts must be on a switched network and have interface adapters that support full-duplex operation. Ethernet hubs only support half-duplex mode.

Ethernet is a broadcast networking technology. Every Ethernet NIC possesses a globally unique 48-bit identifier called a MAC address. Network devices transmit data in small chunks called frames with headers that contain source and destination MAC addresses. By default, each network device continually "listens" to the network and ignores all "frames" except those containing a MAC address matching its own.

Ethernet adapter Also known as a *network interface card (NIC)* or *network adapter*, this component allows a computer to communicate with other devices on an Ethernet network. Most new computer systems have Ethernet adapters built in. FreeBSD natively supports most makes and models.

Ethernet hub A *hub*, also known as a *concentrator*, is a device that connects multiple devices together. A hub takes an incoming signal from any connected device and rebroadcasts the signal to the other connected devices.

Ethernet broadcasting can be compared to shouting a person's name into a crowd. Everyone hears the announcement, but only the person whose name was called listens to the subsequent message. When there is a lot of traffic, this constant shouting can cause a lot of extraneous traffic that a different device, called a *switch*, attempts to mitigate.

Ethernet switch A *switch*, also known as an *intelligent hub*, is a device that connects multiple network devices together. A switch is called an intelligent hub because it employs a MAC address table to store the identities of devices connected to it. When data enters a switch, it is examined for its destination information. The switch will then check the MAC address table for the location of the destination device and forward the data through the appropriate port instead of broadcasting it to everyone. This reduces overall network traffic and increases efficiency.

Think of this as the boss finding an employee's extension in a directory; the employee may then be directly contacted by telephone rather than by shouting his name over a maze of cubicles.

Router This device connects separate networks together much like a junction connects different highways. A router employs a *routing table* to intelligently send packets in the direction of their destination. Routers may also communicate with each other to update these routing tables when needed.

Think of this as an operator at a phone company responsible for routing international phone calls to the appropriate national networks. Most routers sold to consumers combine both a router and a switch into one device to interconnect the local network and route traffic to the Internet. These combined devices are also known as *NAT routers*.

NAT   Network Address Translation is the process by which a device translates local private IP addresses into that of a single public IP address. Most home network routers perform NAT to give multiple users access to the Internet without having to pay for another IP address. A possible drawback to this process is the lack of individual accessibility from the Internet to computers behind the NAT device; for example, each computer cannot run its own publicly accessible web server. Devices behind the NAT device can initiate connections to other hosts on the Internet but cannot accept unsolicited requests from outside the NAT device. NAT can be thought of as a one-way valve. As a side effect, NAT is also a good security measure, since it can keep out attacks and unwanted traffic. Most home NAT routers feature a port-forwarding feature to allow traffic from the Internet to be forwarded to a specific computer in the private network.

Wi-Fi   Wireless Fidelity, or 801.11x, is a set of IEEE (Institute of Electrical and Electronic Engineers) standards used to define wireless local area networks. Wi-Fi uses short-range radio transceivers in the 2.4 GHz band to transfer data. The same rules for data transmission and collision apply as with half-duplex wired Ethernet (CSMA/CD).

A Wi-Fi configuration usually consists of a central access point or *wireless hub* that communicates with clients using broadcasts similar to that of an Ethernet hub. A standard access point broadcasts its identification or *SSID (service set identifier)* "beacon" to notify potential clients of its presence. Access points can be configured to authenticate all connections, or enforce access rules based on the client's MAC address.

The 802.11b standard is the most widely deployed of the 802.11 standards. It specifies a maximum throughput of 11 Mbps. Depending on whether TCP or UDP is used, 802.11b clients can expect an actual throughput of 700 to 900 KB/s. The newer 802.11g standards specify a maximum throughput of 54 Mbps. Actual throughput is usually in the 3,000 KB/s range.

Security of data transmitted using Wi-Fi is provided by one of two mechanisms. The first is called *WEP (wired equivalent privacy)*; the second is *WPA (Wi-Fi protected access)*. These two mechanisms encrypt data between clients and the access point. Security flaws in the WEP mechanism were discovered, which prompted the development of WPA. With the use of a strong shared-key, WPA offers relatively good security to connected clients but is not supported by some older devices.

INDEX

Electronic Frontier Foundation
Defending Freedom in the Digital World

Free Speech. Privacy. Innovation. Fair Use. Reverse Engineering. If you care about these rights in the digital world, then you should join the Electronic Frontier Foundation (EFF). EFF was founded in 1990 to protect the rights of users and developers of technology. EFF is the first to identify threats to basic rights online and to advocate on behalf of free expression in the digital age.

The Electronic Frontier Foundation Defends Your Rights!
Become a Member Today!
http://www.eff.org/support/

Current EFF projects include:

Protecting your fundamental right to vote. Widely publicized security flaws in computerized voting machines show that, though filled with potential, this technology is far from perfect. EFF is defending the open discussion of e-voting problems and is coordinating a national litigation strategy addressing issues arising from use of poorly developed and tested computerized voting machines.

Ensuring that you are not traceable through your things. Libraries, schools, the government and private sector businesses are adopting radio frequency identification tags, or RFIDs – a technology capable of pinpointing the physical location of whatever item the tags are embedded in. While this may seem like a convenient way to track items, it's also a convenient way to do something less benign: track people and their activities through their belongings. EFF is working to ensure that embrace of this technology does not erode your right to privacy.

Stopping the FBI from creating surveillance backdoors on the Internet. EFF is part of a coalition opposing the FBI's expansion of the Communications Assistance for Law Enforcement Act (CALEA), which would require that the wiretap capabilities built into the phone system be extended to the Internet, forcing ISPs to build backdoors for law enforcement.

Providing you with a means by which you can contact key decision-makers on cyber-liberties issues. EFF maintains an action center that provides alerts on technology, civil liberties issues and pending legislation to more than 50,000 subscribers. EFF also generates a weekly online newsletter, EFFector, and a blog that provides up-to-the-minute information and commentary.

Defending your right to listen to and copy digital music and movies. The entertainment industry has been overzealous in trying to protect its copyrights, often decimating fair use rights in the process. EFF is standing up to the movie and music industries on several fronts.

Check out all of the things we're working on at http://www.eff.org and join today or make a donation to support the fight to defend freedom online.

ELECTRONIC FRONTIER FOUNDATION · 454 SHOTWELL STREET · SAN FRANCISCO, CA 94110 · 415.436.9333

ABSOLUTE FREEBSD, 2ND EDITION
The Complete Guide to FreeBSD

by MICHAEL W. LUCAS

The long-awaited and completely revised second edition of what has become the FreeBSD bible. FreeBSD committer Michael W. Lucas has brought the book up to date for FreeBSD 7.*x*, with the help of two dozen expert FreeBSD technical reviewers. This second edition of *Absolute FreeBSD* is sure to remain the perfect resource for FreeBSD system administrators. This straight-forward, practical, and comprehensive book takes the reader through the intricacies of the platform; teaches how to build, configure, and manage a FreeBSD server; and offers friendly explanations, background information, troubleshooting sugges-tions, and copious examples throughout.

NOVEMBER 2007, 744 PP., $59.95 ($65.95 CDN)
ISBN 978-1-59327-151-0

THE BOOK OF PF
A No-Nonsense Guide to the OpenBSD Firewall

by PETER N.M. HANSTEEN

A solid understanding of OpenBSD's PF subsystem is a necessity for any network administrator working in a *BSD environment. *The Book of PF* is a current, no-nonsense guidebook to harnessing the power of PF. Its contents include coverage of NAT (network address translation), wireless networking, spam fighting, traffic shaping, failover provisioning, and logging. This book is written for anyone who has felt lost in PF's manual pages or baffled by its massive feature set. Author Peter N.M. Hansteen helps readers confidently build the high-performance, low-maintenance net-work they need.

DECEMBER 2007, 184 PP., $29.95 ($35.95 CDN)
ISBN 978-1-59327-165-7

WICKED COOL SHELL SCRIPTS
101 Scripts for Linux, Mac OS X, and UNIX Systems

by DAVE TAYLOR

This useful book offers 101 fun shell scripts for solving common problems and personalizing the computing environment. Readers will find shell scripts to create an interactive calculator, a spell checker, a disk backup utility, a weather tracker, a web logfile analysis tool, a stock portfolio tracker, and much more. The cook-book style examples are all written in Bourne Shell (sh) syntax; the scripts will run on Linux, Mac OS X, and Unix.

JANUARY 2004, 368 PP., $29.95 ($43.95 CDN)
ISBN 978-1-59327-012-4